T0067353

The Troopers Are Coming

New York State Troopers
1917-1943

By

Albert S. Kurek - NYSP Retired

authorHOUSE®

AuthorHouse™
1663 Liberty Drive
Bloomington, IN 47403
www.authorhouse.com
Phone: 1 (800) 839-8640

© 2005 Albert S. Kurek - NYSP Retired. All rights reserved.

No part of this book may be reproduced, stored in a retrieval system, or transmitted
by any means without the written permission of the author.

Published by AuthorHouse 05/10/2016

ISBN: 978-1-4208-1327-2 (sc)
ISBN: 978-1-5246-0809-5 (e)

Library of Congress Control Number: 2004098906

Print information available on the last page.

Any people depicted in stock imagery provided by Thinkstock are models,
and such images are being used for illustrative purposes only.
Certain stock imagery © Thinkstock.

This book is printed on acid-free paper.

Because of the dynamic nature of the Internet, any web addresses or links contained in this book may have changed
since publication and may no longer be valid. The views expressed in this work are solely those of the author and do
not necessarily reflect the views of the publisher, and the publisher hereby disclaims any responsibility for them.

TABLE OF CONTENTS

INTRODUCTION

At the turn of the Twentieth Century, one of the greatest difficulties facing New York State was the establishment of an organized force to police the rural areas that was efficient, honest and free from political influence. For several years, a group of New York State citizens calling themselves the Committee for a State Police had lobbied the states legislators to introduce legislation for a State Constabulary. Finally in 1917, their efforts were rewarded with legislation introduced and passed. The New York State Constabulary was established. The men of the Constabulary were known as "TROOPERS" which is simply a term defined as a mounted policeman. This publication covers the years 1917 to 1943 with emphasis on occurrences and events that took place in Western New York State.

The first twenty-five years were a test of the organization's, as well as the individual trooper's strength, dedication and fortitude. Long hours, insufficient manpower and an increasing workload took its toll on many. Almost daily social, natural and economic changes altered the trooper's daily duties testing his ability to the fullest. Newly enacted laws gave troopers increased authority and enforcement empowerment along with added responsibility. The newly formed troopers also had to contend with two World Wars, mass production of the automobile causing increased traffic problems, a depression, strikes, riots, floods and other natural disasters.

Four troops were initially established to insure full police coverage of the rural areas with a Troop Headquarters established at Batavia, Onondaga Valley, White Plains and Colonie, N.Y. The procedures and events described herein were typical of a trooper's workday and could have occurred anywhere in the state. Hopefully the reader will come away with a better understanding of the hardships endured by the early troopers who stood alone.

The contents of this book are as historically accurate, as could be determined through my several years of research. It should be noted that newspapers at the time, more than occasionally misspelled names relying on the "it sounds like system", when printing their reports. I hope to provide the reader with a more detailed and slightly different view of the early history of the State Police. The events described are incidents that actually occurred, however, many case arrest dispositions could not be determined due to poor or inadequate record keeping, lost files, destroyed or misfiled documents and human error.

Unless otherwise indicated, the majority of articles in this publication were found in archived Batavia Daily Newspapers located at the Genesee County, N.Y. History Department, Batavia, N.Y.

This book would not have been possible without the assistance of the many men and women who provided access to library records, court records, vital statistics, scrapbooks, newspaper files and personal interviews. My eternal gratitude to Lois Brockway, Town Historian, Pembroke, N.Y., Susan Conklin, County Historian, Genesee County N.Y., Donald Read, County Clerk, Genesee County, N.Y., Sergeant Kevin Kailbourne, New York State Police, Wellsville, N.Y., John Sikora, Editor, Batavia, N.Y. and my good friend, Keith Hammond, Technical Consultant, Pembroke Enterprises, Corfu, N.Y. for their many hours of personal assistance and inspiration. Last, but not least, my wife Anne for her support and encouragement.

BOOK I – BIRTH OF THE TROOPERS

CHAPTER ONE
THE NEED FOR AN ORGANIZED POLICE FORCE IN THE RURAL COMMUNITY

The advent of the automobile greatly enhanced the ability of the criminal to commit crimes successfully out of the domain of his environment. What took a week for a hard riding horseman to travel could now be accomplished by automobile in a day. With the ever increasing network of inter-connecting highways, the danger of criminal activities outside the cities was greatly increased.

The criminal justice system, as it existed in 1917 provided practically no protection to the rural citizen. Town constables and county sheriff's were elected to limited terms and were hampered by jurisdictional boundaries. No matter how willing, they were under educated and ill trained to effectively perform their duties.

The chief purpose a police department is the prevention of crime. The advocating of a state police department to provide these services in the rural community was not a theory, but was in place, as an efficient organization for more than ten years in Pennsylvania. The establishment of a state police in New York would provide a force of trained men empowered to aid established law enforcement officials without additional cost to the local community. A system of patrols would provide the most isolated areas of the state the protection afforded those residing in cities.

Every community had an element that was lawless and unrestrained. They preyed on the weak relying on fear and intimidation to avoid prosecution. This method of patrol in Pennsylvania had proven effective in controlling the lawless element. The state police kept them under surveillance to a point where no escape from detection was possible. Arsonists, petty thieves, trespassers, auto thieves and bootleggers would think twice before committing a crime.

Legislation was prepared to provide such a force in New York. A survey was addressed to grange officers in Pennsylvania asking for their experience with the state police there. It was overwhelmingly returned with high praise giving instances of their aid and efficiency, as well as commenting favorably as to the high character of each officer. Subsequently, the New York State Agricultural Society, the Automobile Association, the Fish, Game & Forestry Association as well as the many local grange organizations endorsed the establishment of such a force for New York. (This is an edited version of a news article as it appeared in the Oneida Dispatch on 9 February 1917)

CHAPTER TWO
HISTORY OF THE NEW YORK STATE POLICE

The idea for a New York State Police organization was germinated in the minds of two women who fostered the idea after the murder of an employee. During the summer of 1912, Samuel Howell employed on the estate of Miss Moyca Newell located at Bedford Hills, Westchester County, New York, was murdered while carrying the payroll for his employees. Riding a motorcycle, four men attempted to rob him. Refusing to stop, Howell drove through the armed quartet, was fired upon and seriously wounded. He managed to hang on, steering the motorcycle to the Newell estate where he told fellow employees of the attempted holdup. He died three days later of seven gunshot wounds. He identified two of his assailants, as men who previously worked on the Newell estate. An attempt to have the local constable investigate the crime showed how inadequate police protection in the rural areas of the state was, as fear prevailed due to lack of training and loyalty to the position. The constable was a grocer who had been appointed to the position. When an attempt was made to form a posse of Newell employees and local residents, fear for their well being and safety resulted in the killers escaping and never being apprehended. Miss Newell and other community members were outraged at the lack of police protection and security afforded them, as rural residents. This eventually led to the forming of a "Committee for a State Police".

Miss Kathryn Mayo, a prominent writer along with her friend, Miss Newell, vowed to actively lobby for a State Police organization in New York State. They traveled to Pennsylvania and studied the Pennsylvania State Constabulary that had been organized in 1905 under the late Major John C. Groome. It was the only State Police organization in the United States at that time. Miss Mayo authored a book entitled " Justice For All ", a story of the Pennsylvania State Police. Colonel Teddy Roosevelt, the 26th United States President and a Rough Rider during his Army days wrote the forward. The dedication told the story of Sam Howell and his unjust demise. Reaction to the book was so overwhelming that, many prominent rural citizens organized and became active in a campaign to establish and form a "Committee for a State Police" which was realized in 1915. Speakers were hired who had fiery and persuasive manners to speak for the campaign. Labor strongly opposed the committee, proposing that they would be the tools of Wall Street and Big Business. This fear was based on the experiences in Pennsylvania where Coal and Iron Police were called in to suppress strikes in the coal and steel industries.

The year 1917 brought the "Preparedness" program which was an effort to speed up the recruitment of new members into the National Guard because of the impending involvement of the United States into World War I. Recruiting was hindered by the fear of laborers that they might be used for strike duty, if they volunteered for guard service. To offset this sentiment was an additional reason for the prompt creation of a State Police. Support was strong from the farmer with many small rural donations the backbone of the fight, for a State Police. New York Governor Charles S. Whitman, a former District Attorney in New York City proved a strong supporter for a State Police and spoke in favor of its creation. He pointed out that National Guard recruitment would be enhanced, if relieved of police duties then imposed upon it. The State Police could be an effective force when the militia was needed for other purposes. He stated that if a bill establishing a constabulary passed the Legislature, he would sign it. On April 11, 1917, the Mills-Wells Bill passed the legislature by one vote, was signed and became Law creating a Department of State Police. Under Chapter 161 of the Laws of 1917, $500,000.00 was appropriated to acquire horses, uniforms, suitable equipment, supplies, to

3

pay salaries and to select sites for Troop Headquarters. An original amendment provided that the state police not enter a city unless being ordered to do so by the Governor. On May 2, 1917, Governor Whitman appointed George Fletcher Chandler, a Major in the New York Army National Guard and a prominent physician, as the first Superintendent of this newly created police force. Chandler posted a $25,000.00 bond, as required by law.

While serving in the State Assembly, Alfred E. Smith had earlier led a bitter fight against the formation of state police. In 1918, Smith defeated Governor Whitman in the Gubernatorial election. During his inaugural address, Smith recommended the abolishment of the State Police. He felt there was no justification for their existence as the return to the state was not commensurate with the cost. He recommended they be attached to the office of the Attorney General and placed under his control. Superintendent Chandler met with the Governor and succeeded in changing his mind. This was done through accurate documentation of expenses versus revenues received, from arrests with conviction records and letters of support from a multitude of rural organizations. Smith became completely supportive during the strikes of 1919 when the state police quelled major rioting throughout the state with no additional cost to the state. In the past, the National Guard at great expense was activated to quell strikes and rioting.

(Justice For All) (History of NYSP)

COMMITTEE FOR STATE POLICE

LEGAL COMMITTEE

Hon. Henry L. Stimson   Hon. Wm. Church

EXECUTIVE COMMITTEE

Dr. Lewis Rutherford Morris,   William T. Hornaday,   Edwin G. Merrill,
  Chairman   Vice-Chairman   Treas
Richard Warren Barrett   Benjamin B. Lawrence   Frederic R. Couder
Oswald G. Villard   Tomkins McIlvaine   Robert L. Bacon
Edwin G. Merrill   Miss M. Moyca Newell   Charles Elliot Warr
William C. Le Gendre   Edwin O. Holter   H. Lindley Hosford
Henry Marquand   Frederick H. Allen   Miss Katherine Ma
Frank R. Chambers   Theodore Douglas Robinson   William Jay Schieff
                                 W. Newton Giles

Dr. Lyman Abbott   W. P. Capes   F. C. Fay
Charles C. Adams   F. L. Carlisle   Joseph E. Fell
I. Reynolds Adriance   Francis M. Carpenter   John G. Ferres
C. L. Andrus   Lewis G. Carpenter   Dr. Albert Warren
Charles Adsit   Maurice J. Carr   M. L. Fisher
John G. Agar   Louis P. Church   Lewis A. Foote
Richard Aldrich   C. W. Clapper   E. R. Ford
Edward D. Appleton   George G. Clarabut   A. E. Foster
Dr. S. T. Armstrong   C. K. Clark   Northrup Fowler
C. W. H. Arnold   James L. Clark   William K. Frank
Henry D. Babcock   M. Eugene Clark   Allen B. Fraser
Louis L. Babcock   William H. Clark   Samuel Fraser
Dr. Hugh P. Baker   H. W. Clarke   Dr. James L. Fuller
Anson Baldwin   A. T. Clearwater   William Giblin
Edward R. Baldwin   Henry J. Cochran   Newton W. Giles
LeRoy W. Baldwin   Stephen W. Collins   Clayton E. Gill
J. F. Bargfrede   Richard C. Colt   Anson C. Goodyear
Eugene F. Barnes   Charles G. Colyer   Madison Grant
Thomas W. Barrett   Samuel S. Conover   R. P. Grant
Harry W. Barnard   Herbert E. Cook   Niel Gray, Jr.
Walter J. Barrows   James Fennimore Cooper   Gen. Francis V. Gr
Curtis J. Beard   F. W. Crandall   A. W. Gregory
J. E. Beardsley   John D. Crimmins   John H. Gregory
Samuel H. Beach   George A. Crocker, Jr.   E. Morgan Griffin
Gerard Beekman   David Cromwell   H. H. Grimm
Imlay Benet   Mrs. Ernest Crosby   George Bird Grinne
Charles H. Betts   Dr. W. L. Cuddeback   Frederick P. Hall
Charles W. Bingham   Dr. C. M. Culver   Myron S. Hall
Charles H. Bissikummer   S. R. Cunningham   Charles N. Harris
Miss Anne W. Booth   James G. Cutler   R. E. Haven
Frederick Boschen   Miss Elisabeth Cutting   Edward H. Hall
F. A. Bosworth   Churchill H. Cutting   R. W. Hayes
Irving G. Botsford   Leonard Dakin   F. R. Hazard
Arthur F. Bouton   Louis J. Davis   J. H. Heim
C. W. Bower   Howard Davison   A. J. Hemphill
Gen. Oliver B. Bridgman   I. Francis Day   J. H. Herzog
F. E. Bridges   William A. Day   Mrs. G. D. Hewitt
Merritt Bridges   Dr. F. T. De Lano   Nathan T. Hewitt
Philip J. Britt   Kirk B. De Lano   Mrs. Albert H. Hild
Russell Brittingham   Warren Delano   Charles D. Hilles
B. Cook Broadfoot   W. I. Dey   Anton G. Hodenpyl
Charles T. Brockway   J. B. Deyoe   A. M. Holden
Franklin Q. Brown   Herbert Lowell Dillon   Mrs. Henry Osgood
James E. Brown   William B. Dinsmore   John S. Holloran
John H. Brown   R. J. Donahue   M. H. Hoover
Lathrop Brown   Robert Arthur Downey   Charles V. Hopkins
Thomas Brown   Augustus S. Downing   Daniel M. Hopping
Wilbur F. Brown   Harold K. Downing   Ralph S. Hosmer
S. S. Bullions   H. W. Dunlap   C. E. Housel
Rt. Rev. Frederick Burgess   B. C. Durland   Frank E. Howe
C. C. Burns   Edmund Dwight   William L. Howland
Robert M. Bush   Gen. George Dyer   F. J. Humphrey
Nicholas Murray Butler   J. M. Edwards   A. R. Hunt
H. James Cadwell   George W. Fairchild   Thomas Hunt
Farnum Caird   B. H. Fancher   Carry T. Hutchinson
W. E. Candee   Jacob S. Farlee   J. C. Hutchinson

5

Fred W. Hyde
Grenville M. Ingalsbe
C. E. Inman
Charles O. Ireland
William S. Irish
S. S. Jamieson
Dana L. Jewell
C. S. Johnson
John H. Johnson
F. M. Johnston
Otto H. Kahn
V. P. Kennedy
William Winthrop Kent
Franklin B. Kirkbride
Ralph W. Kirby
G. W. Knowlton
Charles E. Knox
Francis H. Lamon
Rev. Lewis Lampman
J. C. Lawrence
Michael A. Leahy
Charles W. Lee
William E. Leffingwell
V. A. Lersner
Herman Livingston
Arthur W. Loasby
William J. Lovejoy
Mrs. Seth Low
Arthur A. C. Luders
F. E. Lyford
Gard. T. Lyon
George L. Lyon
William K. Lyon
Thomas McCave
C. A. McCreery
A. J. McGrath
James McKee
William McNair
P. R. McPhail
Alrick H. Man
Albert Manning
W. H. Manning
Alfred E. Marling
Joseph M. Marrone
H. S. Marvin
L. G. Mattison
D. Irving Mead
Joseph H. Mead
S. E. Medbery
F. H. Meeker
John W. Mellen
Howard C. Miller
John W. Miller
Frederick Franklin Moon
F. L. Moore
Luther W. Mott
David Muirhead
William Muldoon
H. V. Mynderse
Richard H. Nelson
Alfred H. Newburger
C. J. Obermayer
Dudley Olcott
Rt. Rev. Charles Tyler Olmsted
Theodore F. Olmsted
F. G. Olp

Samuel Hanson Ordway
Henry Fairfield Osborn
Howard Opdyke
H. M. Painter
H. H. Parish
A. J. Parsons
J. B. Pease
F. W. Peck
George L. Peck
J. Marshall Perley
William H. Peters
Dr. Frederick Peterson
B. F. Petheram
H. F. Phelps
Jordan Philip
Lee F. Philips
James P. Pitcher
W. G. Pollard
Anson A. Potter
John Craig Powers
Arthur S. Pratt
Wm. Ross Proctor
John J. Pulleyn
Howard M. Quint
W. D. Race
deLancey Rankin
Blake S. Raplee
Major Latham G. Reed
Walter C. Reid
James Adger Reynolds
Dr. Rush Rhees
Adelbert P. Rich
Theodore Douglas Robinson
A. F. Robson
Col. Archibald Rogers
Charles B. Rogers
A. L. Rohrer
William J. Roome
Franklin D. Roosevelt
W. Scott Root
H. B. Rundall
O. N. Rushworth
William Cary Sanger
C. Royce Sawyer
J. Louis Schaefer
Mortimer Schiff
Jacob Gould Schurman
Miss Louisa Lee Schuyler
Montgomery Schuyler
Gen. William H. Seward
F. S. Sexton
Dr. Wm. T. Shanahan
J. O. Sheldon
T. M. Skivington
Adon N. Smith
Charles Smith
Dean Smith
Frank L. Smith
H. P. Smith
John Smith
R. M. Smith
W. E. Smith
B. E. Smythe
Alexander B. Snyder
J. Stanley-Brown
Edwin Allen Stebbins
William M. Stephans

Mark D. Stiles
Giles M. Stilwell
E. B. Sterling
H. R. Stratemeier
John L. Strickland
M. W. Stryker
Darrell D. Sully
Richard Sutro
John T. Symes
Lawrence M. Symmes
Horace S. Taber
W. I. Taber
John Tatlock
John B. Taylor
H. A. Tellier
L. E. Terry
Bert H. Terwilliger
J. L. Thayer
Mrs. Frederick F. Thompson
D. W. Tomlinson
B. Tompkins
Ray Tompkins
G. T. Townsend
W. S. Truman
Paul Tuckerman
William J. Tully
Robert C. Turnbull
S. G. H. Turner
P. A. Twichell
George Underwood
L. K. Vail
Thomas Vail
T. I. Van Antwerp
Dr. Albert Vander Veer
Irving G. Vann
Eugene A. Van Nest
Henri J. Van Zelm
Calvin P. H. Vary
Mrs. Henry Villard
Oswald G. Villard
E. B. Vreeland
J. Mayhew Wainwright
Alexander Walker
Commodore A. V. Wadhams
Major Wm. Austin Wadsworth
Col. Charles Elliot Warren
Benjamin L. Webb
B. J. Wells
Edward Wells
Frank L. White
George H. White
Gilbert C. White
Henry J. Whitehouse
George Whitman
Geo. W. Wickersham
Ansley Wilcox
G. B. Williams
Roger B. Williams
T. C. Williams
G. R. Wilsdon
F. R. Winant
Newell B. Woodworth
I. E. Worden
Benjamin J. Worman
Charles S. Wright
C. T. Wright
Wm. P. Youngs

CHAPTER THREE
GEORGE FLETCHER CHANDLER
FIRST SUPERINTENDENT

Governor Charles S. Whitman's selection of George Fletcher Chandler, as his first superintendent, was more by design than chance. They were lifelong friends having shared quarters while both attended college in New York City many years earlier. Whitman was aware of Chandler's forthrightness, his sense of fair play and military background. He also knew that his high ideals could withstand the pressures of political and social influence in order to move this new creation in a direction to meet the needs of the citizens of New York State, particularly the rural areas. When summoned to

Albany, N.Y. by Governor Whitman in late April 1917, Chandler was unaware of the establishment of a state constabulary. Governor Whitman asked him to look over the proposed legislation with its appropriations and make his recommendations as to what kind of organization it should be. After discussing his ideas with the governor, Whitman looked at him and said " Chandler, you're the man I want to organize this new force". Chandler initially declined, as he wanted to join his National Guard unit for service in the war. Several days later, he was again summoned to Albany to attend a luncheon that included Colonel Theodore Roosevelt, Senator Douglas Robinson, Major General Wotherspoon, Major Frank Hoppin and Governor & Mrs. Whitman. Roosevelt wanted to organize a division to fight in the great war, but had been spurned by Washington.

Whitman announced that under the Militia Act of the State of New York, he would grant Roosevelt authority to raise a division for the purposes of war. Delighted, Roosevelt told General Wotherspoon that he would be his chief of staff and later turned to Chandler and told him that if he organized a constabulary, he would request its assignment to him making Chandler his Chief of Cavalry. Chandler accepted the appointment at once and was confirmed by the senate on May 2, 1917. As it turned out, Roosevelt could not pass a required physical examination and was told by Washington D.C. that even if he raised a division, it would not be accepted for duty. Chandler now found himself with a commission as Superintendent of State Police and an appropriation of $500,000.00 to implement the new constabulary. On May 6, 1917, he traveled to Pennsylvania where he consulted with Major John Groome, the Superintendent of the Pennsylvania State Police viewing their organization and methods. He then traveled to Ottawa, Canada where he studied the organization of the Royal Northwest Mounted Patrol. Upon his return to Albany N.Y., he found that political pressures had mounted to an unacceptable level in an effort to influence the organizing of the new force. He immediately tendered his resignation, but Governor Whitman refused to accept it, quickly putting an end to all outside interference.

George Fletcher Chandler was born December 13, 1872 at Clyde, N.Y., the son of a Methodist minister. He spent his early childhood in Lockport, N.Y. where his father was pastor of the First Methodist Episcopal Church. He was educated at Syracuse University from 1890 to 1892 and attended Columbia University (College of Physicians & Surgeons) Medical School graduating in 1895.

The standards and ideals Chandler established are still the cornerstone of the State Troopers. The horse patrol days are long gone, but the original style of uniform is still in use. Chandler introduced the herringbone style parking at the 1917 State Fair. This allowed maximum use of space for parking and easy in and out access. Chandler also determined that his troopers would carry their firearm on the outside of the uniform contrary to established methods of the time.

His military training began, when he enlisted as a 1st Lieutenant in the 10th New York Infantry, as an assistant surgeon. He later served as a Major of the 1st New York Provisional Brigade during the Mexican border skirmishes of 1916. He served as the first State Police Superintendent from May 2, 1917 to November 30, 1923 resigning to return to the practice of medicine in the Kingston, N.Y. area, where he spent most of his life. He   died on November 6, 1964.

CHAPTER FOUR
TROOPER APPLICANT
REQUIREMENTS

Superintendent George F. Chandler established the following standards in 1917.

A citizen of the United States
Pass a physical examination
Pass a mental examination
Be of good moral character
Between ages 21 & 40
Height not less than 5'8" in bare feet
Weigh not less than 140 lbs. Stripped
Honorable discharge from Army, Navy, Marine Corp or National Guard
(1924 Annual Reports)

In 1931, an examination was scheduled with over 4500 applications received. This was due to economic conditions of the time. To bring this number down to a workable figure, Superintendent John Warner raised the height requirement from 5'8" to 5'10".

In spite of this change, 1500 applications were received with only twenty-five applicants appointed.

(1931 Annual Reports – PG 5)

On March 10, 1938, the State Court of Appeals ruled that selection of state police candidates would be made on a strictly competitive basis. The ruling held that the Superintendent of State Police must conduct competitive examinations. Previous practices required applicants to be citizens between 21 and 40 years of age; able to ride a horse; of sound mind and character. He must pass a rigid physical and mental examination based on the superintendent's standards. A written intelligence examination and oral interview to ascertain ability to reason, judgment, quality of language, attention to detail, self reliance, appearance and manner.

CHAPTER FIVE
THE FIRST EXAMINATIONS

The first examination was given to 420 candidates that appeared from applications on file that numbered 1592. The examination was given at the executive chamber, Albany, New York on June 11, 1917 to fill 232 allotted positions. Only 168 passed. A second examination was given on July 2, 1917 to 512 candidates that appeared from a list of 825. Only 62 passed. Governor Whitman, Major Chandler and the Civil Service Commission were present in an advisory capacity.

Many applicants were eliminated if they had no horsemanship experience. The examination was a practical, written examination. Those candidates that passed the written exam were then examined for physical defects. Major Chandler personally conducted each physical examination. Candidates were then required to write a 200-word letter to ascertain if they could write legibly, were imaginative and were able to express themselves. This was followed by a three-minute psychological test on printed-paper and a memory test where 30 objects were placed on a table and after a 3-minute study; the candidate was required to write down 20 of the objects. A few practical questions about the horse and his care concluded the examination.

Exam Date	Applications	Appeared	Failed Physical/Mental		Passed
June 11, 1917	1592	420	146	106	168
July 2, 1917	825	542	76	204	62
Oct 8, 1917	730	108	28	40	41
April 25, 1918	420	251	58	148	45
	3567	1322	508	498	316

FIRST TROOPER EXAMINATION

This is believed to have been the original test given to become a trooper authorized by Major Chandler in June 1917. The main purpose was to determine if an applicant could read, write and comprehend complicated instructions:

With your pencil make a dot over any one of these letters f g h

And a comma after the longest of these words; boy   mother   girl, then if

Christmas comes in March; make a cross right here _____ but if not pass

Along to the next question and tell where the sun rises _____ . If you believe

That Edison discovered America cross out what you just wrote, but if it was

Someone else, put in a number to complete the sentence: "a horse has _____

Feet." Write, "yes" no matter whether China is in Africa or not _____ and then

Give a wrong answer to this question: "how many days are there in the week.

_____ write any letter except g just after this comma, _____ and then write

"no" if 2 times 5 are 10 _____ . Now, if Tuesday comes after Monday, make two

Crosses here _____, but if not, make a circle here _____, or else a square here

_____. Be sure to make three crosses between these two names of boys George

_____ Henry. Notice these two numbers 3. 5. If iron is heavier than water, write

The larger number here _____ but if iron is lighter write the smaller number

Here _____. Show by a cross-when the nights are longer: in summer _____ or in

Winter _____ give the correct answer to this question: "does water run

Uphill?" _____ and repeat the answer here _____. Do nothing here 5 x 7 is _____

Unless you skipped the preceding question; but write the first letter of your

First name and the last letter of your last name at the end of this line _____.

CHAPTER SIX
ORIGINAL ELIGIBLE LIST FOR TROOPER APPOINTMENTS – 1917

The following data was obtained from documentation researched by Winfield W. Robinson (Troop "A" Commander 1918 To 1944)

Robinson indicated that he made copies of the eligible lists of the first two trooper examinations as they were reported in various newspapers. In many instances, names were incorrectly spelled and many initials were incorrect. However, it was the best that could be had with few exceptions. Robinson believed that all the men listed accepted appointments. Robinson very much doubted that the Division of State Police had any such records because they were destroyed by fire.

On January 29, 1925, The Department of State Police Headquarters was located on the second floor of the five story Wooster Building, South Pearl Street, Albany, N.Y. A rapidly moving fire destroyed the entire building with all state police records and photographs being destroyed. Staff were fortune to get out of the building without injury.

There were a number of men in Troop "G" at Camp Newayo whose name did not appear on either list. Robinson believed that when headquarters prepared a list of appointments, they found an insufficient number eligible for appointment. He believed the examination papers of previously rejected applicants were re-evaluated and approved for appointment.

The first group, 23 men that included Robinson were appointed in the middle of June 1917. The first big group arrived at camp On July 2nd or 3rd with the last group arriving on July 10th.

In May 1917, Superintendent Chandler appointed his headquarters staff as follows:

Barbour, Percy E.	Deputy Superintendent	
Dutton, George P.	Sergeant Major (Chief Clerk)	
Jones, James C.	Sergeant (Clerk)	
Beagle, Stanley F.	Corporal (Stenographer)	

In June 1917, Chandler appointed his officers:

Linn, Willis	Captain	"Troop A"
Warner, John A.	Lieutenant	"Troop A"
Barnes, Hamilton H.	Captain	"Troop D"
Meachum, J.F.S.	Lieutenant	"Troop D"
Rosboro, Herbert G.	Captain	"Troop G"
Gleason, Andrew H.	Lieutenant	"Troop G"
Richman, Ray D.	Captain	"Troop K"
Starks, Howard H.	Lieutenant	"Troop K"

Eligible List From The First Examination Held June 14, 1917

Alesie, Thomas A.	Rochester, NY
Allen, George B.	Manhattan, NY
Allen, U.B.	Evans Mills, NY
Arganza, Anthony	Manhattan, NY
Avery, Herman V.	Ashokan, NY
Barnes, F.L.	Syracuse, NY
Bauer, Clarence	Erie, Pa.
Belknap, Leslie H.	Albany, NY
Benedict, J.H.	Syracuse, NY
Bennett, W.J.	Poughkeepsie, NY
Bortz, James L. ("A" Saddler)	Trumansburg, NY
Boyce, Arthur F.	Manhattan, NY
Boyce, Burton	West Shokan, NY
Bray, William A.	Manhattan, NY
Bracebridge, Sanford	Canajoharie, NY
Brennan, J.M.	Alexandria Bay, NY
Broadfield, Arthur P.	Manhattan, NY
Brown, Ralph D.	Bolton Landing, NY
Browne, James V.	Yonkers, NY
Buckley, D.N.	Lincolndale, NY
Burke, Peter	Port Carbon, Pa.
Byk, Hirsch	Manhattan, NY
Campbell, F.H.	Manhattan, NY
Carlin, J.D.	Albany, NY
Carner, George W.	Rochester, NY
Cashin, W.D.	Kingston, NY
Cashion, William J.	Glens Falls, NY
Chrisman, George F.	Syracuse, NY
Colligan, Joseph P.	Manhattan, NY
Corcoran, M.A.	Brooklyn, NY

Costine, N.B.	Bridgeport, Ct.
Croadsdale, Walter	Oswego, NY
Crowell, Elmer B.	Syracuse, NY
Cruger, William H.	Manhattan, NY
Culver, Charles H.	Manhattan, NY
Decker, D.D.	Buffalo, NY
Defreest, Halbert L.	Watervaliet, NY
Degraff, R.A.	Kingston, NY
Delaney, L.E.	Albany, NY
Delmont, A. C.	Manhattan, NY
Derouche, A.H.	Rochester, NY
Donnelly, Charles F.	Albany, NY
Duff, John E.	Manhattan, NY
Durfee, Ralph	Millerton, NY
Edison, J.P.	Manhattan, NY
Erickson, Edwin R.	Circleville, NY
Ey, Everett H.	Buffalo, NY
Fahnkow, William (K Saddler)	Manhattan, NY
Fellows, Leo D.	Rochester, NY
Fox, Daniel E.	Fort Plain, NY
Flynn, James J.	Manhattan, NY
Fulton, William H.	Waterford, NY
Gaddis, James J.	Lake Katrine, NY
George, Walter	Rochester, NY
Gillece, J.H.	Manhattan, NY
Goetzman, Benjamin	Sodus, NY
Goodale, G.W.	Cortland, NY
Gorenflo, Herman H.	Elma, NY
Greene, Charles O.	Rochester, NY
Gunn, Henry E.	Rochester, NY
Gunner, H.O.	Manhattan, NY
Harms, Edward F.	Wellsville, NY
Hebron, F.F.	Manhattan, NY
Heim, Edward F.	New Brighton, NY
Hickey, Francis M.	Stillwater, NY
Hopkins, John A.	Rochester, NY
Hovaney, Peter	Yonkers, NY
Horvatt, Michael	Binghamton, NY
Husted, E.G.	South Cairo, NY
Jensen, Frank	Brooklyn, NY
Jones, W.H.	Schenectedy, NY
Keating, A.A.	Manhattan, NY
Kelly, R.J.	Manhattan, NY
King, Floyd W.	Rochester, NY
Knight, Paul	Schenectedy, NY
Lamb, John J.	Brooklyn, NY
Lansing, W.H.	Amsterdam, NY
Lengman, Nelson E.	Rochester, NY
Levine, J.T.	Mechanicsville, NY

Lord, N.C.	Manhattan, NY
Luscenberg, G.J.	Manhattan, NY
Magilton, Frank M.	Albany, NY
Marquart, Alfred	Rochester, NY
Matter, William	Brooklyn, NY
Mccreedie, W.M.	Albany, NY
Mcdougal, Harry	Scotia, NY
Mcguire, J.E.	Yonkers, NY
Mcmullen, C.A.	Buffalo, NY
Mcnally, Edward F.	Bath, NY
Mcquade, Thomas	Albany, NY
Meyer, R.A.	Brooklyn, NY
Miraglia, E.J.	Perth Amboy, NJ.
Moe, Clarence T.	Ashokan, NY
Needham, John	Albany, NY
Noehlau, F.M.	Buffalo, NY
O'melia, Charles H.("G"Saddler)	St. Johnsville, NY
Ottman, John R.	Rochester, NY
Panzlau, Rudolph H.	Rochester, NY
Phillips, R.K.	Brooklyn, NY
Price, John W.C.	Albany, NY
Rafferty, George	Kingston, NY
Rausch, Joseph C.	Albany, NY
Reilly, R.F.	Bennington, Vt.
Risely, J.H.	Glens Falls, NY
Robinson, Winfield W.	Ossining, NY
Rogers, M.R.	Manhattan, NY
Romkey, Arthur B.	Manhattan, NY
Runser, Joseph M.	Buffalo, NY
Runt, E.J.	Rome, NY
Ryan, W.J.	Brooklyn, NY
Salzman, C.S.	Manhattan, NY
Schneider, W.H.	West Point, NY
Schremp, Theodore A.	Utica, NY
Sharrott, H.S.	Manhattan, NY
Sheehan, Edward J.	Amsterdam, NY
Sheehan, John A.	Albany, NY
Skiff, James N.	New Rochelle, NY
Smith, Henry R.	Sheridan, NY
Steinmiller, Ray C.	Rochester, NY
Storr, C.J.	Bridgeport, Ct.
Stout, Orrie W. (Ora F.)	Rochester, NY
Strictland, J.O.	Brooklyn, NY
Striegel, Robert F.	Buffalo, NY
Sullivan, Michael	Yonkers, NY
Townsend, Gus	Buffalo, NY
Walton, John F.	Connecticut
Wernesbach, P.S.	Brooklyn, NY
Wexler, Isador	Brooklyn, NY

Albert S. Kurek - NYSP Retired

Whalen, J.E.	Manhattan, NY
Wilson, James E.	Manhattan, NY
Zeh, Frank L.	Schoharie, NY

Eligible List From The Second Exam Held July 3, 1917:

Almar, J.G.	Niverville, NY
Baldwin, E.H.	Syracuse, NY
Barnes, R.W.	Syracuse, NY
Bishop, Clarence W.	Rochester, NY
Boyce, K.D.	Kingston, NY
Broadfield, Charles J.	Manhattan, NY
Brophy, C.W.	Kingston, NY
Brown, L.I.	Mt. Vernon, NY
Brown, O.A.	Vienna, NY
Butler, Arthur E.	Syracuse, NY
Cappon, Martin J.	Rochester, NY
Casey, C.M.	Tully, NY
Cooper, John H.	Troy, NY
Coots, Henry H.	Middletown, NY
Corr, John W. ("D"Blacksmith)	Troy, NY
Cullen, W. James	Brooklyn, NY
Daley, Dennis B.	Glens Falls, NY
Devine, Frank E.	Amsterdam, NY
Doane, Harlow ("A" Blacksmith)	Gouvernor, NY
Dougherty, J.W.	Manhattan, NY
Doyle, William A.	Albany, NY
Dubois, Kenneth B.	Albany, NY
Dumka, G.L.	Alexandria Bay, NY
Dunn, H.L.	Dewitt, NY
Ebel, F.W.	Woodhaven, NY
Farnum, Frank J.	Oswego, NY
Freeman, Samuel	Manhattan, NY
Forst, Henry	Kingston, NY
George, William J.	Macedon, NY
Gibbs, Warren A.	Rochester, NY
Griffin, Samuel	Geneseo, NY
Guerin, Emmet L.	Rochester, NY
Granning, George L.	Rochester, NY
Granville, E.A.	Rochester, NY
Hames G.C.	Albany, NY
Henry, William H.	Rochester, NY
Herrick, Harold C.	Albany, NY
Hupman, Byron E.	Whitehall, NY
Hussey, Nicholas J.	Albany, NY
Jones, H.W.	Albany, NY

14

Karchar, D.	Syracuse, NY
Keeley, John M.	Geneseo, NY
Kelly, Robert A.	Albany, NY
Kelsey, Gordon E.	Comstock, NY
King, Robert A.	Rochester, NY
Klein, Arthur F.	Buffalo, NY
Leddy, James V.	Manhattan, NY
Linney, W.M.	Binghamton, NY
Linscott, Earl P.	Rochester, NY
Lockman, Jacob B.	Albany, NY
Maguire, Charles F.	Rochester, NY
Maloy, William J.	Rochester, NY
Manhold, William P.	Rochester, NY
Mcgarvey, Francis S.	Manhattan, NY
Mcgovern, Mark N.	Catskill, NY
Mcgrath, Stephen (G" Blacksmith)	Troy, NY
Mcvey, S.	Manhattan, NY
Meyers, William F.	Meriden, NY
Moore, Albert B.	Schenectedy, NY
Morris, Richard William	Albany, NY
Murphy, ("K" Blacksmith)	New York, NY
Nagell, Harold J.	Rochester, NY
Nelson, Raymond H.	Piffard, NY
Ohara, M.L.	Manhattan, NY
Parker, E.G.	Manhattan, NY
Piper, Glenn R.	Rochester, NY
Richter, Arthur W.	Amsterdam, NY
Robinson, Paul H.	Howes Cave, NY
Rooney, Peter	Manhattan, NY
Root, Lynn P.	Rochester, NY
Ryan, T.H.	Manhattan, NY
Salmon, David	Whitehall, NY
Schlansker, H.C.	Schenectedy, NY
Smith, Abram S.	Big Indian, NY
Snyder, Harry R.	Kingston, NY
Spiegel, Charles W.	Albany, NY
Stanwix, Anthony M.	Manhattan, NY
Starks, Ralph J.	Troy, NY
Stockfish, W.H.	Brooklyn, NY
Strassenberg, J.H.	Rochester, NY
Sundheim, G.M.	Manhattan, NY
Swarthout, H.W.	Milo, NY
Taylor, Alfred A.	Rochester, NY
Toole, Walter.E.	Geneseo, NY
Vanzandt, W. Kirby	Albany, NY
Voelker, Charles J.	Albany, NY
Voris, A.L.	Lewiston, NY
Warner, John J.	Amsterdam, NY
Webber, John E.	Kingston, NY

Welch, James G.	Manhattan, NY
Welter, G.E.	Syracuse, NY
Whitbeck, George E.	Rensselaer, NY
White, A.J.	Manhattan, NY
Wightwick, F.A.	Harrison, NY
Wynkoop, George A.	Albany, NY

CHAPTER SEVEN
EARLY TROOPER REQUIREMENTS

Many men entered the service with the idea that it was a glorified national guard unit especially favored by the governor for his private protection and special duty during the duration of World War I. When it dawned on them that the constabulary was to be a rural police force with no particular glory or romance, they dropped out.

Trooper enlistments were for two years. Resignations had to be approved by the superintendent in accordance with law. The trooper was a man who was able to swim, dive, ride a horse, drive a motor vehicle, knew the penal code, knew how to present evidence and be a good witness. He was physically perfect and fairly well educated in order to be able to make a good report. He required the courage to go anywhere and get the man he was after, even though the worst type criminal was armed or an insane man with a gun. He was absolutely honest, of good morals, a soldier and a gentleman.

Because of their high standards and training, varying high paying jobs were constantly being offered to the troopers. Many valuable men accepted these positions to their own advantage at great loss to the department. Troopers were on call 24 hours a day with an occasional twenty-four or forty eight-hour leave following an extended duty. Each trooper received two weeks vacation each year, almost always in the wintertime, when travel was slow. The basic trooper salary was $900.00 per year.

$7.00 a day per man covered every expense of the trooper. Troopers doing extra duty kept down the cost. Superintendent Chandler, a physician, personally conducted all physical examinations of troopers. Troopers with previous experience were utilized as mechanics in the care of motor vehicles and motorcycles. Troopers held in reserve at the barracks maintained the stables, cared for the horses, did lawn care, building cleaning, re-modeling and plumbing repairs.

(1919 NYSP Annual Reports)
(Captain Robinson Letter 5/28/57)

CHAPTER EIGHT
CAMP NEWAYO

Troop "D", First New York Cavalry, National Guard farm at Manlius, New York was selected, as the site for the mobilization and training of the first New York State Troopers. This was an ideal location because it was centrally located with pasturage, good water, buildings and railroad facilities. Enough tents were purchased from the army to accommodate the men. The farm was leased for a three-month period at a cost of $250.00. Training commenced on June 20, 1917 and continued through September 5, 1917. The farm was equipped with a state shooting range, which was of great benefit. Troopers drilled and trained during the day and studied law in the evening through addresses by lawyers, police officials and magistrates. Lecturers included Judge Alton B. Parker, Judge Ben V. Shove, Deputy Attorney General Edward G. Griffin and Inspector Cornelius F. Culhane, New York City Police School Director.

Officers appointed by Major Chandler conducted and supervised military drill and rifle instruction. Under the watchful eye of these officers, those who showed any inclination to flinch or quail were dismissed. Being appointed non-commissioned officers upon completion of training camp rewarded trainees who proved their ability.

On September 2, 1917, the Syracuse Post Standard published the following article.

"Two hundred thirty two troopers are being turned into one of the finest police organizations in the world at the Troop "D" Farm at Manlius, New York. During the last week in August, Miss M. Moyca Newell presented a silk cavalry guide-on to Captain Percy Barbour, the Camp Adjutant. Camp Newayo was named in her honor, as well as Miss Katherine Mayo, using a combination of the two names.

The uniform is distinctly military. The flare on the trousers is twice the size of the flare of a cavalryman. The tunic, blouse or coat has very wide skirts with pockets similar to the Canadian officers fashion, a snappy wide belt and a rolling collar, which exposes a purple tie, which is the squadron's official color. The men carry Winchester rifles and .45 caliber colt revolvers.

The best horses available were bought from the British Remount Commission at a cost of $150.00 per head delivered. The 250 untamed horses were received from Lathrop, Missouri and four weeks later, could go through any military maneuver or formation on command of the rider. The task of giving each horse a name was solved, when Major Chandler directed that each trooper name his mount. The only stipulation was that all horses would have names beginning with the initial letter of the troop to which they belonged. This proved practical, as horse on record would show at a glance what troop he was assigned. A an example, horses from Troop A were named America, Arrow, Abe, Adare, Troop D were named Doc, Dixie, Dude, Dooley, Troop G were named Gail, Ginger Golly, Gall and Troop K named Kick-in, Kentuck, Kop, and Krazy-Kat. Major Chandler's horse was named Purple after the squadron color.

Major Chandler had personally selected the horses including brood mares with the idea the department would raise there own future mounts. A short time after delivery of the horses to Camp Newayo, a colt was born to the amazement of the troopers. He was appropriately named "Gee Whiz". Governor Whitman upon inspection of the camp made the comment that this was the first time that he was aware of the state getting something for nothing."

The Troopers day consisted of constant drill, target practice, first aid, classes in law, procedure, and riding with and without saddles. Classroom instruction was given during evening hours.

First call was at 0:645 AM with reveille at 0:655 AM. Then it was off to the stables to feed their horses and stable chores. Breakfast was from 0:730 to 0:815 AM followed by roll call and close order drill on horseback. Lunch was from 12:00 Noon until 01:15 PM. Classes and review followed until 5:00 PM. Dinner was served at 05:45 PM with evenings spent tending to their equipment and classes in law with a bit of relaxation.

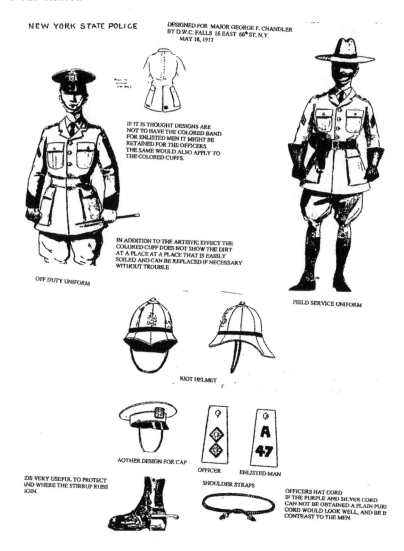

NEW YORK STATE POLICE

DESIGNED FOR MAJOR GEORGE F. CHANDLER
BY D.W.C. FALLS 16 EAST 60ᵗʰ ST. N.Y.
MAY 18, 1917

IF IT IS THOUGHT DESIGNS ARE
NOT TO HAVE THE COLORED BAND
FOR ENLISTED MEN IT MIGHT BE
RETAINED FOR THE OFFICERS
THE SAME WOULD ALSO APPLY TO
THE COLORED CUFFS.

IN ADDITION TO THE ARTISTIC EFFECT THE
COLORED CUFF DOES NOT SHOW THE DIRT
AT A PLACE AT A PLACE THAT IS EASILY
SOILED AND CAN BE REPLACED IF NECESSARY
WITHOUT TROUBLE

OFF DUTY UNIFORM

FIELD SERVICE UNIFORM

RIOT HELMET

AOTHER DESIGN FOR CAP

OFFICER   ENLISTED MAN

SHOULDER STRAPS

DS VERY USEFUL TO PROTECT
AND WHERE THE STIRRUP RUBS
iGIN.

OFFICERS HAT CORD
IF THE PURPLE AND SILVER CORD
CAN NOT BE OBTAINED A PLAIN PURI
CORD WOULD LOOK WELL, AND BE IN
CONTRAST TO THE MEN.

CHAPTER NINE
UNIFORM

The selection of uniform, its color and design were drawn up and selected by Major George F. Chandler. He felt there had to be a reason for the color of the uniform and came to the conclusion that white was usually employed to depict right, while black was the symbol of evil. He selected a cloth fabric that contained equal parts of white and black thread resulting in a neutral gray. It was the only cloth made in this way so Chandler had it patented. (The patent could not be confirmed.) He added a purple necktie because the color had never been used before and it distinguished the troopers from other police departments.

Because the design of the new uniform was so radical, as many as nineteen different firms bid and made samples for the uniform. None satisfied Chandler until finally, James Russell, owner of the Russell Uniform Company, 1600 Broadway, New York City said he could reproduce any design and did so in a day.

Troopers were measured and the uniforms manufactured. On July 6, 1917, a bill was submitted in an amount of $3,555.00 for 237 uniforms that included an extra pair of breeches. After delivery, a few troopers went into the City of Syracuse, N.Y. in the new uniforms. As it was wartime, several thousand troops were stationed in and around Syracuse. The soldiers including officers seeing the new uniform stood at attention and saluted thinking the troopers to be foreign officers.

The uniform coat had an open neck showing the gray flannel shirt above. It was tight fitted at the waistline, then widened to a full-skirted effect. The breeches had their greatest flair just above the knee being tight around the hips. They wore puttees or high-laced boots reaching almost to the knee and a wide brown leather belt with cartridge pockets. A bit of royal purple lended distinction to the uniform. In 1920, Chandler had black stripes added to the trousers and coat. He also directed that all state police correspondence be sent on gray color-coded paper so it could be distinguished from other correspondence.

Major Chandler also ordered that the revolver be carried outside the uniform. This was a first and radical idea in police practices, as police departments adhered to the practice of having their weapons concealed. He wanted the trooper to be able to draw his revolver instantly, if needed. This would place him on equal or an advantageous position with the criminal element.

A fourteen-pound knee length sheepskin coat was issued for winter and foul weather wear.

The Hat

The J.B. Stetson Company of Philadelphia, Pennsylvania having in excess of fifty years of experience was chosen to produce the hats for the troopers. A high crowned grey felt with a single purple band was selected. The purple band only used by the New York State Police instantly identified the wearer, as a New York State Trooper.

To maintain uniformity, all uniforms and equipment were provided by the state. Underwear were the only items that the individual trooper was required to purchase.

Troopers were issued, a riding crop, a .45 caliber colt revolver carried from a wide brown leather belt and a Winchester 30-30 rifle. The rifle was carried in a scabbard from the saddle, however this practice was discontinued for fear of it being stolen from an unattended mount. The riding crop was later discontinued replaced by the riot stick.

In 1920, Major Chandler introduced a service ribbon that was worn over the left breast pocket. It was of a deep purple color with a gray stripe one-quarter inch wide at one end denoting two years of service, the term of a trooper's enlistment. Every subsequent enlistment would result in the addition of another stripe.

Chandler further wanted every detail of the trooper uniform to be distinctive. Officers were identified with elongated silver, diamond shaped shoulder insignia, one for Lieutenant, two for Captain with Major being designated by an elongated gold colored insignia.

In January 1923, Several Assemblymen from Erie County initiated an effort for the troopers to wear a badge on the uniform. Chandler had considered an exposed badge while designing the uniform, but decided against it. Instead, troopers wore a bronze badge (collar ornament the size of a nickel) on their shirt collar that indicated the officers troop number and troop designation. This collar badge was always conspicuous with the coat on or off.

The popular McClelland military saddles were purchased from the Army and provided for each mount. Office furniture, bedding and miscellaneous necessary items were purchased from the New York State Prison Department where they were manufactured.

(Dawn Days of the State Police)
(1918, 1919 NYSP Annual Reports)
(Grey Riders, The Book)
(State Trooper Magazine September 1920)

CHAPTER TEN
FIRST TROOPER APPEARANCE

On September 1, 1917, a picked squad of the New York State Constabulary under the direction of Captain Hamilton Barnes made their first official public appearance in their new uniforms during a drill of mounted maneuvers that bespoke their fine training.

Five hundred farmers attended the farmer's picnic at Edwards Falls near Manlius, New York where the troopers gained the farmers admiration for their dash and vim during the drills.

On September 5, 1917, the troopers left Camp Newayo and moved to Syracuse, New York to police the state fair. This duty had previously been performed by about 100 members of the mounted New York City Police Department at a cost to the state of $5000.00. This would be the last time that all members of the New York State Police would work together, as one unit, at the same location, at the same time.

At the conclusion of the state fair, the troopers in four groups of fifty -eight headed on horseback to their respective assigned troop barracks. Troopers assigned to Troop "A" at Batavia, N.Y. traveled by rail so that they might arrive in time to police the Genesee County Fair held at Batavia.

The original troopers that trained at Camp Newayo are respectfully referred to as, "Campmen".

(Syracuse Times Union)
(1918 NYSP Annual Reports)

CHAPTER ELEVEN
ORGANIZATION AND INITIAL TROOP
HEADQUARTER LOCATIONS

Governor Charles Whitman appointed George Fletcher Chandler, as Superintendent of the new State Police Department after posting $25,000.00 bond, as required by the State Police Bill. His first task was to build a nucleus for the department. He succeeded in having fifty-one soldiers released from active duty with the Army that had passed the examination for appointment. His officers were selected from New York National Guard units of the state who were expert horsemen and disciplinarians with whom he had served on the Mexican border.

The following are the original officer appointments made by Major Chandler:

Deputy Superintendent – Captain Percy E. Barbour, 22nd Engineers

Troop "A" Headquarters – Dyke Skating Rink, Batavia, New York
Captain - Willis Linn, 1st NY Ambulance Company
Lieutenant – John A. Warner, 1st NY Cavalry

Troop "D" Headquarters - Valley House, Onondaga Valley, New York
Captain–Hamilton H. Barnes, 1st NY Cavalry
Lieutenant – J.F.S.Meachum, 1st NY Cavalry

Troop "G" Headquarters - Flynn Estate, Colonie, New York
Captain – Herbert G. Rosboro, 1st NY Cavalry
Lieutenant – Andrew H. Gleason, 1st NY Cavalry

Troop "K" Headquarters - Gedney Farms Estate, White Plains, New York
Captain – Ray D. Richman, 1st NY Ambulance Company
Lieutenant – Howard Starks, 1st NY Cavalry

Constabulary Headquarters were located at room 100, Capitol Building, Albany, New York and staffed by the superintendent, deputy superintendent and two stenographers.

The initial legislation provided for an allotment of 232 troopers.

Each troop consisted of a:

Captain at $1800.00 per year
Lieutenant at 1500.00 per year
First Sergeant at 1200.00 per year
Four Duty Sergeants at 1100.00 per year
Four Corporals at 950.00 per year
One Blacksmith at 950.00 per year
One Saddler at 950.00 per year
Forty-five Privates at 900.00 per year

Troop areas of responsibility from 1917 to 1921

Troop "A" area.
All counties west of a line from the east border of Wayne County continuing south along the west shore of Seneca Lake and south in a straight line from the south end of Seneca Lake to the Pennsylvania border.

Troop "D" area.
All counties east of the Troop "A" area bordered on the east by the western borders of Franklin, Herkimer, Otsego and Delaware Counties north to the Canadian border and south to the Pennsylvania State line.

Troop "G" area.
All counties east of the Troop "D" area bordered on the east by Vermont, Massachusetts and Connecticut State lines north to the Canadian border and south to a point across the center of Sullivan, Ulster and Duchess Counties.

Troop "K" area.

All of Long Island north to the southern border of the Troop "G" area bounded on the east by Connecticut and on the west by Pennsylvania and New Jersey.
(1918 NYSP Annual Reports)

CHAPTER TWELVE
RULES OF CONDUCT

Governor Charles Whitman approved the rules proposed by Major George F. Chandler for the governing and conduct of the department on June 3, 1917. Whitman intended to give the new State Police Department his personal attention, because he believed the people throughout the state would watch with great interest its formation and its work.

The department would be free of political influence. It was to be a department made up of men with brains, courage and tact. No bullies, ex- private detectives and emphatically, no users of alcohol would be retained. There was no place for a drinker in the department. The Governor desired to have competent, careful and intelligent men on the force. Officers who would be of service not only in times of trouble, but who would assist and accommodate citizens whenever and wherever possible and by their demeanor, impress people generally with their desire to be of assistance and service.

Legislation directed that it was the duty of the state police to prevent and detect crimes and apprehend criminals. Troopers were subject to the call of the Governor and were empowered to cooperate with any other department of the state or with local authorities. They had the power to arrest without a warrant any person committing or attempting to commit a crime in their presence or view, a breach of the peace or other violation of law. They were given the power to serve and execute arrest and search warrants anywhere in the state, when issued by proper authority and to exercise all the powers of Peace Officer of the State of New York. They shall not exercise their power within the limits of any city to suppress rioting or disorder except by direction of the Governor or upon request of the mayor of the city with approval of the Governor.

(Syracuse Post Standard-June 4, 1917)

In August 1917, the New York State Attorney General ruled that members of the New York State Police were exempt from military draft, because they were considered executive officers of the state.

(Syracuse Post Standard-August 25,1917)

The Committee once more desires to call attention to the bulletin issued by Major George F. Chandler, Superintendent, on November 1, 1917, for the guidance of his men:

A physician aims to save life and cure disease; a lawyer helps people out of trouble; a clergyman tries to make people better; a soldier fights for his country in time of war. These are fine professions, all of them. They are professions of service.

The service a State Trooper renders to his community is an auxiliary to all these, and his duty in a measure embraces the work of these four great professions.

You who wear the uniform of the State Troopers must be ready to render first aid pending the arrival of the doctor; you must maintain the law which the lawyer expounds; you must instruct people to do right, and, if the need arrives, you must fight.

You must have the confidence in yourself which comes from knowing you are a trained horseman, a good shot, and a judge of what is right and wrong in the matter of simple laws. . . .

Go about with the idea of helpfulness and a friendliness that wins the confidence of the people. Never permit a child to be afraid of you. . . .

Never hesitate to render assistance of any kind, and let nothing be too much trouble which you can do for the people you come in contact with.

Always be a gentleman, courteous, kind, gentle, fair, keep yourself clean and neat, you and your horse equally well groomed, stand erect, put snap and vigor into your movements. Avoid the appearance of lounging. Keep your mind calm and free from excitement. Do not be carried away by rumors but investigate every story and hear both sides before you believe it.

Remember that you represent the authority of the Governor, that you are an executive officer and a State official. Be proud of it, live up to it, work in harmony with your officers and the other troopers for the good of the service and for the honor of the great State of New York.

CHAPTER THIRTEEN
HORSE PATROL DAYS

Initial duty consisted of mounted patrols traveling in pairs, traveling 20 to 25 miles a day unless detained by court appearances or investigations. Patrols might be away from the barracks for a month or more depending on what they encountered.

A patrol itinerary was laid out prior to departure of the patrol with the home barracks apprised daily by either postcard or telephone where the patrol expected to be for the next 24 hours. When a complaint came in, the barracks having a fair idea where the patrol might be made contact through telephone operators in a grapevine system. The operators would contact subscribers asking them to keep an eye out for the gray riders.

This system of extended patrols involved traveling long round about routes during the first two years of the organization. Patrols followed one another a week apart. In this manner, the same trooper was seldom seen twice conveying the impression that the force was larger than it actually was. No one could be sure when a trooper would appear, but the certainty that one would, sooner or later had a moderating effect upon the rough elements, local bullies and wife beaters.

This system prevailed into 1919, when the county zone system was put into effect ending the extended patrol system. Under this plan, a pair of troopers were assigned to a single county making their headquarters at a hotel or rooming house. At the end of three months, the troopers would be replaced by another patrol and move to another county. The reasoning was that a man would do better work where he was not too well known.

When a trooper went on patrol, he mounted up in the back barracks yard, with a toothbrush in one saddlebag and an extra feed of oats for his horse in the other. He was completely on his own. He made his own decisions on all matters that he came in contact with. He rode the highways and byways, stopped to visit when and where he wanted to, stopped at farm houses for lunch and to feed and rest his horse and while there often solved the family problems. He acted, as a veterinary in caring for the farmers stock and in many cases took junior out to the barn to teach him the facts of life. In general, the trooper did everything he could to assist the people he came into contact with.

Passing through each of the villages and towns, local residents, unfamiliar with the trooper in uniform would give him the once over. A few unwise bullyboys would challenge his authority. They were quick to learn that lawlessness and criminal activity would no longer be tolerated. He would always contact the local telephone operator to make his presence known in the community and to learn if there were any complaints requiring his attention in the area.

The troopers were loyal to his job and one another. Using common sense, early troopers brought law and order to the rural area. Lawlessness no longer prevailed. They earned a reputation still enjoyed today by teaching respect for the law.

The horse was essential in the work of the state police, particularly in rioting, handling of large crowds and for patrolling in bad weather through isolated portions of farming areas.

In 1918, the troopers entered into a co-operative agreement with the American Horse Association and the American Jockey Club to improve the breed of the state police cavalry mounts. The Jockey Club placed several high-class stud horses at each troop headquarters. Troopers cared for and maintained these stud horses while in their care. Local farmers were able to take advantage of this high class breeding for a nominal fee. This resulted in no new mounts having to be purchased. Having no suitable pasture land, colts born in the troop were sent to Troop "K" at White Plains, N.Y. where in the fall of 1919, thirty colts were being cared for.

It would be interesting to determine just when law enforcement in the rural areas would have developed, if it were not for the creation of the state police. There had always been an office of County Sheriff and Town Constable both doing little, if any, law enforcement. It would appear that those offices became more active after the troopers started to patrol. Troopers were now available to support them, if needed during arrests either through their presence or through inference that they were coming to assist.

(1918 & 20 NYSP Annual Reports)

CHAPTER FOURTEEN
JOHN ADAMS WARNER – SECOND
SUPERINTENDENT – 1921 to 1943

John Adams Warner was born at Rochester, New York on September 17, 1886 the son of Rochester Architect J. Foster Warner. At four years of age, he started playing the piano becoming a child prodigy. At age 16, he was the organist at Christ Episcopal Church, Rochester, N.Y. After graduation from Harvard University in 1909, he traveled abroad studying in Paris, Vienna and Italy with Widor, Harold Bauer, Vladimir de Pachmann and Leopold Godowsky. Prior to his military enlistment, he was a renowned concert pianist at New York's Carnegie Hall and the Rochester Eastman Theatre. In 1934, he played a nationwide radio broadcast of a Schumann Concerto from WHAM radio, Rochester, N.Y. While assigned at Batavia, N.Y., he played the organ at the First Presbyterian Church and St. James Church and gave several recitals including one at the New York State School for the Blind. He served in the New York National Guard, Old Troop H, replaced by Troop F, 1st Cavalry serving on the Mexican border.

On June 5, 1926, he married Emily Josephine Smith, daughter of New York's Governor Alfred E. Smith at Albany, N.Y. Troopers from Batavia attending the reception were Captain Robinson, Lieutenant William George, Corporals George Tetley and John Bembuista, Troopers Donald Guerin, Harvey Gregg and Charles Stanton. Each of the six troops had a similar number as guests.

John Warner enlisted in the State Police on June 11, 1917 as a Lieutenant and was the fourth person sworn into the Department. His first assignment was as a Lieutenant at Batavia, N.Y. Promoted to Captain in 1918, he was assigned to Troop "K". His appointment as Superintendent came at the recommendation of Major Chandler and lasted until December 1943. He was a disciple of Major Chandler's and continued the operations of the department as laid out by Chandler.

In 1924, Warner raised the enlistment height standard for applicants from 5'8" To 5'10". This was done to attract long-term job oriented applicants. Most officers and non commissioned officers had been in the department since its inception. Only 30 % of the original force remained. The legislature in the meantime had authorized trooper manpower of 468 and gave a 10% salary increase to all that had been with the department since 1919, $60.00 for each reappointment plus $100.00 for each year of service up to 4 years.

In 1943, newly elected Governor Thomas E. Dewey felt the state police needed re-organizing and that leadership should be designated to younger, more energetic men. Although publicly lauding Warner, it was generally felt that Dewey was responsible for the transferring of popular Troop Commanders resulting in forced retirements with Warner pointed to as the bad guy. Warner found this distasteful, as these officers were his close personal friends from Camp Newayo days. He resigned his position taking a commission, as a Lieutenant Colonel in the US Army. He died on August 19, 1963 at Southampton, Long Island, N.Y.

1917-Major Chandler Captain Barbour

T. JAMES ROSBORO - ORIGINAL UNIFO

TROOP A - CAMP NEWAYO 1917 - WILLIS LINN - JOHN WARNER FRONT CENTER

BOOK II – TROOPERS IN WESTERN NEW YORK

CHAPTER FIFTEEN
THE TROOPERS ARE COMING

BATAVIA DAILY NEWS – AUGUST 16, 1917

Major George F. Chandler, of Kingston, N.Y., head of the New York State Troopers, as the State Constabulary was to be officially known, toured the Batavia locality, as well as the Hornell, Avon, Leroy, and Dansville areas, seeking a suitable location for a headquarters and troopers barracks to house the first state troopers in Western New York. Under consideration in Batavia was the Agricultural Park at the fair grounds, the Brisbane House and Barn, the West End Hotel and the Dyke Skating Rink. The Dyke Rink was looked at favorably, as there was room on the ground floor for the horses under the skating floor and the main floor could be readily converted to sleeping and living quarters with administrative offices in the front. Fred B. Parker, a State Fair Commissioner from Batavia, N.Y. along with the Chamber of Commerce led by President Edward H. Leadley, Messers Lou Wiard, Crane, Gubb and Torrance were successful in their active pursuit for the location of the constabulary in Batavia. Dyke Rink owners Samuel J. Houseknecht and Elmer J. Cook agreed to an option taken for the troopers that had been prepared by Attorney Albert J. Waterman on behalf of the Chamber. On August 17, 1917, Major Chandler advised the Chamber of Commerce of his selection of Batavia, as his troop headquarters.

On January 9, 1933, Fred B. Parker provided the following information that was printed in the Batavia Daily News.

During the summer of 1917, I was a Commissioner with the State Fair Commission and had conversed with Major Chandler on several occasions. During one of those conversations, I asked where the troops were to be located? He mentioned several locations one being Western New York. He said that he had requests from Hornell and Avon, with Captain Linn who would be the Captain of Troop "A" being partial to Avon. I asked "what about Batavia"? His reply was that Batavia looked good geographically, but he had no request from there. Well major, I replied, you have one now. I am sure the Batavia Chamber of Commerce will invite you to Batavia. When are you ready to inspect? He said he had an appointment at Hornell for 4 o'clock the next day. I replied "why not come to Batavia tomorrow morning". We will show you Batavia and take you to Attica where you can catch an Erie train arriving at Hornell in time for your appointment. He agreed so I caught the first train home and along with the Chamber of Commerce, met that evening. We arranged to show Major Chandler the West End Hotel, the Fair Grounds Buildings and the East Main Street Skating Rink. The major arrived the next morning and was shown the three sites. He said the rink property had the earmarks of a barracks. We then had lunch at the Batavia Club. Chandler said he was committed to Hornell for a tour later that day, but due to lack of transportation, could not leave there until the next day. With that, I said, that would be an unfortunate condition, If you had to ship men and horses out in a hurry call. Lou Wiard with his perpetual pep said, Major, I will drive you to Hornell by way of Avon. You can look over both places and I will return you to Batavia in time to get a train for Syracuse tonight. The Major gladly accepted and was driven to Hornell by way of Avon. The next day, Wiard and I called on Chandler at Manlius, N.Y. He made us an informal proposition that was immediately approved by the Chamber of Commerce. The Major said he would make a final decision within three days and advise us. Captain Linn protested on a contract with Batavia arguing for Avon. A few days later, Lou Wiard obtained a signed agreement from Chandler and Troop "A" came to Batavia to make their home. .

On August 18, 1917, the Batavia Daily News Headlines read " STATE MOUNTED TROOPERS ARE COMING TO BATAVIA" - This City to be Headquarters of Western Division. The location of the Troop in Batavia, N.Y. means that at least 58 men none of whose salary is less than $1000.00, will take up residence here, many with their families. Much of the purchasing for troopers will be done in Batavia as well as feed and supplies for the 58 or more horses.

Troopers are chosen not only for their fearlessness, but because they represent a high type of manly Americanism. Each trooper is a gentleman and Is bound to be a credit to Batavia.

The Dyke Skating Rink was selected, as the site for the headquarters. The building is 210 feet long by 75 feet wide, the narrow side facing north. It was built for a skating rink with the rink floor 180 feet by 75 feet. In front of the skating hall are several rooms. On the east side are the skate room, check room and ladies room. On the west side are the kitchen, dining room and men's room. Beneath is a basement, which rises 14 feet above the ground. The highest point in the roof is about 36 feet from the ground.

In remodeling, about half the skating hall will be cut off. A partition will be erected leaving a gymnasium to the south that will measure about 75 by 60 feet. An equal amount of space, to the north will be divided by a partition erected at right angles and dividing the north half in two equal parts. In turn, partitions will be built which will give a bedroom for every eight troopers and a dining hall and kitchen. The rooms now used for skates and checks will be turned into shower rooms and officers quarters. There is a furnace in the basement with a second furnace to be added. The horses will be quartered in the basement requiring little remodeling.

On August 24,1917, Major Chandler sent the following telegram to Batavia Industrial Commissoner Wiard, "Lease signed and forwarded to you". Architect advised to communicate with you at once for immediate action. In reply, Wiard sent the following: "Local architect already engaged as per arrangement, plans practically completed, figures ready early next week and will start on September 1st. Expect to be completed on September 30th."

The troopers arrived by rail on September 17,1917 for duty at the Genesee County Fair at Exposition Park. Arriving at 3:18 PM, at the Central Station, the troopers were greeted by Chamber of Commerce President Leadley and Secretary Crane, Industrial Commissioner Wiard and several other citizens. The train backed to the siding east of Ellicott Street near the freight house where it took more than an hour to unload horses and equipment. At about 5:15 PM, the mounted troopers in columns of twos and threes went up Jackson Street and east on Main Street to their new headquarters. Frank Thomas drove his car at the head of the column with Police Chief McCulley, Newell K. Cone and a trooper, as passengers. Commissioner Wiard's car followed. The Dyke Rink was not ready for full occupancy with the troopers only sleeping there while their horses were rested in the basement stalls.

Batavia Daily News - September 27,1917 "Troop Home Transforming Former Rink - Housekeeping Job Going on With Alterations"

The still uncompleted interior of the Dyke Skating Rink would hardly be recognized. On the main floor, as one enters, officers will have their quarters in three rooms to the left of the main entrance. The front room is their bedroom with office and bath to the rear. On the right side are the First Sergeants bedroom, office and bathroom. A kitchen, pantry and dining room, as well as seven bedrooms have been built in what was formerly the main skating rink. Each bedroom will accommodate ten troopers. The rooms were all built from wall board and present a neat appearance even before painting.

Troop A's chef is here and it is hoped that the serving of meals can start tomorrow. The feeding of 58 men is quite a task.

Batavia Daily News November 14, 1917 -" State Trooper Barracks Now Nearly Furnished " " Old Dyke Rink Now A Comfortable Place"

After ten weeks, the barracks of Troop "A" on East Main Street have been finished and the new furniture placed. Since September 1st, stables, troopers & officers quarters have been built, heating and plumbing installed and the building painted within and without. Delays in the receipt of materials shipped by freight held up the work in several instances.

Furniture was moved in, much of it made by prisoners at the states prisons, in conformance to a provision by the state which insists that state institutions buy as many articles as possible, from shops maintained at the various prisons.

Batavia Daily News December 5, 1917 - "Immense Crowd Saw Troop Home" "Public delightfully entertained at the East Main Street Barracks"

No big event at the old Dyke roller skating rink ever drew so many people to it, now the barracks of Troop "A" of the New York State Police Department, as did the grand opening and public reception held yesterday afternoon and evening. Not even when former President Theodore Roosevelt made a progressive campaign speech at the old rink were there so many people in the building at one time, it seemed, as there were between 8 and 9 PM last evening.

It was the first affair of the kind ever held by the New State Police Department. The Troop "A'" invitation to the people to inspect its quarters and to delightfully entertain the visitors, will undoubtedly be followed by the other three troops in the state. An invitation was extended to people throughout the troop with an estimate of from 1500 to 2000 visiting the barracks. Automobiles lined the front of the barracks the entire day and the trolley cars did a big business.

Those familiar with the skating rink were hardly able to grasp the transformation. Everything was in apple pie order for the reception and no part of the troopers home was closed to visitors. They were shown where troopers slept, ate and spent their recreation hours. The chef showed off his kitchen even allowing a glance into the refrigerator where big roasts and other foods were stored for his family of 58 men.

Everyone was anxious to see where the horses were kept. The basement stables were as clean as could be and tacked up over each stall was a white card containing the name of the horse and the name of the trooper who rode him. The name of every horse begins with a letter "A", which is the letter of the troop. In one box stall were a mare and her colt, not many weeks old. In another was Fashion Plate, a thoroughbred which won $18,000.00 in purses during the past year. The horse is owned by the American Jockey Club and is being kept at the stable for the winter.

At the end of the evening, spectators were entertained in the rear dance hall by a five-piece orchestra, where young people danced until 2 AM. John L. Rider had charge of the checking stand with no charge being made. During the afternoon, lunch was served to visitors in the dining hall at a nominal sum. Fifty pounds of sausage were disposed of with the $45.00 receipts, as well as voluntary contributions donated to buy tobacco for the soldiers at Camp Dix, New Jersey.

All but three of the Troop "A" men were at home for the visitors. Corporal James L. Bortz, Troopers Herman Gorenflo and Walter Toole were too far from Batavia to make the reception.

A contest for the best appearing sleeping section was conducted. Many decorated their sections by placing colored paper over the light bulbs and putting up bunting. Section two with Sgt. James Rosenburgh in charge won first prize with Section four with Sgt. Walter Croadsdale in charge taking second place and Headquarters Section third place. Section one with Sgt. George Carner in charge did no decorating, but hoped to win a prize on the strength of the following statement hung from a large card on the ceiling. " We are seldom in, outside service our motto. Interior decorations unnecessary, we only sleep here."

Major Chandler, head of the State Police Department and Mrs. Chandler were among the visitors with a dinner in his honor given at the Batavia Club. Also present were Captain Percy Barbour & Sgt. Button of the Albany Headquarters, Captain Willis Linn, Troop A, Batavia, Captain Hamilton Barnes of Troop D, Syracuse, Captain Gleason of Troop G, Albany, Captain Richman of Troop K, White Plains and the directors of the Chamber of Commerce. President Leadley, Major Chandler and Capt Linn and each of the Captains made brief speeches. Each Captain expressed the wish that the Chamber of Commerce in their area would take as much interest in the troopers, as Batavia had.

Visitors to the barracks included State Senator Knight of Arcade who brought cigars for the troopers. The Chamber of Commerce Committee that arranged for the reception consisted of Frank Thomas, Frank W. Garnier, Laurence W. Griswold, R.C.Scatcherd, D.W. Tomlinson Jr., & R.C. Williams. A committee of 35 assisted during the afternoon and evening, as the troopers were busy every minute showing people through the building doing these honors in a courteous manner.

(The Dyke Skating Rink was located in the vicinity of the present day Miss Batavia Diner on East Main Street, Batavia, N.Y.)

CHAPTER SIXTEEN
ORIGINAL 1917 TROOP "A" ROSTER

The following is a list of the original troopers roster for Troop A, Batavia, N.Y., as appeared in the Batavia daily news on 27 September 1917.

Name	Rank	Home
Linn, Willis	Captain	Rochester, N.Y.
Warner, John A.	Lieutenant	Rochester, N.Y.
Skiff, James F	First Sergeant	New Rochelle, N.Y.
Carner, George W.	Sergeant	Park Ridge, Illinois
Rosebaugh, J. R.	Sergeant	Groveland, N.Y.
Miller, Edward B.	Sergeant	Williamsville, N.Y.
Croasdale, Walter	Sergeant	Oswego, N.Y.
Tobey, Elihu F.	Corporal	Kingston, N.Y.
Panzlau, Rudolph	Corporal	Rochester, N.Y.
Gunn, Henry H.	Corporal	Rochester, N.Y.
Barnes, F.L.	Corporal	Syracuse, N.Y.
Bortz, JamesL.	Saddler	Trumansburg, N.Y.
Doane, HarveyA.	Blacksmith	Gouverneur, N.Y.
Weinstein, Julius	Asst.Blacksmith	Rochester, N.Y.
Taylor, Alfred A.	Bugler	Rochester, N.Y.
Alesi, Thomas C.	Trooper	Rochester, N.Y.
Bishop, Clarence W.	Trooper	Rochester, N.Y.

Colligan, James P.	Trooper	New York City
Coots, Henry H.	Trooper	Middletown, N.Y.
Crowell, Elmer B.	Trooper	Brockport, N.Y.
Freest H. J.	Trooper	Buffalo, N.Y.
DeRight, Weldon J.	Trooper	Marion, N.Y.
Erickson, E.	Trooper	Circleville, N.Y.
Gorenflo, Herman H.	Trooper	Townline, N.Y.
Goetzman, Benjamin B.	Trooper	Sodus, N.Y.
Goetzman, Edward H.	Trooper	Sodus, N.Y.
Griffin, J.L.	Trooper	Rochester, N.Y.
Granning, Ggeorge L.	Trooper	Rochester, N.Y.
Gibbs, Warren A.	Trooper	Rochester, N.Y.
George, William J.	Trooper	Macedon, N.Y.
Guerin, Donald L.	Trooper	Rochester, N.Y.
Hopkins, John A.	Trooper	Rochester, N.Y.
Harms, Adolph A.	Trooper	Wellsville, N.Y.
King, Floyd W.	Trooper	Rochester, N.Y.
King, Robert A.	Trooper	Rochester, N.Y.
Klein, Arthur F.	Trooper	Buffalo, N.Y.
Keeley, John M.	Trooper	Geneseo, N.Y.
Lengeman, Nelson E.	Trooper	Rochester, N.Y.
Longway, Leonard E.	Trooper	Blossvale, N.Y.
Manhold, William F.	Trooper	Rochester, N.Y.
Nelson, Raymond C.	Trooper	Geneva, N.Y.
Runser, Joseph M.	Trooper	Buffalo, N.Y.
Smith, Henry R.	Trooper	Dunkirk, N.Y.
Steinmiller, Ray	Trooper	Rochester, N.Y.
Stout, Ora F.	Trooper	Rochester, N.Y.
Striegel, Robert F.	Trooper	Buffalo, N.Y.
Tarbox, M.	Trooper	Rochester, N.Y.
Taylor, Arthur G.	Trooper	Rochester, N.Y.
Toole, Walter H.	Trooper	Geneseo, N.Y.
VanLengen, Jacob A.	Trooper	Syracuse, N.Y.
Welsh, James W.	Trooper	New York City
Whipple, Harry F.	Trooper	Morton, N.Y.
Young, Guy R.	Trooper	Lebanon, Pa.

There existed one vacancy due to a resignation prior to arrival at Batavia, N. Y.

The following three resignations from Troop " A" occurred on 30 October 1917:

Maloy, William J.	Trooper	Rochester, N.Y.
Root, Lynn	Trooper	Rochester, N.Y.
Ohara, M.L.	Trooper	New York City

They were replaced on 2 November 1917 by the following:

Taylor, J.A.	Trooper	New Berlin, N.Y.
Sullivan, Gerald R.	Trooper	Palmyra, N.Y.
Knudson, H.A.	Trooper	New York City

CHAPTER SEVENTEEN
WILLIS D. LINN

FIRST COMMANDER OF TROOP "A"
BATAVIA, NEW YORK

Captain Willis Linn had served with Superintendent George F. Chandler in the New York State National Guard, seeing duty with him during the 1916 Mexican Border Campaign searching for border bandits. He was a Lieutenant in the 2nd New York Ambulance Company.

Linn was born August 14, 1889 at Rochester, New York the son of Dr. Samuel H. and Edith Linn. The Linn's resided at 46 Vick Park B with Dr. Samuel Linn practicing medicine at the Hayward Building, and later, at 243 Alexander Street, Rochester, New York. Willis was also an accomplished physician practicing medicine with his father. On June 3, 1917, he accepted a commission in the New York State Constabulary. He was an excellent horseman and while attending Colgate University, his alma mater, was named an All American in Football. He was a striking man standing six feet six inches tall and while serving in the Army was voted the best looking soldier in uniform. An undisciplined individual, Linn's activities eventually led to his short tenure in the State Police.

On January 9, 1918, Captain Linn was seriously injured when the automobile he was riding in struck a trolley car head-on near Vine and East Main Streets, Batavia, New York. The car, owned by the state, was wrecked beyond repair. Also riding in the car was Trooper Arthur Taylor and two unidentified women. Linn suffered leg and facial injuries and was removed from duty for two weeks. Councilman Casey, the trolley motorman, said that Linn and the passengers were removed to the Sherwin residence at 415 East Main Street and later attended to by a physician. The driver of the car was never identified.

In his annual report to Albany, New York dated June 8, 1918, Captain Linn reported that Batavia was not a proper location as Troop "A" Headquarters. He felt the outlying areas could be better served from the Livingston Inn at Geneseo, New York, a more central location in the troop area. It was also the home of the influential Wadsworth family. Needless to say, his suggestion was not heeded.

On June 16, 1919, Linn was charged with attempting to take fish by means of explosives at Fuller's Pond, Elba, New York. (Near the five corners intersection of Bank Street Road north of Batavia, New York) Game Protector Morris Brackett brought the charge alleging Linn placed lye or lime into a bottle and threw it into the pond expecting an explosion, which would kill fish. No explosion occurred. On June 30, 1919, Linn signed a statement admitting to the incident. He was fined $100.00 under civil compromise and released. Court proceedings were held before Batavia City Justice Burroughs at the trooper's barracks in Batavia, New York. It should be noted that Trooper Harlow Doane, the Troop "A" Blacksmith had paid a $100.00 fine a week earlier for the same incident

On June 20, 1919, complaints were laid by Genesee County District Attorney James L. Kelly with the Governors Office on behalf of residents of Morganville Road, Stafford, New York. The complaints concerned allegations of misconduct at a farmhouse near Horseshoe Lake used by the troopers. Trooper Michael Serve on behalf of Captain Linn rented the farm from owner Chris Casey of Batavia, New York. Linn said it would be used as a "Club for the Boys" and to pasture Troop "A" horses. The governor's office sent an unidentified trooper to investigate the allegations. He interviewed Horseshoe Lake and Morganville Road residents with most stating they observed troopers with women going to the farmhouse at all times of the day and night. They referred to the farm as the "Lonesome Promise

Parlor". It was also reported that no horses had ever been seen pastured there. Several complained of troopers riding their horses through their crops, an occurrence that was discontinued after several complaints to the Captain. Residents interviewed included Walter A. Peters, Milo Clark, Joseph Rath and Charles Coniber.

Many of the trooper's two-year enlistments would soon be expiring with troopers openly saying they would not re-enlist unless a re-organization of the troop was made. Many had already resigned with the few veterans that remained stating their dissatisfaction. On June 28, 1919, Linn was to be transferred to Troop "G", Albany, New York. While investigative results of Linn's alleged misconduct were pending, Captain Winfield W. Robinson, Troop "G" Commander was reassigned to Batavia effective July 1, 1919. The troopers hailed Robinson's arrival with delight because of his excellent reputation of fairness and honesty.

Captain Linn's career as a constabulary officer was concluded on July 5, 1919, initially by suspension, then termination, after it was learned by Major Chandler of the conviction for illegally taking fish by means of explosives. Some accounts indicate Linn resigned at Chandler's request. Major Chandler, a man of high ideals, expected his officers and men to lead by example, to be model citizens and to enforce all the laws, not violate them. He found Linn's conduct unacceptable. No matter what the outcome of the present hearing, Linn was terminated.

Allegations of misconduct charged by District Attorney Kelly resulted in hearings being held at Batavia and Rochester, New York from July 14 thru 28, 1919. Commissioner Joseph A. Lawson, an Albany Attorney appointed by the governor, presided over the hearings. Lawson's investigative results were directed to be made in a sealed report provided to the governor for his determination and recommendation for punishment, if any.

Linn retained John McInerney, a well-known Rochester, New York Attorney to represent him. They promised disclosure of a plot to oust Linn because of his knowledge of police protection given a certain disorderly house and his raiding of this establishment. District Attorney Kelly was retained by Lawson, not as a prosecutor, but tasked with only questioning witnesses.

Testimony started with Corporal Henry Coots testifying of Captain Linn taking state furnishings and food to the rented farmhouse. He described the farmhouse, as a 1-½ story frame building with three bedrooms and a kitchen. He stated that it was generally understood that none of the men were to go to the farm. He testified of having seen women and girls entering and remaining in the Captain's barracks bedroom. He stated that Linn would take these girls on automobile rides with him. On one occasion, Linn requisitioned two pair of trousers for Trooper Henry S. Brennan. Brennan had resigned some time earlier with the trousers being given to the girl who visited Linn. He further saw the Captain intoxicated at the barracks on several occasions and believed Linn had shot pheasants from his bedroom window. Linn also requisitioned lumber for an oat bin that was never built. The lumber was used to make jumping hurdles for horses Linn was keeping for friends.

Henry D. Prole, a produce dealer and James O. Bolt, a farmer testified as to the reputation of the farmhouse and having seen Linn, troopers and women enter the farmhouse on many occasions.

Testimony was given that Linn stopped Walter A. Peters, a farmer while driving by the farmhouse. Linn asked Peters to drive a girl to Batavia, because his car had gotten stuck in the mud. She was described as being about 16 or 17 years old.

Milo Clark, a farmer, stated that on one occasion, Linn came to his home located a short distance from the farmhouse at 2:30AM asking to use the phone. He called the barracks requesting assistance, as he had been in a car wreck. Clark also reported seeing women at the farmhouse on more that one occasion.

Charles F. Thornell, a farmer, testified that on November 3, 1918, he stopped Linn, a woman and a second trooper, as they started to ride their horses across his clover field. He told them they could ride across for business, but not for pleasure or else he would take his shotgun to them. When asked if he would indeed use the shotgun, he stated no, but the threat had worked earlier with a Batavia resident so he thought he would try it on Linn. He said it must have worked, as no troopers rode across his field after that.

Corporals Henry Smith and George Tarbox both testified that on June 13, 1919, two women in a car visited the barracks. Captain Linn left with them returning some time later. They all appeared to have been drinking alcohol. One woman tried to ride an unbroken horse in the corral, but was thrown from the mount. Attorney Kelly introduced an expense voucher submitted by Linn for meals at Watkins, Corning and Hornell, New York for May 23, 1919. Smith testified that Linn had been in Batavia that day having delivered a recovered stolen car to Heveron's Hotel in East Pembroke, New York.

Linn discharged former Trooper Henry S. Brennan, because of political statements he had made. Brennan admitted that they did not like one another and that Linn, showing his authority would make him go on patrol on an unbroken bucking horse. He testified that he had observed young women visit Linn at the barracks, observed him in an intoxicated condition on more than one occasion and had seen an expense voucher submitted by Linn for out of town meals, when in fact, he had not left Batavia.

Corporal George Tetley advised of seeing Linn drunk in uniform on several occasions while in Buffalo, New York. On three occasions, he assisted him to the car returning him to Batavia. On one occasion, Linn was so intoxicated, that he left him at the Lenox Hotel in Buffalo. On two or three occasions, he drove Linn and a girl, aged 16 or 17, to the Bachelor Apartments at West Tupper and Franklin Streets, Buffalo, New York where they would remain for several hours. He would then return them to Batavia. On one occasion, Linn had him drive to East Pembroke, New York, just a few miles from Batavia, where they picked up Bill Heveron and Tom Cowler, a few bottles of whiskey and continued on to the Bottomless Lake at Indian Falls, New York where the consumed the whiskey.

Sergeant Edward A. Miller, Linn's aide, testified he never saw Linn intoxicated and never saw women go in or out of Linn's room. He recalled Linn giving a young girl two pair of riding breeches, because she rode Jockey Club Horses at horse shows in Hamburg and Geneseo, New York, which were under the Captain's charge. When queried about the pheasants taken out of season, he said that he and Linn would feed the birds near the Horseshoe Lake, in a conservation effort to maintain them. He said that on one occasion, they found a bird in the snow and gave it to Corporal Coots. Coots later told them that it tasted pretty good. He further described former Trooper Brennan as a poor trooper example. He described Linn as a beloved commanding officer, fair with his men, an able and efficient man and above reproach, as a gentleman. Observers later described Miller as a splendid example of loyalty to a superior officer.

Trooper John S. Hopkins and Corporal Edward Goetzman testified about repairing and painting the farmhouse and while there, finding empty whiskey, gin and beer bottles.

Troopers Ora F. Stout and James F. Borst testified of seeing women visit Linn at the barracks and seeing him intoxicated on several occasions. They did not feel he was fit to command the troop.

Troopers West, Harry G. Warner and Corporal John Keeley described Linn, as an all right officer while Trooper Albert I. DeFreest had no comment.

On August 28, 1919, Commissioner Lawson's report to the governor was made public. The recommendation was for Linn to be removed.

Linn returned to his medical profession practicing at 243 Alexander Street, Rochester, New York where he was listed as a physician from 1916 to 1919. He then practiced at Brockport, New York from December 1919 to August 14, 1920, relocated to Avon, New York for a short time, then on to Binghamton, New York in about 1921 or 1922.

Linn's wife, Ethel H. Linn, sued for divorce as the plaintiff, which was granted in January 1920 at Rochester, New York.

In January 1924, Linn was charged with False Marriage. Miss Mildred Westbrook, a nurse of Washington, D.C. was the victim of the false marriage that was followed by a honeymoon in the south. She alleged that a friend of Doctor Linn's performed a mock wedding at the Continental Hotel, Washington, D.C., posing as clergy. Linn was held on $5000.00 bail on a charge of violating the federal Mann Act. The charge was not actively pursued. On March 28, 1924, Doctor Linn and Miss Westbrook were married at Montrose, Pennsylvania.

On August 12, 1925, Linn was shot and admitted to the Binghamton Hospital in serious condition. His wife Mildred was held for questioning. Investigation revealed that two shots fired from a 22-caliber revolver entered Linn's chest just below the shoulder. Linn's wife contended that she did not shoot him while he contended that she did. Mildred was charged with Assault 2nd Degree on August 15th, posted $2500.00 bail and was released. A county Grand Jury failed to indict her resulting in her complete release. A divorce followed.

Linn married for a third time and moved to Garrison, Kentucky where he established a medical practice. On May 2, 1927, he closed his flamboyant career with a self-inflicted knife wound. His wife Naomi and a neighbor, Howard Behimer were present when he displayed a knife and plunged it into his throat. He was thirty-seven years old. His wife Naomi Townsend Linn of Glenora, New York, a son from a prior marriage and his mother Edith Linn Forbes of Rochester, New York survived him. Burial was at Glenora Cemetery, Yates County, New York.

(Binghamton Newspaper)
(Batavia Daily News)
(Annual Reports)

CHAPTER EIGHTEEN
CAPTAIN WINFIELD W. ROBINSON

Winfield W. Robinson was born on February 15, 1886 at New York City, New York where he attended public schools, as well as The College of New York. He was employed for many years at the offices of the New York Central Railroad, the Continental Fire Insurance Company and later, was Assistant Secretary to Commissioner Arthur M. Woods of the New York City Police Department. While there, he studied the Bertillon system becoming an expert in the field. Commissioner Wood went on to become Assistant Secretary of War.

Robinson was an original Campman being in the first group to arrive at Camp Newayo. In 1918, Robinson was Troop Commander of Troop "G" at Troy, N.Y. where he was ranked as the most efficient troop commander in the state. He developed an efficient records system, which was put in place throughout the state. Captain Robinson came to Batavia, N.Y. in July 1919 replacing Captain Willis Linn, as Troop Commander. He served as the Troop "A" Commander until his retirement in 1944.

An impressive figure, Robinson during the 1920s & 30s annually led the Batavia Memorial Day parade astride his favorite horse, Gray dawn.

In 1921, Senator John Knight of Arcade, N.Y. presented Robinson's name to Governor Nathan L. Miller, as a replacement for Major Chandler who was returning to his physicians practice. Active boosters included John G. Baukat, President of the Batavia Car Works, Inc. and Fred B. Parker, Secretary of the Genesee County Fair.

At the suggestion of Captain Robinson, the 1922 Batavia Directory devoted a page to the personnel of the troop, giving the name, rank and address of each member. Most of the troopers lived at the barracks, but several had other addresses in the city. The directory noted that there were 3122 houses within the city limits and 445 in the town. It gave an alphabetical listing of the city and town residents over fifteen years of age. There were 28 lawyers, 26 physicians, 12 dentists and 58 meat markets and grocery stores.

Captain Robinson was a member of the First Baptist Church of Batavia, N.Y. and member and Past President of the Holland Historical Society. He was also affiliated with the Sons of the American Revolution, Sons of Union Veterans of the Civil War, The Genesee County Draft Board and Board of Ethics for the City of Batavia, N.Y. He also served as President of the Genesee County Chapter of the American Red Cross and Genesee County Civil Defense Director.

He was married to the former Ruth Coolidge with whom he had two children. A daughter Nancy and a son, George Chandler. George died in 1947 at age of 24 the result of contracting meningitis while serving in the US Army.

Sergeant John Long recalled that on several occasions, Captain Robinson would direct First Sergeant Joe Brandstetter to have the station housekeeper, Mrs. O'Grady make up the bed in his room, as he would be staying the night due to a sore back. Brandstetter would chuckle because the Captain would only stay at the barracks, when he fought with his wife Ruth.

On one occasion, Captain Robinson had Sergeant Eddie Rimmer and two troopers obtain four wooden barrels from the Colgrove and Ryan Meat Market in Batavia, N.Y. He directed that the barrels be filled with plain horse manure and to make sure there was no straw in it. When filled, they were to be taken to his home on Redfield Parkway and spread about his front lawn. John Long was one of the troopers and referred to himself as a stable rat. There were about sixty horses in the stable at the time. When a horse's tail went up, a trooper would dash behind it with a scoop shovel to try and catch its deposit to fill the barrels. They had little success, but eventually filled the barrels with whatever lay around. Sergeant Rimmer had the troopers take it and spread over the lawn. The next day, the Captain came in fuming. He wanted to know from Sergeant Rimmer what it was that had been spread on his lawn and had blown all over the neighborhood. "Horse-crap" replied Rimmer. "Horse-crap" yourself sergeant. With that, Robinson demoted Rimmer to the rank of Corporal. The demotion only lasted for about a month. It wasn't the first time Rimmer had been demoted. He had considered getting snap-on chevrons for his uniforms.

He was an active member of the Batavia Red Cross and took employment in the Security Department at the Doehler Die Casting Company, Batavia, N.Y.

The Batavia Daily News printed the following in testimony to his many years of service, upon retirement.

The state and all of Western New York will lose what might be termed one of the finest police officers that we believe is in the entire state police service. He has been the head of Troop "A" for 24 ½ years and is taking advantage of the 25 years service retirement that he is eligible for.

No finer man that possesses all of the qualifications of so high a position in the state police work could ever have been sent to Batavia. He was a thoroughly trained official, a man among men, a man who did his work in a way that brought nothing but high praise to him and his force.

It will be recalled that when Captain Robinson first came to Batavia, he came to relieve another captain who had gone wrong and who caused all kinds of scandal and what not. From the moment he took over the office, things were different; the morale of the men under him was greatly improved and never once in the long period of time did anything ever arise again to belittle this prominent organization.

He has been fair and honest in all his dealings with the men under him. His retirement will be a severe loss, not alone as we have to the state, but to the people of Western New York and everyone hopes for him the very best of success in anything he might choose to do following his retirement.

At age 82, Captain Robinson died on October 18, 1978 at Batavia, N.Y. where he had resided with his family at 56 Redfield Parkway.
(Batavia Daily News – 10/18/78)

(Bertillon system – a system of identifying persons, particularly criminals by a record of individual measurements and physical peculiarities especially by fingerprints.)

CHAPTER NINETEEN
A MODERN BARRACKS

On October 19, 1919, a campaign was launched by the Batavia, N.Y. Chamber of Commerce for the erection of a modern and adequate barracks for the state constabulary. It was announced that the present barracks were unfit for use as a quarters. The lower part was used for a stable and upper part for a sleeping quarters. Both heating and ventilation were almost impossible in the winter. The men were using small gas and oil stoves for heat and all were crowded into one room to take advantage of what heat was available. Stable odors and the unpleasant dampness of the building were considered objectionable. Secretary Coley of the Chamber announced the chambers support of a new barracks in the city.

Plans to build a new $80,000.00 barracks with separate stables and garage were reviewed by the chamber. The City of Batavia would have to build the new barracks, which would be rented to the state for a long term of years. Troop "D" at Oneida, N.Y. moved into a new barracks recently with the plans used to build their barracks being utilized for the Batavia Barracks.

Lobbying efforts were made in Albany, N.Y. to relocate the barracks to Hamburg or Williamsville, N.Y. On January 9, 1920, Colonel Chandler decided on the four-acre site of the Philip Hartnell estate on East Main Street as the location for the new barracks. James J. Green, a realtor acting for the chamber took a three-month option of the property for $4,500.00 from owner, Mrs. Jennie Trick of Stafford, N.Y. The property consisted of a ten-room house and two barns with four- acres of land. It was located 600 feet west of the New York Central Railroad line, with 300 feet of frontage on the north side of the road. This site also had access to city water and sewage.

Ground for the new barracks was broken on May 1, 1920. The Barracks Committee met with Architect I.V. Van Duser of Cazenovia, N.Y. to review changes to the original barracks plans. The first floor would provide for offices, file rooms and officer's quarters. The second floor would have the first sergeants quarters and one large dormitory. The third floor would have two dormitories, shower baths, washrooms and toilets.

On May 13, 1920, R. Norton Reed was awarded the contract to build the new barracks. Frank H. Homelus was engaged as the supervising architect. Arrangements were also made to have a private fire alarm box placed in front of the barracks site.

It was determined that $75,000.00 would be required for the financing of the barracks. Of this, The First National Bank, Judge Washburn, Director, the Bank of Batavia, William Miller, President and the Bank of Genesee, William G. Pollard, President provided $50,000.00. Endorsed demand notes were issued at six- per cent conditional upon the investment of $25,000.00 by the stockholders of the proposed Batavia Barracks Corporation. Chamber Director Frank Thomas was placed in full charge of securing subscriptions for the $25,000.00 to be raised. C.A.K. Pistell of Pistell, Trubee and Company, Inc made arrangements for a bond issue.

Elected as officers of the Barracks Corporation on 14 June 1920 were Frank Thomas, Treasurer, Lewis D. Collins, President, Edward H. Leadley, 1st Vice President, Charles H. Honeck, 2nd Vice President, P.J. Marion, Secretary. Directors included James L. Bean, Walter W. Buxton, Judge Newell Cone, Laurence W. Griswold, Charles H. Honeck and Oren C. Steele. Subscribers were W.E. Woodbury & Co., The Genesee Light & Power Company and Batavia Dry Cleaning Company.

A contract between the Batavia Barracks Corporation and the State of New York was entered into with the following terms noted. Beginning July 1, 1921, a return of ten- per cent per year or $7500.00 for rental to the state for ten years, which could be renewed for an additional ten years was guaranteed. The state had the option to purchase the barracks at a price of ten per cent above the final cost at any time.

R. Norton Reed, General Contractor who bid just under $65,000.00 for the contract sublet the plumbing to Goade & Flohr and the heating to the Steele & Torrence Company. R.A. Wentworth conducted surveys. Construction on the outer buildings was started immediately.

On October 1, 1921, troopers moved to and spent their first night at the new barracks location. The room above the newly erected stables was used for a reserve of three troopers, a corporal and first sergeant. All other men were sent out on patrol. The stables themselves were used to store equipment until the barracks itself was completed. Captain Robinson took a room with Fred G. Coolidge of 12 Union Street. Dyke rink owners Cook and Housenecht sold the building to the Coots brothers who turned it back into a skating rink that was known as the "Palace Roller Rink".

The barracks building accommodated eighty-five men and was constructed of concrete block with a tile roof. The building measured 60 by 40 feet with a wing for a kitchen, cold storage and laundry. The first floor had general offices, a large recreation room, captain's room, lieutenant's room, dining room, pantry, kitchen, cold storage and laundry. A well-lighted large dormitory occupied the entire front part of the second floor. Neat, white cots, covered with blankets of the official gray color of the troop and a dressing table for each man were uniformly placed. There was a smaller dormitory for emergency use in the rear. Also in the rear were the sergeant's rooms, clerk's rooms and dormitories for civilian employees of the troop with shower baths and toilets. The third floor had a dormitory room, showers and toilets. In the basement were the quartermaster's room, storeroom, canteen room and a large boiler room with adjoining smaller rooms for a root cellar and coal bins. All interior woodwork was of hardwood finish.

The garage measured 40 feet long by 30 feet wide and had a capacity for 15 to 20 cars. It was also constructed of concrete block with a poured concrete floor and fireproof roofing shingles.

The stable was a wood framed building measuring 90 feet long by 40 feet wide with two wings. The entire building was covered with fireproof shingles, fireproof roof materials with a concrete floor. There was a saddle maker's room, blacksmith shop and saddle room. Thirty-six horses could be accommodated in the stables.

On June 4, 1923, legislation was passed authorizing the state to purchase the newly constructed barracks. On April 12, 1924, stockholders in the Batavia Barracks Corporation were rewarded with a $59.00 or $60.00 interest earned besides each $100.00 invested.

The last Troop "A" horse patrols were utilized during the winter 1935 – 1936. Having no further use as a stable, it was converted into a parking garage during the winter of 1936.

(The original garage is the only building still in existence and is the current home of CR Auto Sales owned by Richard Donk and James Clor)

(Batavia Daily News)

CHAPTER TWENTY
APRIL 1921 TROOP "A" ROSTER

Captain	Winfield W. Robinson	
Lieutenant	Daniel E. Fox	
First Sergeant	John M. Keeley	
Sergeant (Troop Clerk)	Joseph P. Colligan	
Sergeants	Walter Croadsdale	William J. George
	Rudolph H. Panzlau	Gerald R. Sullivan
CORPORALS	John H. Lockhart	Milton F. Nurenmberg
	Michael Serve	Henry C. Wagner
Privates	Ellis H. Bannkratnz	Albert J. Barton
	Carl D. Baxter	John J. Bembuista
	Leslie C. Benway	Elmer C. Bovee
	Gordon W. Brush	Charles G. Burnett

Raymond C. Clark	James J. Corrigan
Nathan R. Foody	Everett C. Giles
Armon P. Gunnison	George E. Hofer
Joseph E. Holcomb	John F. Howard
William L. Ireland	Robert B. Jones
John J. King	William Larson
C.Leo Lunney	Maryan J. Maciejewski
JohnT. Melvin	John S. Metzer
Frank J. Miller	Howard P. Miller
Ralph W. Miller	Thomas J. Murphy
Raymond H. Nagell	Laurence C. Nelson
Clarence A. Pitt	Fred M. Pitt
William H.Rhubottom	Walter D. Richardson
Edward A. Rimmer	Freeman Sprague
Ora W. Stout	George E. Tetley
Harold H. White	George E. Winne
Frank W. Yates	

From Batavia Daily News / 02 April 1921

CHAPTER TWENTY-ONE
TWO TROOPERS KILLED – 1927

RASMUSSEN – ROY MURDER

Two New York State Trooper of Troop "A" barracks in Batavia, New York were shot and killed at Caneadea, Allegany County, early this afternoon. So read the headlines of local newspapers on September 8, 1927, describing the murder of two State Troopers that led to one of the largest manhunts in Western New York history.

THE CRIME
The dead troopers, Robert Roy, aged 24 of New York City and Arnold T. Rasmussen, aged 26 of Jamestown, New York, were shot by Wilmont Leroy "Roy" Wagner, aged 25 of Caneadea, New York.

Troopers Roy and Rasmussen assigned at Rushford, New York had gone to execute a warrant on Roy Wagner for Petit Larceny. The warrant was issued earlier in the day, when Wagner had left a service station in Fillmore, New York without paying the garage employee, Clarence Mower for six dollars worth goods and gasoline. Mary Cox, owner of the Maple Inn on the Rushford Road, also complained to the troopers that Wagner had taken articles from her without paying.

Wagner was located at the home of his father, William and the warrant served. Having worked all day in the fields, Wagner asked if he could change his clothes for better appearance. Known by both troopers as being non-violent, they allowed this request. Wagner went upstairs to his room unescorted. Trooper Roy went to the front lawn where he was in conversation with Wagner's sister,

Margaret. Trooper Rasmussen went into the back yard engaging another sister, Mrs. Grace Miller in conversation. She related that she stood in the yard talking with Trooper Rasmussen, when suddenly, she heard a shot and a moment later, Trooper Rasmussen lay dead on the ground. None of the shot struck her. As she turned looking toward the house, she saw her brother Wilmont standing at an upstairs window. A moment later, he disappeared and she heard a second shot fired. Wagner's father just entering the yard from the barn saw Trooper Rasmussen fall to the ground, ran to the house just as Trooper Roy was starting up the stairs. He warned the trooper not to go up, but his warning went unheeded. Wagner fired at the approaching trooper from close range with some of the paper wadding from the shot becoming imbedded in the wounds. Wagner immediately fled the scene on foot. The location of the killings was a farm about one mile northeast of Caneadea across the Genesee River owned by B.D. White, the Wagner's being farm tenants.

THE MANHUNT

First news of the shootings came from Daniel Wagner, an uncle who ran to a neighbor and called the local sheriff's office. Deputy Monroe Day was the first to arrive on the scene. The time of the crime was fixed at 1:30PM with the Batavia barracks notified at 2:20PM. Captain Winfield W. Robinson, Troop "A" Commander immediately dispatched Lieutenants Samuel Freeman and William George along with fifty troopers who aided by dogs searched the countryside for Wagner. Troopers John Faulkner and Lyman Fortner, two of the first to arrive guarded the murder scene.

On September 9, 1927, Wagner was observed by his uncle Daniel, in Dalton, New York driving a truck that had been reported stolen. The truck owned by George Chamberlain of Belfast, New York bearing New York license plates numbered 638-933 was stolen the previous day. At about 8:00AM the same day, Daniel found the shotgun with which Wagner shot the two troopers, hidden behind a door where Wagner had evidently placed it. He turned the shotgun over to two troopers he came across along the road. It was believed Wagner was now headed for Pennsylvania. William Wagner, the father, was jailed without bail, held as a material witness.

On September 10, 1927, a $1000.00 reward was offered for the capture of Wagner from monies collected among state troopers. Allegany County also offered a $1000.00 reward with L.H. Schultz, President of the Blue Bus Lines offering a $250.00 reward and the Western New York Motor Lines offering a $250.00 reward.

On September 11, 1927, District Attorney Walter N. Renwick of Cuba, New York issued two warrants for Wagner charging murder in the First Degree. One warrant was given to the troopers and the other to Sheriff Edson A. Bingham. The troopers established their local headquarters at Kelly's Hotel in Caneadea, New York. Troopers, deputies and citizens searched near Caneadea, Belfast, Belmont, Corning, Addison and Dalton without success. Reported sightings had proven futile with Wagner successfully eluding searchers in the heavily wooded hills.

THE CAPTURE

On September 26, 1927, the search for Wagner came to an end, when troopers at the outer fringe of the dragnet captured him. The eighteen-day search ended at 4:00PM, when Corporal Herbert Southworth and Trooper Jacob Topolski of the Batavia barracks took him into custody at gunpoint. He was located and taken into custody at the John Allen farm in Tioga County, Pennsylvania. He had been employed there since September 13, 1927 using the alias Frank Harte. He was taken to the home of his sister, Mrs. Thomas Hughes of Tioga for positive identification. Mrs. William Lewis of Morris Run, Pennsylvania was praised by troopers for the clue that led to the arrest. She contacted Lieutenant George at Tioga telling him that a man answering Wagner's description had stopped at her home on September 13, 1927 looking for farm work. She had none and sent him on his way. After reading accounts of the murders and Wagner's description, she was sure the man was Wagner and believed he had taken work at the Allen farm.

THE TRIAL

Wagner was arraigned and jailed without bail at the Allegany County Jail. Motions for a change of venue were heard and granted on November 2, 1927. It was determined that a fair trial could not be given locally due to deep personal feelings. The case was moved to Buffalo, New York with testimony to commence on November 14, 1927. Supreme Court Justice Charles H. Brown of Belmont, Allegany County was selected to preside over the trial. Thomas F. Rogers of Corning, New York was counsel for the defense and Attorney William T. Moore, appointed as special prosecutor.

On November 18, 1927, testimony began with the first witness, Mrs. Ella Stephens of Shongo, New York, an aunt of Wagner's wife, Doris, telling of his cruelty to his wife and his threats to kill any troopers that came after him.

Trooper John B. Lynch provided testimony of an oral confession given to three people by Wagner admitting to the shootings.

On November 21, 1927, Doris Wagner's testimony contradicted her aunt's previous testimony stating that she never heard her husband threaten to kill any troopers.

Sergeant Charles G. Burnett, Troopers Jacob Topolski and Thomas H. Corbett and Auburn Criminologist Albert H. Hamilton gave crime scene testimony. They testified about body locations, spent shells and witness statements negating any defense theory of self-defense.

During his testimony, Wagner complained that while confined to the Allegany County Jail, state troopers would throw firecrackers into his cell and that Undersheriff Schuyler wouldn't give him any tobacco, because he wouldn't talk.

THE VERDICT

On November 25, 1927 at 5:00PM, Justice Brown charged the jury. In recess until 7:30PM, they re-convened and at 10:15PM, announced their verdict. Wagner was found guilty of Murder in the First Degree in the killing of Trooper Robert Roy. On November 30, 1927, he was transferred to Sing Sing Prison where he was sentenced to die in the electric chair. On May 1, 1928, Wagner's conviction was affirmed by the Court of Appeals.

THE SENTENCE

On June 21, 1928, Wilmont Leroy Wagner, protesting his innocence, "Rode the Bolt to Eternity". He sat in the electric chair smoking a cigarette and announced in a low tone, "Gentlemen, I am innocent, I shot Robert Roy in self defense." At 11:08PM, the switch was thrown ending the life of a killer.

ROBERT "ROB" ROY

Rob Roy was born Theodore Steinbock at Foxboro, Massachusetts on June 24, 1903. His family moved to New York City where he attended public schools. At age fourteen, he traveled to Quebec, Canada where he enlisted under the name of Rob Roy in the First Depot Battalion, First Quebec Regiment. He was transferred to the 42nd Canadian Highlanders, fighting in France during WW I where he was slightly wounded. He was discharged at Montreal on February 20, 1919. He joined and served with the Canadian Northwest Mounted Police from June 29, 1920 until June 28, 1923. He joined the New York State Police in October 1926 serving at White Plains and Batavia, New York. He was buried at Mount Olivett Cemetery, Maspeth, New York.

ARNOLD T. RASMUSSEN

Arnold T, Rasmussen was born in 1901 at Wilcox, Pennsylvania. He was a two-year veteran of the United States Navy and resided at 12 Seventeenth Street, Jamestown, New York with his wife, Margaret and two infant daughters. Burial was at Lakewood Cemetery, Jamestown, New York. An annual pension of $750.00 was awarded the widow.

CHAPTER TWENTY-TWO
1929 STATE TROOPERS FIELD DAY – BATAVIA, N.Y.

On October 19, 1929, the Batavia Troopers held their first ever rodeo, aerial show and field day for the benefit of the Genesee County Children's Health Camp. It was held at the Batavia Fair Grounds with an admission of 50 cents. In addition to raising funds for the children's camp, it was an opportunity for the troopers to demonstrate their skills and promote good will with the citizens of Western New York. General chairman of the event was Captain Winfield W. Robinson, Troop "A" commander. The days activities featured trick and fancy horsemanship, aerial acrobatics, roman riding, motorcycle trick riding and races, tug of war on horseback, band concerts and athletic events.

Participating guests were the Troop "D" rough riders, Rochester, Buffalo, Batavia, Jamestown and Leroy police departments, Donald Woodward airport pilots, Leroy, N.Y., Larkin Womens Fife, Drum and Bugle Corp, Erie County Fife and Drum Corp, Batavia and Buffalo American Legion bands, Buffalo Police motorcycle squad and Leroy High School band.

The program opened with presentation of colors by the Glenn S. Loomis American Legion Post accompanied by their band. Field events started with roman riding races (a rider standing on the backs of two racing horses) by Troopers Leslie P. Button and Earl R. Wilkinson won by Wilkinson. Next came the county high school boys 100 yard dash won by Lawrence Wright , Batavia, N.Y. in 11.00 seconds, second was Louis Russo, Leroy, N.Y. and third, Harry Idenrick, Oakfield, N.Y.

The crowd enjoyed a vaudeville skit introduced by Corporal Richard (Trixie) Lemay and David Mousseau of a hick cop stopping a speeder (10 mph) and winding up singing song favorites with Lemay playing the piano.

Local troopers won the mounted horseback tug of war. The mounted wrestling match (where the riders tried to wrestle an opponent to the ground) was won by Troop "D".

The Buffalo, N.Y. Police Department took honors in a 2-½ mile motorcycle race with first going to Officer, Youknot, second Officer Shea and third to Officer Demerling. The 100-yard motorcycle dash was won by the Rochester, N.Y. Police Department with first to Officer Van Auker, second Officer Winfield and third Officer Lees.

The motorcycle races were followed by the aerial carnival from the Donald Woodward Airfield, Leroy, N.Y. consisting of three planes that looped the loop, made slow and snappy rolls, intricate upside down flying formations and speedily plunged their planes earthward only to pull up at the last moment.

Mrs. Charles Poplin, wife of Trooper Poplin from Oneida, N.Y. did a display of trick horse riding and acrobatic feats while at full gallop. Her skills equaled that of the troopers.

The highlight of the day were the team of 10 Troop "D" rough riders with an exhibition of rodeo, rough riding, pyramid building and jumping through a ring of fire. Under the direction of Captain Stephen McGrath, they rode in amazing unison while performing stunts, then each individual trooper gave an exhibition of his own riding mastery. The horse show finished with a ½ mile bare back riding race, which was won by Trooper Paul Mellody, with Troopers Sam Vint second, and Eugene Hoyt third.

The program ended with music by the Leroy High School Band, Buffalo American Legion Band and the Larkin Drum Corp.

Sergeant Sam Dunlap of Troop "A" noted that $3500.00 in all had been raised from the benefit with all monies going to the local children's camp.

(Batavia Daily News)

CHAPTER TWENTY-THREE
CAPTAINS TRAIN

Captain Robinson having worked briefly for the New York Central Railroad developed a great love for railroads and was a great believer in trains. During the early 1930s he had troopers lay a track adjacent to the Erie Railroad Spur located at the rear of the corral behind the barracks on East Main Street, Batavia, N.Y. Utilizing a saddle horse, the troopers hooked up a scoop shovel to level the track bed. The horse ran away several times, fortunately not injuring itself by the scoop shovel striking it's legs. The ground was eventually leveled with the railroad ties and rails placed in position. The Captain had obtained the ties and rails from an Erie Railroad work crew and created his own rail spur.

Robinson located a small quarry locomotive that was obsolete at a stone quarry in Clarence, N.Y. The locomotive was given to him free of charge. He then found a Caboose that was also donated. The engine and caboose were hauled to the barracks in a low flat bed truck borrowed from the Department of Transportation and set onto the rails. He had the troopers paint the engine with black enamel paint with red trim and the caboose with red enamel.

In his memoirs, T/Sgt. John Long recalled Captain Robinson's 12-year-old son, Chandler playing on the train. He was pretending to be an engineer blowing the train's whistle. Sgt. Long happened to be outside at the time, when Chandler said how nice it would be if there was smoke coming from the engine just like a real train. Long got some newspaper and old rubber footwear from the stable and started a fire in the locomotives boiler. The black smoke poured out in bellowing clouds, but the heat from the fire also peeled off the paint showing the rust beneath. Long told Chandler not to tell his father, as there would be big trouble for both of them. The boy never said a word. A few days later, Captain Robinson was heard to say that if he found out who started the fire, he would be fired.

The final resting place of the "Captain's Train" could not be determined. A reasonable assumption is that it was scrapped, melted into steel and used in the war effort.

Viola Roblee, Captain Robinson's secretary from May 1943 until his retirement in January 1944 never saw the train, as it had already been removed. She remembered him talking about his "Shawmut Line" which was what he named it.

According to Rowena Wood, wife of deceased former Senior Investigator George Wood (29 to 69), Robinson was told to have the train removed by the superintendent in about 1940. The Captain was tight-lipped and not very happy about it, but there wasn't anything he could do. She didn't know its final disposition.

Sometime after Robinson's retirement in January 1944, Governor Thomas E. Dewey visiting Batavia Trooper Headquarters asked if this was the location of the famous railroad. Captain Joseph Lynch now commanding told him it was, but it had been removed several years earlier.

W.W. ROBINSON - 1917

1919 BATAVIA TROOPERS

1921 TROOP "A" MOTROCYCLE INSPECTION

1921 TROOP "A" FLEET

1923 TROOP "A" ROLL CALL

1923-CHARLIE BOLTS GRAVEL PIT

CAPTAIN ROBINSONS TRAIN - 1939

1920 DYKE RINK-CAPTAIN ROBINSON IN CTR.

1919 - ASSISTING A MOTORIST

NEW TROOP HQ., BATAVIA, NY -1921

1918 HOTEL RUSSELL -WEBSTER, N.Y.

BOOK III – STRIKES AND RIOTS

CHAPTER TWENTY-FOUR
LABOR UNREST 1919 TO 1921

Labor unrest dominated the news headlines beginning with the Rome, N.Y. Brass Strikes in May 1919 followed by Lackawanna Steel Strike, the Olean Carmen's Strike of August 1919 and the United Traction Company Strikes of 1921. Troopers were sent to maintain law and order, when local authority required support after losing control of the rioting crowds. They performed their duties in small groups, many times facing several thousand strikers, restoring order and maintaining patrols to insure the peace was kept. Under threatening and dangerous conditions, troopers maintained such restraint from provocation, that not one person was killed. As the strikes waned, the reputation of the troopers as an organization was established, as a group of men that could enforce the law impartially with integrity and courage against overwhelming odds.

Beginning in May 1919; the Rome Brass Works strike escalated to the point of violence and rioting on East Dominick Street, the industrial center of Rome, N.Y. On July 14, 1919 Governor Alfred E. Smith at the request of Rome Mayor Midlam ordered the troopers to Rome to assist local authorities in preserving the peace. Rioting strikers from the Rome Brass and Copper Company, the Rome Hollow Wire and Tube Company, Spargo Wire Company and the Williams Brothers Manufacturing Company using rocks, guns and other missiles caused serious injury to company officials and non-strikers. Automobiles were wrecked as the mobs roamed the streets day and night. There was a band playing and marching back and forth in support of the strikers. Special Police hired for the strike resigned walking off their posts out of fear of serious injury or death to themselves.

The first troopers to arrive were from Troop "D" led by Captain Hamilton Barnes. Headquarters was established at the police headquarters, with horses and cars quartered in the jail yard. The courthouse was turned into a sleeping quarters. This first contingent of 65 men, through prompt answering of the emergency call and use of their skills, training and ability were able to turn the tide of 3000 rioters. During the night, each troop sent men with a total of 200 troopers arriving for duty. Troopers on foot and horseback were armed with their service revolver, a heavy club and 30-30 carbines that were put to use if the occasion required. Shots were fired and stones thrown at troopers by the striking crowd with no serious injury resulting.

Licenses that had been issued to many foreigners (migratory workers) to carry revolvers were revoked. Suspicious persons were searched and weapons confiscated. Roads were patrolled by the troopers with no gathering of persons permitted on sidewalks or front porches for more than a few minutes. Troopers rode their mounts several abreast and occasionally charged at full gallop clearing the streets of malcontents. They would ride their horses onto porches and into gathering places to break up gatherings. Many arrests were made for Possession of a Revolver, Rioting, Assault 2nd, Disorderly Conduct and Open Charges.

Striker Antonio Frank drew a revolver on a state officer, was disarmed, and then attempted to take the troopers gun away. He was subdued with the troopers club resulting in a scalp wound. Adolpho Stagliano was also injured from a troopers club when he tried to take away the troopers revolver.

On July 16, 1919, everything was reported quiet in the city. A few men went to work unmolested. Captain Barnes issued the following warning: "any person who has in his possession any rocks, stones, bricks or other missiles or who attempts to throw them commits a felony violation. All persons are cautioned to keep away from rock throwers." Police issued an order for all firearms to be turned in for safekeeping. Arrests would result for anyone that did not comply. A large number of residents brought their shotguns, rifles and pistols to the local police department. Each weapon turned in was identified and a receipt issued. Illegal revolvers turned in were destroyed without penalty to the owners.

This was the first time that troopers were asked by the mayor of city to help quell disorder and were ordered by the governor to do so.

The troopers met this duty, their first real test of their ability with fairness and impartiality to the Citizens of New York State. In addition, the City of Rome saved many thousands of dollars in expenses that would have been incurred had the militia been called out and the city placed under martial law.

(Batavia Daily News) (Rome Daily Sentinel)

CHAPTER TWENTY-FIVE
STREET CARMENS STRIKE OLEAN, NEW YORK – 1919

Strikes by trolley drivers on August 12, 1919 escalated to the point that on August 18, 1919, the City of Olean, New York experienced its wildest night of violence. A frenzied mob of 5000 took the law in their own hands and acted in absolute disregard of city and county authorities. Police Chief John C. Dempsey and R. O. Griffin, President of the Trades and Labor Council led strikebreakers out of the Western New York and Pennsylvania Traction Company car barns in a police wagon through an angry crowd to police headquarters. Other officers formed a lane, as they exited the police wagon, but the crowd was still able to throw stones and beat the strikebreakers with their fists, causing some serious injuries. Chief Dempsey returned to the car barns for a second, third and fourth group of strikebreakers. These men were all beaten and stoned by the crowd, just as the first group had been. A local physician, Doctor J.P. Garen gave immediate attention to the injured. Many of the strikebreakers required hospital attention for their injuries.

The unrest started in midday, when an automobile was seen traveling on Union Street toward the Traction Company car barns located at Main and Union streets. A second automobile with fifteen men in it gave chase with nuts, bolts and stones thrown back and forth between the two cars. The automobile escaped to the safety of the car barns, but was followed by a huge crowd, chasing on foot, who were also throwing rocks, stones & eggs at the automobile. At the car barns, nuts and bolts were thrown in return and the battle was on. During the melee, a shotgun was stuck out of a car barn window and a shot fired. Douglas Denning, a Pennsylvania Railroad (PRR) Brakeman was hit by small shot in the leg; John Campbell was hit in the foot and another PRR employee hit in the arm. Police soon arrived, quieted the crowd and advised them that the shooter was in custody. The shooter was never seen being brought out of the car barn. The crowd soon dwindled only to return in masse later in the evening. Lawrence Page, son of Traction Company President Wilson R. Page entered the car barns with provisions for the strikebreakers. A short time later, he exited armed with a shotgun. The crowd gave chase and caught him in a nearby potato patch beating him severely. Police interceded, undoubtedly saving his life and rushed him to Higgins Memorial Hospital. The crowd also mistook taxicab driver Joe Mongorono, as a scab strikebreaker. He was beaten by the crowd and also taken by police to Higgins Hospital. Others injured and treated at the hospital were Frank Batista, shot twice in the back, C.J. Brady, a fractured skull, Charles Simpson, head wounds and Clarence Wilbur, head wounds.

During the night of August 19, 1919, Chief Dempsey and Sheriff Raymond T. Mallery quietly removed 39 strikebreaker prisoners to the county jail in Little Valley, New York. It was expected that the strike breakers would be released one or two at time to return to their homes in New York City and Philadelphia, Pennsylvania.

The first contingent of state troopers arrived at 10:30 pm under the command of Lieutenant E. J. Sheehan to protect life and property. Lieutenant Sheehan denied that the troopers were brought here to protect the company's property. He stated that "we are neutral all the way" "We don't know anyone connected with the strike and don't want to." "We are here to put down disorder". "Both sides of the strike look alike to us". "We are only here to deal with law breakers". Colonel Chandler, head of the state police said the troopers would stay, as long as they thought it was necessary. Troopers now patrolled the city fully armed.

No more trouble was anticipated unless the traction company tried to run with scab help. Unrest was in the air, when it was rumored that the traction company was going to bring in 150 Negro strikebreakers. The traction company gave no comment when asked if more strikebreakers were being brought to Olean. In the meantime, various city organizations circulated petitions asking the city powers not to allow any strikebreakers into the city. An attempt was made by the State Industrial Commissioner and United States Labor Department to meet with President Page of the Traction Company. This meeting ended abruptly by Page, when the committee told him they had come, as representatives of the Trolleymens Union.

August 20, 1919 was payday at the Traction Company. Prior to being paid, striking motormen, conductors and others were asked to turn in their keys and other company belongings. They were told they were no longer employees, their employment was terminated and that they would not be rehired, when the strike ended.

District Attorney Archibald M. Laidlaw started an investigation of the Monday night rioting. The car barns at Main and Union Streets were boarded and nailed with all cars inside. Only a work car with section crew left the car barns in the morning returning at night with no interference by the strikers. Various unions voted that each union member would donate fifty cents towards the pay of the strikers from Olean, Salamanca and Bradford.

On August 20, 1919, Mister Page, Mayor Studholme and State Police Lieutenant Sheehan met to discuss protection of the company property. Page stated that as far as he was concerned the strike was off and none of the former strikers would be taken back. It was also determined that although there was strong opposition, strikebreakers could not be prevented from coming in to the city. With no traction cars running, only enough power was manufactured to supply the Rocky Crest Sanitarium.

On August 25, 1919, the troopers left returning to their barracks. The strike became a tame affair after the strikebreakers left. Lieutenant Sheehan was the last to leave staying until district Attorney Laidlaw finished his investigation. This resulted in arrest for rioting of many involved.

(Olean Times Union - August 12-19, 1919)

CHAPTER TWENTY-SIX
LACKAWANNA STEEL STRIKES – 1919

On September 23, 1919, Governor Alfred E. Smith ordered the state troopers to strike duty at Lackawanna, N.Y. where life and property was being threatened. Captain Winfield Robinson and 46 troopers from Batavia arrived by horse and automobile. Orders were sent out for all surrounding patrols to also report to Lackawanna as soon as possible. Details of ten men each were dispatched to Lackawanna from Troop "D", Oneida, N.Y. and Troop "G" Albany, N.Y. The men from Troop "A" and "G" were housed in the basement of police headquarters and Troop "D" housed at the firehouse. The sleeping rooms were not heated and at night, the tired men shivered themselves to sleep making the best of the situation while doing their duty well.

On September 24, 1919, a squad of twelve troopers on horseback demonstrated their efficiency in cleaning up street crowds when they charged the full length of Ridge Road along the sidewalks. They rode into saloons along the Ridge Road driving out strikers seeking refuge. The crowds were quickly dispersed. A few that stood their ground were hit with the troopers clubs into a change of mind. No serious injuries resulted and no firearms were used.

On September 25, 1919, troopers kept the streets clear and were credited with preventing a riot and bloodshed. Lieutenant Edward J. Sheehan was placed in charge. Using his experience from strike duty at Olean, N.Y., he laid down stringent rules that forbid the assemblage of more than two strikers in the district adjacent to the plant and required that meetings of strikers be restricted to halls designated by city officials. Saloonkeepers and poolroom owners were told that their places would be closed, if strikers were permitted to talk of rioting. Union leaders demanded an investigation saying that the steel plants private police force provoked the strikers and fired shots in an effort to intimidate the workers back to work. Troopers broke up gatherings in the streets, especially the Hamburg Turnpike and Ridge Roads in the vicinity of the steel plant. Troopers met violence head on with the injured treated at Moses Taylor Hospital. Every conceivable insulting epithet was hurled at the trooper, as well as stones, bricks, bottles, kerosene lamps and pepper thrown into trooper's eyes.

Many revolvers and guns were taken from rioters including a browning machine gun that was probably a war trophy, but not used. On December 24, 1919 just three months to the day that they had arrived, the troopers were ordered to discontinue further duty. They returned to Batavia arriving early on Christmas Day after an eight-hour march through a snowstorm.

It was claimed that reds fostered the recent strikes at Lackawanna with three strikers filing civil suits against Trooper Sergeant Henry Tarbox, a former guard on the University of Rochester football team. Tarbox was tackled by three of the strikers resulting in the three assailants requiring considerable patching prior to being arraigned in court on an assault charge. The three then sued Tarbox for personal damage at Lackawanna City Court in an amount of $1000.00. Attorney Lyman Tilden of Buffalo, N.Y. represented him with a February 13, 1920 return date. No determination could be found.
(Batavia Daily News)

CHAPTER TWENTY-SEVEN
TRACTION STRIKES OF 1921

On January 28, 1921, workers of the United Traction Company went on strike over wages and work hours. Violence erupted first at Albany, New York and eventually up and down the Hudson Valley where communities were linked by the Albany trolley tracks and wires. Daily attacks by strikers and retaliation by the company grew into savage violence. Cars were stoned, strikebreakers beaten, wires pulled down and tracks ripped up.

On February 8th, 1921, Albany Mayor James R. Watt, realizing that his local policemen could no longer handle the situation asked for assistance. Governor Miller ordered mobilization of the troopers as soon as possible for duty in Albany. Deputy Superintendent George P. Dutton, Acting Commander, as Major Chandler was away tending to his critically ill son, ordered the Troopers to Albany to hold the revolt in check. If the troopers could not restore order, Governor Miller would have to activate the New York State Guard to strike duty at great expense.

The first contingent of troopers from Troop "G" arrived that evening. Troop "D" arrived at 3:45 in the morning, with Troops "A" and "K" arriving at 8:00am by train for a total manpower of one hundred sixty troopers. The Troop "A" contingent was led by Lieutenant Dan Fox and Sergeant John Keeley along with Corporals Milton Nuremberg, Henry Wagner, John Lockhart, Herman Gorenflo, James Bortz & about 20 troopers. They were quartered at the 10th Regiment Armory.

Early on February 9th, Lieutenant Raymond Nagell of Troop "G" led twenty troopers on horseback and relieved the Albany Police that were guarding property at the car barns in the northern part of Albany. Shortly after noon, a repair wagon guarded by troopers with Sergeant McGarvey in charge started out to repair downed wires two blocks from the car barns. As the workers started their repairs, strikers on the rooftops began throwing cobblestones at the troopers and workers hitting the horses, causing them to bolt. Sergeant McGarvey went forward ordering the strikers to stop only to be met with jeers and increased throwing of missiles. McGarvey drew his revolver and ordered one of the strikers on a rooftop to move back. He fired one shot from his revolver, with the bullet hitting where the striker had been standing. McGarvey now stood in his stirrups and shouted that he always hit what he aimed at and the next shot would be fired at the next man to throw a cobblestone. At this the strikers scurried from the rooftops. As the repair wagon returned to the car barns, strikers in an ugly mood blocked their passage again hurling rocks. The troopers put spurs to their mounts and charged the strikers who broke into flight. When the pursuit and flight were over, the troopers returned with three of the striking leaders who were arrested and held without bail. The remainder of the day was without incident.

Captain George Dutton ordered the Traction Company to withdraw their detectives and strikebreakers from the street for any agitation would result in their arrest.

On February 11th, Governor Miller extended jurisdiction of the troopers to Troy, New York with fifty troopers on horseback assigned to the city. Troopers were quartered in the Washington Volunteer Fire House. Strikers had gathered at Franklin Square daring the police to intervene. Lieutenant Nagell led a squad of mounted troopers to the head of the square. Nagell then rode alone into the milling mass of strikers telling them they had forty-five minutes to clear the square. If they did not, the squad would charge. This was met by laughs and jeers. Another warning was given with five minutes left to clear the square. We dare you to charge the crowd yelled, and the troopers did. In less than ten minutes, the square was cleared and the riot was over. The same situations arose in Watervaliet, Cohoes,

Waterford, Green Island, Hoosick Falls, Ogdensburg, Tonawanda and East Syracuse, N.Y. In each instance, the violence was met and overcome. Eventually, the enthusiasm of the strikers for direct action waned in the face of the trooper's presence. Less than 200 troopers had quelled the riots and returned to their assigned troops. They had restored order. The strike continued, but in a more serene atmosphere.

In Albany, the strike dragged with tension felt by all sides. Strikers felt provoked because of a dispute between jitney drivers and police. Jitney drivers were used early in the strikes to carry stranded passengers. When transportation resumed, the jitneys continued to operate. Traction Company Officials complained to officials that jitneys were being operated on streets through which car lines ran in violation of their franchise. Police were ordered to withdraw the special licenses of the jitneys. On May 19, 1921, when streets were crowded with sympathizers of the strikers and jitney drivers, police proceeded to tear up the jitney licenses that had been issued. In less than fifteen minutes, a riot was in progress. Traction cars were stoned and were left deserted by strike breaking crews who were chased by the rioters. In less than an hour, Governor Miller again called for the state police to intercede. Ten mounted troopers from Troy, N.Y. responded immediately. They took a position abreast of one another at the head of the street where fighting was still going on and bore down upon the rioters. Under the surge of horse and man, the mob broke and fled. Ten troopers had broken a riot that was thought would require the National Guard. By morning there were twenty troopers patrolling the city by horse, automobile and motorcycle breaking up groups and keeping everyone on the move. No one raised a hand against the troopers. In the morning paper, Major Chandler announced that he had issued orders to the troopers to shoot to kill, if they saw anyone with a weapon or a missile in their hand. There was no trouble that day with re-enforcements arriving from Batavia, Oneida and White Plains. High profile troopers patrolled the city without incident for a week. Then on June 1, 1921, they withdrew, turning the city over to local police.
(State Troopers Magazine April & July 1921)

DEPARTMENT OF STATE POLICE
GEORGE F. CHANDLER
SUPERINTENDENT

GEORGE F. DUTTON
DEPUTY SUPERINTENDENT

NEW YORK STATE TROOPERS
STOP 39, SCHENECTADY ROAD
MAILING ADDRESS: ROOM 100, CAPITOL BUILDING
ALBANY

E. F. TOREY
CAPTAIN

H. J. NACELL
LIEUTENANT

March 10th, 1921:

From: Trooper J. D. Maroney, Troop D., Oneida, N. Y.

To: C. O. Strike Detatchment, Albany, N. Y.

Subject: TROUBLE ON JITNEY BUS IN NORTH ALBANY:

1.   On the night of March 7th at about 12:30AM I boarded
a Jitney Bus(Hudson Super-six) at corner of Garbrance Lane
and Broadway. I was going to the New York Central Station
to take a train to Oneida. There were two men and a girl
on the back seat and two men and a girl in the front seat.
I stood up in back of the front seat, resting my hands on
the back of the front seat. When about opposite the
Hudson Valley Ice Company, one of the men in the rear seat
said in a loud voice"Do you allow rats to ride in this car?"
I turned and said to the man on the right hand side of the bac
seat"Did you say that?" He replied"No, the other fellow said
By this time I had my Black Jack in my hand and I struck the
man on the left hand side of the back seat on the forehead
between the eyes. The blow drew blood. At this time the man
passenger in the front seat said"We'll throw him to Hell out",
and drew back his hand as if to strike me, whereupon I struck
the said man in the front seat, on the back of the head with
my Black Jack. He slouched down in his seat and I am not able
to say whether he was unconcious or not. I told the driver to
drive on and let me out at the New York Centrall R.R. Station,
which he did. I took the 1AM train for Oneida.

2.   My reason for not arresting the above mentioned men was
that I had recently been discharged from the Hospital and
could not have made the arrest without assistance, I was
in such a weakened condition.

             Respectfully submitted,

                  J. D. Maroney.

CHAPTER TWENTY-EIGHT
TRANSPORTATION STRIKES AT
BUFFALO, NEW YORK – 1922

On July 2, 1922, the International Railway Company went on strike at Buffalo, Corning and Hornell, New York. Rioting broke out at Buffalo, with all trolley transportation disrupted. Large loads of dirt, piles of boulders, iron girders, billboards and debris of all kinds were dumped squarely in the center of the trolley tracks. When the cars were forced to stop, the trolleys were showered with rocks and the crews beaten including policemen that rode escort. In anticipation of being called to strike duty, Major Chandler concentrated a total of 35 horses at Batavia, N.Y. that could be rushed into use by men from other troops, if the situation required. Extra patrols were stationed in the villages outside of Buffalo.

At the request of Sheriff Waldrow, but opposed by Mayor Frank X. Schwab and Police Chief Burfield who believed they had the situation under control, the order was given to the troopers to provide assistance at Buffalo.

On July 20, 1922, 250 troopers from across the state were mobilized and sent to Buffalo for strike duty. Their sole purpose was to preserve the peace. Housing was provided at the 106th National Guard Armory. Troopers were issued steel helmets, cots, blankets; heavy riot sticks and carried pistols and rifles. Major Chandler on the scene and in charge had the troopers working independent of other departments.

After one night of duty, it was reported that troopers had the situation well in hand with almost all trolley routes opened without incident. No attempt had been made to resist or injure any troopers. Complaints against troopers were minimal. People claimed that troopers rode along the street on horseback pointing pistols at windows and houses, had ridden their horses into stores, used their riot clubs for no good reason and were being unduly harsh. Major Chandler declared that troopers were "teaching respect for law and order" and every blow struck was the result of a vile remark aimed at a trooper. "Until the spirit of lawlessness that manifested itself in the early stages of the strike dies down, we must be strict. Troopers resort to force only as a last resort, and then without kid gloves."

On July 25, 1922, Boselaus W. Bialecki, 166 Lovejoy Street, Buffalo, N.Y. claiming to represent 10,000 Poles complained to Sheriff Walrow to protest the outrages, cruelty and unwarranted violence on the part of the troopers. On July 28, Sheriff Waldrow made the following statement in support of the troopers. "I prefer the present rule to the mob rule that existed on the east side just before the troopers came and I am sure that law abiding citizens of Buffalo prefer it to". On August 1, troopers left Buffalo, N.Y. for Batavia, N.Y. without giving notice of departure. There, they awaited further orders to return to their home troops.

On August 19, 1922, troopers were sent to patrol the high-speed trolley line between Buffalo and Niagara Falls. The high-speed line had been dynamited the day before resulting in the derailment of three-car trolley that injured fifty passengers. Buffalo Police Chief of Detectives Zimmerman arrested Bert Wilson and John W. Simme who had 500 sticks of dynamite in their possession.

HORNELL, NEW YORK

On July 24, 1922, eighteen troopers under the command of Sergeant Gerald Sullivan arrived at Hornell, N.Y. because trouble was feared from strikers and sympathizers. Mayor Fred A. Robbins made the request from Governor Miller after the arrest of Mark Valentine, Tony Puski and Vincent Kershbner, three Erie Railroad Detectives being held for the killing of Erie shop striker Frank Ardivino. No confirmation of disposition could be located, but it was believed the detectives were not held for trial. Calm prevailed with only a few incidents reported. On September 21, 1922, Sergeant Sullivan arrested 18-year-old Jennie Massi on charges of Inciting a Crowd to resist police authority, but she was later acquitted after a jury trial. On June 29, 1923, Sebastian Sall, guardian for Massi sued for damages at Supreme Court in Hornell, N.Y. claiming Assault, False Imprisonment & Malicious Prosecution. After a short trial, a verdict of "no cause for action resulted." Testifying in behalf of Sergeant Sullivan was former Trooper Peter Larsen, now Police Chief at Westfield, N.Y. (Batavia Daily News)

CHAPTER TWENTY-NINE
PRISON RIOTS

CLINTON PRISON, DANNEMORA, N.Y.

On July 22, 1929, a mass inmate attempt was made to storm a prison wall, form a human ladder and escape. Sirens sounded with all available guards reporting for duty on the walls. Guards were supplemented by a detail of troopers from Malone, N.Y. and U.S. Customs Officers. The rioting inmates were turned back and secured in their cells. Order was restored, but not before two inmates lost their lives.

AUBURN NEW YORK PRISON RIOTS

On July 28, 1929, inmates at Auburn Prison rioted for seven hours before being subdued and returned to their cells. Warden Edgar Jennings said there had been an air of tension since the rioting the week before at Clinton Prison. Heat of the summer and overcrowding conditions contributed to the disorder.

The Auburn Prison population was at 1772 inmates crowded into twelve hundred cells with many inmates sleeping in corridors. Inmates had overpowered guards, taken their keys and secured sub-machine guns and other weapons from the prison armory. Using a guard as a shield, inmates stormed the main gate with four inmates succeeding in escaping. Fires had been started within the prison work areas as a diversion. Troopers responded to the call for assistance. With trooper sharpshooters on the walls for cover, a six-man detail led by Lieutenants Franklin D. Orser and John D. Cosart entered the prison yard with weapons drawn. They went among the inmates and disarmed them. The searched inmates were then taken to their cells and locked in. Early morning found the unrest had ended. The escapees were identified as Henry Sullivan, from Erie County, Ernest Pavesi, King County, Joseph Bravsta and Stephen Pawlak. All were recaptured and returned to the prison. They were subsequently charged and convicted of Escape.

On December 11, 1929, a gang of twenty long-term, violent inmates spread terror and death at Auburn Prison, when they killed Principal Keeper George A. Durnford and took Warden Edgar Jennings and seven guards hostage. Fifteen hundred other inmates although curious, stayed out of harms way. The alarm was spread, when Guard David Winney escaped flying bullets to reach the main gate. Within a short time, the prison was an armed camp of troopers, citizens and soldiers from the Army National Guard 108th Infantry ordered there by acting Governor Herbert Lehman. The convicts demanded safe passage through the gates or they would kill the hostages. Corrections Commissioner Dr. Raymond Kleb ordered that if they came out, shoot, if they don't come out, go in and get them. There would be no compromise. The twenty mutineers responded by barricading themselves and their hostages at the rear of a main hall within the prison. Under cover of darkness, a detail of troopers led by Captain Stephen McGrath, stormed the main hall with the use of tear gas bombs. Warden Jennings and four guards rushed through the gas followed by a hail of bullets.

Injured and sent to the hospital were; Guards George Atkins, shot through the neck, James F. Van Housen, shot in the eye, Albert C. Holzhauer, shot in the mouth, Claude Dempsey, Walter Failey, Lucius Hugunin and Milton Riker, treated for gas effects.

The National Guard Troops and a majority of the troopers were returned to their posts the next morning. Eight inmates killed during the revolt were identified as Perry Johnson, Broome County, sentenced to life, Alex Tucholka, Erie County, sentenced to life, Steve Pawlak, Erie County, sentenced to double life, Stephen Sporning, Erie County, sentenced to sixteen years, Duke J. Bonnell, Queens County, sentenced to 30 years, Henry Sullivan, Erie County, sentenced to 21 years, Ernest Pavesi, Kings County, sentenced to 40 years and James Biancrassi.

The Troop "A" flying squad of sixteen troopers responded to the Auburn Prison riot led by Lieutenants Gerald Vaine and Lawrence Nelson. Five Troop "A" men had been on duty at the prison since the July riots. Led by Lieutenant Vaine, an assault group made up of Sergeant Joe Brandstetter, Trooper Theodore Lewis, Leslie Button and "Blizzard" Gus Nelson was formed. Many remaining rioters were hiding at the end of a tier in a cellblock and continued to shoot and use tear gas against the troopers. Corporal Gus Nelson ordered them to surrender. Riot leader Steve Pawlak yelled for him to go to hell, then poked his head out from the end of the cellblock and was shot dead with one shot by Nelson. Troopers rushed in and subdued the remaining rioters all of whom had suffered gunshot wounds. Other troopers from Troop "A" that responded to the riot were Corporals Arthur Rich and Errol W. Wheeler, Troopers Chester W. Acer, Devillo Chamberlain, Thomas A. Greer, Albert S. Horton, Theodore E. Lewis, Albert E. Perry, Raymond R. Regan, Harley C. Robinson, Sam Vint and Leo J. Miller.

In his memoirs, Sgt. John Long, (1929 to 1969) noted that troopers were assigned to guard duty on the walls at Auburn Prison working in twelve-hour shifts. Long was there from December 12, 1929 with Sergeant Charles Burnett, Corporal Ted Martin, Troopers Donald Girven, Harry DeHollander and Hugh Dougherty and were housed at the local armory. At Christmas time, local families invited every trooper to their homes to enjoy a wonderful Christmas dinner.

Former State Police Superintendent George Chandler was appointed to investigate and report on cause and remedies at the prison. His report noted that in 1913, an inner prison organization called the Mutual Welfare League made up solely of inmates were given authority to hold meetings at anytime in rooms provided by the warden. No outsiders except the warden could attend. There was an executive committee of nine elected from inmate representatives in a ratio of 1 to 85. Other prisoners could be called in to league meetings at their pleasure. They had authority to take away or grant privileges, mete out punishment and run entertainment and baseball games with monies from outsiders kept. In 1929, the League had been taken over by hardened, violent inmates who abused the system. The prison, built in 1816 was antiquated, dark, damp and cold with outdated sanitation systems adding to the unrest. It was also noted that since the July riots, workshops that were burned were still under repair resulting in inmate's frustration over having nothing to keep them busy. Chandler recommended the relief of overcrowding through use of off site rental property adequate for the task. He advocated the hiring of an additional fifty guards, the abolishment of the Mutual Welfare League and establishment of a place for segregation of incorrigible prisoners. A detail of troopers remained on guard duty at Auburn Prison until April 1, 1930.

(Batavia Daily News) (Memoirs of Sgt John M. Long, 1985)

CHAPTER THIRTY
THE MILK STRIKES – 1933

March 29 - Albert Woodhead, Rochester, New York, President of the Western New York Milk Producers Association (WNYMPA) called for a strike that was aimed at the Dairymen's League Co-operative Association. (DLCA) Woodhead felt that the DLCA did not represent the farmer's interest and steadily took a larger middleman profit. With statewide support, the WNYMPA attempted to deal directly with the milk dealers to obtain a 3-½ cents per quart of milk increase. Striking farmers stopped two trucks near Pittsford, New York that were enroute to a Rochester, N.Y. milk plant, dumping out their loads of milk.

March 30 - The strike escalated to the point where thousands of protesting farmers stopped trucks carrying milk, dumping the loads in an effort to cut off the Rochester supply. Milk trucks escorted by state troopers succeeded under their protection, with no milk lost although two striking farmers were injured in an encounter with troopers. Troopers in riot gear dispersed seventy-five strikers that had gathered in front of the East Avon, N.Y. trooper's station in an effort to prevent them from leaving the barracks. Troopers were determined in their resistance to any efforts to halt truckers legally using the highway with many heads bruised in brushes between strikers and defending officers. The highways between Batavia and Rochester bristled with trooper activity, all equipped for riot duty in their assignments of guarding trucks laden with milk. Captain Winfield W. Robinson, Troop "A" Commander stated that the "troopers have no interest in this matter other than the protection of the rights of the traveler of the highway"

March 31 - Twenty-two carloads of troopers escorted a milk convoy from Syracuse to Rochester, N.Y. without incident. At Williamson, N.Y., seventy-five strikers clashed with thirty troopers, when they barricaded the road in an attempt to stop two trucks from reaching Rochester. Troopers traveling to Rochester from White Plains, N.Y. for milk strike duty were involved in an automobile accident, when their automobile left the roadway near Schenectady, N.Y. Sergeant Walter A. Purcell of Richfield Springs, N.Y was killed, the result of a broken neck, Corporal Homer Brown of Schenectady, N.Y. suffered a fractured skull and Trooper Edward F. Merkle of Catskill, N.Y. suffered a head injury.

March 31 to April 8 - Strikers now 90,000 strong remained in abeyance pending a legislative vote on the Pitcher Bill, which would establish a state, control board to determine fair prices for producers and consumers.

April 8 - No action on the Pitcher Bill resulted in a renewal of the strike. Over two hundred troopers were on duty with those assigned at the East Avon barracks led by Lieutenant Gerald Vaine bearing the brunt of the re-newed violence. Milk trucks from surrounding areas were escorted to Webster's

Crossing, N.Y. where the milk was loaded into railroad tank cars for shipment to Brooklyn, N.Y. for processing.

April 9 - One of the most violent outbreaks occurred at the Elba Milk Plant, Elba, N.Y., when 100 strikers attempted to damage the plant and destroy milk. Thirty troopers led by Sergeant Joseph Brandstetter, dispersed the strikers after a rain of blows from riot sticks. Trooper J.T. Murphy was injured, when hit in the face by a rock that split his tooth. One trooper commented, "Every farmer that was rapped with a stick will bear a grudge against the department". We have to live with the farmer's all through the year and it is too bad that this had to happen.

April 10 – Governor Lehman signed the Pitcher Bill into law with no independent representative assigned to the board. This ended the milk strike and the most violent civil disobedience ever encountered in Genesee County and Western New York.

August 1 – Albert Woodhead, now president of the newly formed Empire dairyman's Protective Society (EDPS) called for a statewide strike which grew out of the repeated refusal of the State Milk Control Board to grant disaffected milk producers a larger share of the consumers milk dollar. Sporadic violence erupted at Oneida, Lewis and Herkimer Counties.

August 2 – At Booneville, N.Y., it was called the "Milk War". Over 400 striking farmers, many armed with axes and clubs attempted to stop an escorted milk shipment. Troopers using riot clubs and tear gas resulting in eight farmers being seriously injured dispersed them. Local officials later protested to the governor stating the troopers attacked the striking farmers without provocation, because they were gathered in the vicinity of the highway where the milk was passing. No milk was lost.

August 3 – Genesee County milk producers voted not to participate in the strike having their shipments escorted by troopers who had been ordered to protect all milk shipments, milk plants and milk trains.

August 4 – Violence continued at various locations throughout the state. Troopers Fritz and Kearns were injured near Fonda, N.Y., when attacked by strikers while escorting a milk truck. At Honeoye Falls, N.Y., Sergeant Edward Doody, Troopers Michael Fort and Andrew Fisher were severely bruised, when they were rear ended by one of the milk trucks they were escorting.

August 5 – The fiercest fighting of the strike between troopers and strikers occurred at Vernon and Oriskaney, N.Y. Trooper George Marshall was hospitalized with a brain hemorrhage, when struck by a rock or club. Trooper George Lewis was hospitalized with a brain concussion and Corporal George Coburn lost several teeth, when struck in the face with a metal bar. Hand to hand combat saw at least twenty strikers go down, the result of troopers cracking heads with riot sticks and strikers hurling rocks and swinging clubs.

August 6 to 8 – Only minor outbreaks of violence occurred at various location.

August 9 – Strikers dumped over 6000 gallons of milk on the roads to Syracuse. Firearms were brought into play with an occasional harmless shot fired. Troopers were issued 30-30 rifles for their protection.

August 10 to 11 – Only sporadic dumping and violence occurred. The strike is waning with more than two hundred strikers arrested statewide.

Sergeant John M. Long recalled the 1933 Milk Strikes that pitted farmer against farmer. One group of striking dairy farmers, members of a Milkman's Association, were holding out for more money for their milk. Other farmers that weren't part of the strike tried to deliver their milk to the processing plants. The strikers would carry kerosene jugs, throw it onto the milk cans on the trucks and beat up the drivers. They would loosen lug nuts on the delivery trucks eventually resulting in the truck's wheel coming off.

(Batavia Daily News) (Rome Daily Sentinel) (Rochester Democrat & Chronicle)

1921 STRIKE DUTY - COHOES, NY-TPR SILVERNAIL

1929 AUBURN PRISON DUTY

1933 MILK STRIKES

1933 MILK STRIKE ESCORT DUTY

1929 AUBURN PRISON -GUS NELSON

1929 AUBURN PRISON AFTER RIOT

STRIKE DUTY 1921

STRIKE DUTY 1921

BOOK IV – GROWTH & MANDATES

CHAPTER THIRTY-ONE
LAWS DIRECTLY AFFECTING THE STATE POLICE

Chapter 161, Laws of 1917 – Authorized establishment of a state police.

Chapter 176, Laws of 1921 – Authorized expenditure for a NYS Police School.

Chapter 328, Laws of 1921 – Conservation Law conferred upon members of the state police all the powers and duties of game protectors.

In April 1921, the Mullan-Gage Act gave police agencies authority to enforce prohibition under NYS Laws. This law was repealed in total on June 1, 1923.

Chapter 406, Laws of 1922 – Amended the Labor Law authorizing the state police to make inspections of places of public assembly except where there was a local enforcing agency.

Chapter 671, Laws of 1922 – Placed licensing and enforcement regulations of billiard rooms and imposed specific duties on the state police for enforcement.

Chapter 429, Laws of 1923 – Directed the Superintendent of State Police to co-operate with the Commissioner of Motor Vehicles in the enforcement of the Vehicle & Traffic Law.

Chapter 605, Laws of 1923 – Required members of the state police to act as court officers in courts of special sessions on Indian reservation. (The Attorney General later declared this unconstitutional)

Chapter 668, Laws of 1924 – Authorized the Superintendent of State Police authority to issue commissions for railway policemen within the state.

In 1924, the State Education Department designated all members of the state police as inspectors for the purpose of visiting theatres throughout the state to ascertain if motion picture reels shown carried the proper license or seal as required.

Chapter 7, Laws of 1925 – Authorized the state police to kill any dog found pursuing or killing deer within the Adirondack or Catskill State Parks.

Chapter 523, Laws of 1925 – Permitted the state police to contract for and carry group life insurance.

Chapter 547, Laws of 1926 – Amended the Vehicle & Traffic Law by taking police powers from motor vehicle inspectors and delegating this power to the state police.

Chapter 57, Laws of 1927 – Executive Law changing the "Department of State Police" to "Division of State Police" of the Executive Department.

Chapter 336, Laws of 1928 – Amended the Agricultural Law requiring state police to prevent gambling or obscene shows at agricultural fairs or exhibits.

Chapter 556, Laws of 1928 – Amended the Civil Service Law making the state police eligible to become members of the State Employee's Retirement Fund.

Chapter 610, Laws of 1928 – Required persons finding stray dogs to report same to local police or the Superintendent of State Police.

Chapter 272, Laws of 1930 – Provided for the enforcement of motorboat regulations on the St. Lawrence River. A swift patrol boat was purchased with two troopers assigned.

Chapter 633, Laws of 1931 – Provided funding for the establishment of a teletype system.

Chapter 792, Laws of 1931 – Required all revolver licensing officers within the state to file a duplicate of all applications with the Superintendent of State Police at Albany, N.Y.

Chapter 121, Laws of 1932 – Amended the General Business Law authorizing the state police to obtain and preserve evidence in case of airplane wrecks and forbidding the removal of such wrecks until viewed by a U.S. Commerce inspector.

Chapter 697, Laws of 1935 – Established within the state police a Bureau of Criminal Investigation and laboratory facilities.

Chapter 389, Laws of 1936 – Increased the state police manpower by 100 men.

Chapter 516, Laws of 1938 – Abolished enlistments for a specified number of years (2- years) and made appointments permanent. It also provided for a ½ at salary retirement after twenty-five years of continuous service.

Chapter 881, Laws of 1942 – Required the state police to fingerprint industrial guards utilized at military plants.

CHAPTER THIRTY-TWO
FAIR DETAIL

The first official duty performed by the full complement of the newly formed New York State Constabulary was the policing of the New York State Fair at Syracuse, New York in September 1917. Initially, Pinkerton men conducted policing, but as the fair grew in size, this was taken over by the New York City mounted police at a cost of several thousand dollars each year. Since the troopers took over, there was no additional financial burden placed upon the Fair Commission. Troopers faced two immediate problems, keeping law and order and directing traffic at the fair. Visitors came on foot, by trolley, rail and automobile. Major Chandler determined that in the interest of pedestrian safety, only officials and exhibitors would be allowed on the grounds and then could only use a perimeter road on the outside of the buildings. All others were parked off the fair grounds property. Chandler fashioned a system of fishbone parking that allowed for maximum automobile parking capacity with both easy entry and exit, when needed. Ropes first designated these parking lanes, but as drivers became accustomed to them, only a white stake was needed as a marker. In later years, this parking of thousands of automobiles was acknowledged as one of the trooper's greatest achievements.

Paramount duty of the trooper at the state fair was the handling of large crowds without accident or confusion. Sideshows and entertainment were carefully censored. No immorality was permitted. Known crooks and pickpockets were warned that they were being closely watched. The racetrack was kept clear of visitors to prevent injury. The first year troopers policed the fair, a horse bolted with the driver losing the reins, as it galloped around the track. A mounted trooper gave chase catching the loose horse in front of the grandstand near the box where Governor Whitman was sitting. The crowd gave a standing ovation. On the aviation field, troopers were worn to a frazzle keeping young boys away from the planes and airstrip where planes were landing and taking off. There were many narrow escapes, but no injuries. A trooper was stationed near valuable exhibits and proved better than a thousand do not touch signs. On one occasion, a visitor reported his car with a bulldog pup in it stolen. He reported that he would be at the Onondaga Hotel, if it were located. When he reached the hotel, he found the following message waiting: "Your car is at State Police Headquarters, the thief is held for your complaint, the bulldog pup has had his dinner and is comfortable."

On January 9, 1933, Fred B. Parker of Batavia, N.Y. wrote the following edited article found in the Batavia Daily News regarding the state fair.

I had been a member of the State Fair Commission for several years and one of my activities placed me in charge of policing the grounds and buildings. Policing was done with civilians sent from various parts of the state recommended by politicians. It was quite an unsatisfactory service. I knew Major Chandler was recruiting and training four units of the newly formed state police at Manlius, N.Y. Since they were a state organization, as was the state fair, I thought they might police the annual state fair. This would provide an introduction of the new department to the public and at the same time save the fair the expense of costly security and policing. I called on Major Chandler several times and arrangements were completed for the state police to make their initial appearance at the September 1917 New York State Fair.

Many years later, Corporal Howard Blanding noted the following about the fair in his memories:

He stated that not too many troopers volunteered for state fair duty. The long exhausting hours of duty drained your energy and we were confined to a barracks for the few hours we were off duty. It was hot and uncomfortable, as there was no such thing as air conditioning. A fan was all you had. He remembered the state fair being about two weeks long. He recalled an incident, when he shot a diseased cat in one of the horse stables, with his 45-caliber revolver. No one wanted to shoot it, because it meant a lot of paper work for discharging the weapon. Troopers have policed and provided security at the State Fair every year since.
(State Trooper Magazine 1920-1922)

CHAPTER THIRTY-THREE
NEW YORK STATE POLICE SCHOOL

Authorized under Chapter 176, Part 2 of the Laws of 1921, the first state police school- sessions were held at the Troy, N.Y., Young Men's Christian Association (YMCA). These accommodations were found to be inadequate and were moved to the 105th Regiment Armory, Troy, N.Y., after the second year. This location proved invaluable because of its excellent pistol and rifle range and spacious rooms.
(1921 NYSP Annual Reports)

Troopers were constantly brought up to speed on new changes and methods. From 1917 to 1921, daily classes were held for troopers in reserve at the barracks. In addition to troopers, railroad police, police chiefs and other state police agencies attended the school at no cost to their department.

Recognized as the first certified police school in the nation, the New York State School for Police held its first sessions from November 1 to 30, 1921. Courses given were evaluated and approved by the New York State Board of Regents. Fifty-three troopers graduated from the first session and were awarded a state certificate as a professional policeman.

The first class of graduates had no practical police experience and failed to meet expectations when placed in their assigned duty stations. Major chandler immediately   implemented a policy where all attendees at the school had to first have one year of field experience prior to attending classes. The school was under the direction of Lieutenant Albert B. Moore, a trooper and outstanding instructor. He gathered an excellent staff from the Attorney Generals Office, District Attorneys and other professionals who were willing to donate their time.

In 1922, the school published a training textbook " the Policeman's Art" through Funk & Wagnall's of New York City. This text was sold nationwide with proceeds going to maintain the school. In 1925, sessions were increased from four to six weeks and curriculum increased with classes held during January and February.

Newly hired probationary troopers were on the road for several months prior to attending classes at the police school. Successful completion of courses given at the Academy was required to become a trooper.
(NYSP Annual Reports 1922)

During 1930, Inspector Albert E. Moore was sent to Europe for three months to study investigative methods and systems in use by Scotland Yard and the French Surete. The purpose was to study these techniques, methods and reporting systems for possible use and improvement of courses taught at the State Police School.

1930 also saw the system of statewide bulletins initiated through the Police Academy. This method provided uniformity and was distributed to police agencies throughout the state providing the most recent information pertaining to statutes, amendments to existing laws, court decisions and police procedure. This distribution of information was vastly improved and quickly provided through the new teletype system installed in 1931.
(NYSP Annual Reports – 1930 & 1932)

In 1932, Inspector Moore was assigned to the State of Virginia for one week where he helped inaugurate a statewide system of police training schools. Moore trained instructors and provided them with an initial curriculum. The entire curriculum provided was adopted and approved by the Virginia State Police and used statewide.

In 1932, the service of the New York State School for Police was also requested by the University of Chicago to help formulate a national police-training program.

The January 4, 1937 class was the first session where students were required to enter a gas filled building as part of their training in tear gas. The theory was that the experience would take away any fears they might have. In March 1937, a one-week class was held for troopers assigned to the Bureau of Criminal Investigation and in April 1937, a one-week session was given in traffic investigations.

THE ORIGINAL SCHOOL FACULTY OF 1921

Lt. Colonel George F. Chandler – Department of State Police
Lieutenant Albert B. Moore – Department of State Police

Captain Allan C. Smith – US Army
Doctor G.A. Cornell – Physical Department, YMCA. Troy, N.Y.
Captain Elihu F. Tobey – New York State Police

J. Allan Van Wie – Revolver Instructor
Colonel Roy D. Jones – Smith & Wesson Company
J.P. Fitzgerald – Colt Patent Firearms Company
William T. Moore – Deputy Attorney General, New York State
Edward G. Griffin – Deputy Attorney General, New York State

Honorable Joseph A. Lawson – Albany, N.Y.
Lieutenant J.J. Fitzpatrick - NY City Police Department
Judge Herbert F. Roy – Troy, N.Y.
Lieutenant E.C. Roberts – Department of State Police
Colonel Ransom H. Gillett, Albany, N.Y.

Judge Walter Knapp – NYS Tax Commission
N.J. Walker – State Secretary of Humane Societies
C.L. DeAngelis – District Attorney, Oneida County, N.Y.
G.L. Flanders – Counsel, NYS Department of Farms & Markets

Sergeant J.S. Reap – New York State Police
Captain George P. Dutton – New York State Police
Llewellyn Legge – Chief Division Fish & Game Conservation
J.T. Mahoney – NYS Conservation Commission
Lieutenant H.J. Nagell – New York State Police

Judge Pierce H. Russell – Judge, Rensselaer County
Captain W.W. Robinson – New York State Police
Berne A. Pyrke – Commissioner Department Farms & Markets
J. Allan Wood – Chief, Kingston Police Department
J.J. Sheehan - Federal Narcotic Agent

Matthias Nicoll Jr. – Deputy Commissioner NYS Department of Health
A.W. Hoffman – Managing Editor, Kingston Daily Freeman
(1922 NYSP Annual Report)

CHAPTER THIRTY-FOUR
HORSE RIDING TEAMS

In 1921, Captain Stephen McGrath, Troop "D" Oneida, N.Y. formed a group of troopers into a skilled riding team that he named the "Rough Riders". They were soon followed by the Spotted Horse troop led by Captain Dan Fox at Troop "C", Sidney, N.Y. and the Black Horse troop at Troop "B" Malone, N.Y. Troops "A" and "K" had two and four man horse teams that competed and performed at local fairs. These teams were encouraged for their training value and exposure of troopers to the public during performances at local fairs & expositions, as well as creating inter-troop competition. Troop "G" had a fine riding team that was disbanded in 1926.

Blankets with surcingle (girth belt around a horse's belly) were used initially and the routines were known as "Monkey Drills". They then used the McClellan saddle and as the tricks became more difficult, high class Western saddles were purchased by the men themselves. The Troop "D" trick horses were Palomino's with bridles and breastplates red in color and the saddles studded in silver. The rough riders were regarded as the best in the country. They displayed their skills at the National Legion Convention in Boston, Massachusetts and Detroit, Michigan. They always performed on Governor's day at the State Fair, the Tri-State Fair at Athens, Pa and all county fairs in the troop area. They performed a difficult and dangerous ten (10)-man pyramid maintained aboard four (4) galloping horses for a distance of one half mile.
(1921 NYSP Annual Report)
(History of NYSP)

Members of the 1929 Rough Riders included Captain Stephen McGrath, Lieutenant Tremaine Hughes, Joseph Deveans, J.A. Steeley, Benjamin Butler, J. Buster Todd, John Damrath, William Wheeler, John Mitrzyk, B.M. Sockman, C.M. Poplin, G. Smith and Joseph Fitzpatrick.

Other team members during the existence of the Rough Riders included:

(Believed to be members prior to 1929) Lt. Walter Croasdale, John M. Keeley, Cpl. Gray, Tprs. Grieg, Albrighter, Pfifer, Gonterman, McAleese, Dashway, Cowburn, and Danforth.

(After 1929) Tprs., Murphy, Hackett, Harney, Holmes, Tubbert, and Tupper.

SPOTTED HORSE TROOP
Troop "C" started its brilliant career in 1921 under the guidance of Captain Daniel E. Fox. He assembled 50 colored or so-called spotted saddle horses or pintos. The superintendent permitted him to engage in horse trading, using his judgment, until Troop "C" had the distinction of having all spotted horses. This was no easy task, as they were very scarce at the time. In 1926, he traveled to the Crow Indian Reservation in Montana where he acquired a carload of spotted horses. In 1921, Fox convinced the superintendent to sponsor the presentation of a trophy at the State Fair in Syracuse to the troop displaying the best horsemanship. The riders also used Western saddles that were silver studded with the bridle and breastplate colored white. The tournament was held and won by Troop "C" for seven consecutive years. In 1926, the "Spotted Horses" competed against other states at the Sesquicentennial in Philadelphia and won first prize. They appeared at the Canadian Nation Exposition on two occasions. Appearances were made at the National Horse Show in Madison Square Garden, as well as agricultural fairs throughout New York, Pennsylvania and New England. The trick riding team was composed of eight troopers and their mounts. They rode in unison in a single line at full gallop while engaged in sixteen different maneuvers. Included are acts of crawling under the horse's belly, under the neck, jumping off from the hindquarters, jumping off either side, standing upright on the horse's shoulders and on the saddles followed by individual performances. These appearances were gradually reduced and discontinued due to the increased demand upon the troopers, mostly in traffic control. An agreement existed between Troops "C" and "D" that they would never compete against each other to determine the best team. Both teams finished their careers, as champions.

The 1923 riding team was made up of Captain Dan Fox, Troopers Guy Moore, Tom Mangan, Henry Freer, Russell McLewman, Louis DeCarlo, Oscar Brown, Ed Hulse, John Norton, Paul McMahon, T.C. Weeks, Edward C. Smith and William Packard.

In May 1939, Major Warner eliminated all appearances of the Troop "D" Rough Riders and Troop "C" Spotted Horses from county fairs and exhibitions. Every trooper was needed to supervise traffic because of the anticipated high volume of traffic traveling to the World's Fair held in New York. The horses were eventually sold off or sent to the State Health Farm to remain only a historic memory.

CHAPTER THIRTY-FIVE
CONSERVATION LAW

Troopers were charged with the enforcement of all laws. They were particularly fond of the Conservation Law, as little paperwork was required and dispositions were through civil compromise, a fine paid with no criminal record resulting.

On October 21, 1927, eighteen year old Adolph Zink, Riga, N.Y. was shot and killed during the first day of pheasant hunting season. Corporal James Wolcott investigated the accident finding that the youth was hunting with his father, Cornelius Zink and a brother walking along a heavy hedgerow on the family farm. A second group of hunters were unknowingly hunting across from them, when a pheasant flew up between them. Alexander Yargealitis of Rochester, N.Y. fired through the brush striking the Zink youth. The shot penetrated the right lung. He died almost immediately.

Martin A. Hull, Mechanic Street, Elba, N.Y. while in an open field shot his hunting partner, fifty-two year old Frank H. Squires of Chapel Street, Elba, N.Y. in the legs. Hull heard a shot in the near vicinity and when he turned, his gun discharged with shot striking Squires. Oakfield Doctor A.H. Stein removed four pellets from his legs.

Corporal Charles Stanton and Trooper Stitt arrested Welton Pickett, 42 Waverly Street, Buffalo, N.Y. for having four male pheasants in his possession. He paid a civil penalty of $52.50 before Pembroke Justice C.L.Mallory.

Attica farmer Frank Karpinski was charged with not having a hunting license. Not being a United States citizen, he was not entitled to one. He paid a $17.50 civil penalty before Bennington Justice Henry Lapp.

Robert E. Sanford, Albion, N.Y. was charged by Troopers Laurence Nelson and Earl Pratt with taking a hen pheasant. He paid a $27.50 civil penalty before Albion Justice J.B. Daniels.

Canisteo, N.Y. laborer Clause Hall was arrested for taking a hen pheasant out of season. He paid a $27.50 civil penalty before Hornell Judge George Cotton.

Sergeant John Krick and Trooper Walter Helfeldt arrested four men for hunting on the Tuscorora Indian Reservation. Each paid a $12.50 civil penalty before Lewiston Justice Charles W. Fieldus.

Mrs. Gloria Schemerhorn, age 21, Bemus Point, N.Y. was arrested on October 19, 1928 for hunting without a license. She paid a $12.50 civil penalty before Indian Falls Justice Elmer Passmore.

Troopers during the first few days of the 1928 hunting season checked on 4,642 hunters in the field, made 22 arrests for game law violations and collected $1,342.50 in fines.

CHAPTER THIRTY-SIX
FIRST NEW YORK STATE TROOPER AIRCRAFT

Since Charles Lindbergh's historic flight from New York City to Paris, France in "The Spirit of St. Louis" on May 20, 1927, large numbers of transport and commercial planes had come into use. The 1929 Batavia, N.Y. high school civic class, as a school project, made a recommendation to Major John Warner advocating the use of an airplane by the state police. Major Warner did not believe that the distance traveled by troopers was long enough to give the airplane any advantage of speed. However two years later, the need for rapid travel for field inspection, taking of tear gas bombs to scenes where needed, search for fugitives and lost persons, transportation of prisoners and the taking of fingerprint experts to crime scenes had changed and the first state police aircraft was authorized.

The first trooper airplane was delivered in July 1931 at the Amboy Municipal Airport near Syracuse, N.Y. Company pilot P. Warner flew it there from Buffalo, N.Y. It was turned over to Lieutenant Hughes who flew it on to Oneida, N.Y. where a large delegation of officials awaited its arrival. If the use of the airplane proved successful, other troops would be equipped with planes. The Consolidated Aircraft Plant in Buffalo, N.Y, manufactured the aircraft. It was a "Model 8 Fleet" powered with a 125 horsepower Kinner motor and was capable of a top speed of up to 110 miles per hour. The plane had a three place open cockpit with yellow wings and gray fuselage trimmed in black. Its first use was for patrol work and to carry prisoners from outlying areas. (The description as a three-seat open cockpit plane is directly from an article, as it appeared in the Batavia Daily News. In every other document that I have read, the plane was described as a two-seat open plane.)

The troopers aircraft program was under the direction of Lieutenant Tremaine Hughes. Hughes became interested in flying, when the Oneida Flying Club was organized in 1928. He later transferred to the Utica ground school taking courses and instructions from Dick Botsford of the Colonial Flying School that he completed in 1930. With five brother troopers, a plane was purchased and home training started. He trained the small group, all of who earned transport or limited commercial licenses. They were Sergeant Vincent D. Cooper, Corporal Joseph Fitzpatrick, Troopers Clarence G. Doran, Harry J. Sanderson, William Stevenson and John Wheeler. The legislatively purchased plane was delivered in July 1931 and kept at the Oneida, N.Y. airport, replacing this plane.

On January 15, 1932, Lieutenant Tremaine Hughes and Corporal Theopholis Gaines plunged to their death in their burning trooper plane near Cazenovia, New York while flying from Batavia to Albany, New York. At about 5:15 PM, Mrs. Glendon Blowers who lived nearest the scene heard the crashing of the plane, looked out the window and saw a burning mass on the roadway. She believed it to be an auto accident and immediately telephoned Trooper Lyman stationed at Cazenovia four miles away. Lyman responding to the scene found Lieutenant Hughes still in the burning cockpit and pulled him out of the fire. Seeing the state insignia on the aircraft, Lyman only then realized who was in the plane. He immediately called Captain Stephen McGrath at Oneida, N.Y. who made notifications to division headquarters. It was learned that Corporal Gaines had been making an inspection tour of the states new teletype system. Lt. Hughes had flown Gaines from Sidney to Batavia, N.Y. and both were returning from Batavia to Albany, N.Y., when the crash occurred. It was determined that Hughes was flying at tree top level due to a heavy fog with his landing lights on and was either looking for a place to land or had engine trouble. One wing was found at the base of a tree and the other a short distance away with the fuselage 400 feet away with motor buried deep in the mud along side of the concrete highway.

Major Warner paid tribute to the dead fliers: He said that there never were two finer men in the service. No one could find a better, pluckier man than Lieutenant Hughes. He was a skillful pilot, daring when daring was necessary, but not foolhardy. Corporal Gaines was a man of splendid ability and spotless reputation.

After World War I, the United States Army sold its surplus planes to the public at a cost of $300.00 that also included flying lessons. In 1930, there were 9840 planes in the United States with 1119 registered in New York State. There were 10,215 licensed pilots nationwide with 170 being women. New York State had 1005 licensed pilots.

(Batavia Daily News)
(Rome Daily Sentinel)
(Syracuse Herald)

CHAPTER THIRTY-SEVEN
PISTOL PERMIT BUREAU

Chapter 792 of the Laws of 1931 provided that a copy of all applications to carry or possess revolvers and pistols must be filed with the Division of State Police at Albany, N.Y. by the issuing authority. The pistol bureau was established and started functioning in 1932 with a total of 85,000 applications received for the year. No funding or additional personnel were provided for with the function handled by the Albany staff in addition to their normal duties.

Licensees were card indexed and all licensed revolvers classified under a numerical filing system. This system allowed for every licensed revolver by serial number reference to be classified under a three digit indexing system.

During 1933, help was obtained through the Emergency Unemployment Relief Act that permitted the updating of files. Annual renewal of each license to carry a weapon made all original applications the subject of a yearly search. This was very time consuming. Cross-referencing was extremely valuable in tracing ownership of lost, stolen or weapons found at or near a crime scene. The bureau records were available twenty-four hours a day, every day.

In 1936, Trooper William P. Brefka was designated Chief Clerk of the Pistol Permit Bureau.

During 1937, pistol applications continued to increase by about 3000 a year. Persons licensed by the New York City Police Department were not included, as they maintained their own separate files. Various police agencies made 1,410 tele-type inquiries resulting in 136 positive identifications of a weapon used directly in the commission of a crime.

The most valuable file maintained was that containing information on lost or stolen weapons. In 1938, there were 4,800 weapons listed here.

In 1941, a total of 9,226 were listed as stolen or lost. In addition, files were searched in connection with persons suspected or affiliated with subversive organizations or activities. Chapter 452, Laws of 1941 required that records be kept for applications to manufacture or deal in explosives. These records provide a ready reference in case of stolen or unlawfully used explosives.

CHAPTER THIRTY-EIGHT
COMMUNICATIONS

Through the increasing use of rapid transportation, crime was no longer confined to a local area. A criminal could be many miles away from a crime scene in a short period of time without being apprehended. The need for rapid, coordinated, communication between police agencies was absolutely necessary in the fight against crime.

Chapter 633 of the Laws of 1931 sponsored by State Senator J. Griswold Webb of Hyde Park, N.Y. and Assemblyman Howard N. Allen of Pawling, N.Y. created the new fast service communication system for the New York State Police Department. On June 3, 1931, preparations for the installation of three teletype machines to be part of the state system of police communication were commenced. An office on the first floor of the Albany barracks was set apart for the tele-type department. The American Telephone and Telegraph Company installed the machines in August. Similar equipment was installed in other State Police barracks and was part of a main trunk line system that connected with police departments in the larger cities of the state. Ten lines and three circuit connections were installed from the Batavia barracks to the Hamburg, Friendship and East Avon substations, as well as police departments at Buffalo, Rochester, Olean, Jamestown and Troop "D" Oneida, N.Y. The Batavia Police Department was provided use of the Troop "A" machines. Messages were sent on an ordinary typewriter keyboard and received in written form in all receiving points connected to the system. Switches made it possible to transmit a message to any part or all of the system. It took about seven or eight minutes to broadcast a crime description to anywhere on the system. The machines had a maximum speed of 65 words a minute. 299 teletype machines were in operation with wires extending from Albany to Pennsylvania and New Jersey.

The system was the first installation of its kind for a police department with an installation cost of $100,000.00. The system was installed on September 1, 1931 with control points at each troop headquarters. Sergeant Joseph G. Brandstetter and Corporal Charles Z. McDonald were designated to attend a two-day school at Albany to learn use of the system and provide instruction upon their return to Batavia. Governor Franklin D. Roosevelt sent the first message on the system on September 15, 1931 to the Governors of Pennsylvania and New Jersey with replies received.

In 1934, there were eight states and seven hundred police departments on line with the teletype system.
(Batavia Daily News) (1931/1934 NYSP Annual Reports)

1936 legislation required that any felony complaint where the perpetrator was not apprehended within five hours be reported over the teletype system providing details of the crime. Criminal acts were no longer a local issue and the rapid relay of information was essential in the fight against crime.

The New York State Department of Corrections was connected to the troopers teletype system in July 1937. It became known, as the "Silent Cop" and was on duty 24 hours a day, every day. In less than a year, 1,561 known criminals were identified to police departments in eight states who might have otherwise gone free.

The teletype system processed 142,033 messages and 41,900 automobile license data requests in 1937.

During 1939, several two circuits replaced single circuits permitting continuous two-way operations between two points at all times. A teletype machine was set up and in use at the Worlds Fair connected to a control board at Hawthorne. The entire teletype bureau was re-arranged and upgraded with new radio panels and amplifiers installed.

In 1940, there was a great increase of state police installations. Direct lines were utilized for the first time with New Jersey and Pennsylvania saving valuable transmission time.

In 1941, there were eight states, seventy-three state police points and thirty-two municipalities interconnected on the system. Valuable road conditions were provided during emergencies, storms and disasters. The telegraph bureau was equipped for blackouts permitting it to function in case of air raid. Telegraph operators were designated air raid wardens of the Capitols fifth floor having received training in use of equipment installed to combat incendiary bombs or other dangerous missiles.

RADIO COMMUNICATIONS

1931- The first state police automobile to carry a short wave radio for official police communications was installed in a patrol car at the Avon Precinct under the command of Lieutenant Gerald D. Vaine. The car was used to patrol the area around Rochester, New York getting its news flashes of crime news from broadcasting equipment at the Rochester, New York Police Department.
(Batavia Daily News – 10/7/31)

On January 15, 1932, Albany, New York Radio Station "WOKO", through the courtesy of General Manager Harold Smith, provided ten minutes time daily except Sunday for the state police to broadcast information regarding crimes and messages of general interest to the public. Many instances were documented where these broadcasts helped in the apprehension of offenders, locating of missing persons and property and updating of new laws and safety equipment. This resulted in an attitude of co-operation and assistance by the public with police.
(Annual Report – 1932)

On September 21, 1933, a transmitter built by the General Electric Company of Schenectady, N.Y. was put into service providing radio communications to the eleven counties policed by Troop "G". Twelve patrol cars and twenty fixed stations were equipped with radio receivers.

Designated "WPGC", the transmitter was a 5-kilowatt unit all ac operated, located in South Schenectady, N.Y., RCA Transmitting Radiotrons were used throughout the equipment. It was crystal controlled using a quartz crystal ground to the operating frequency of 1534 kilocycles. General Electric Company maintained a 24-hour a day licensed operator with operation remotely controlled from State Police Headquarters at Albany, N.Y.

In addition to the Troop "G" radio cars, five trooper cars in Erie County were radio equipped operating from the Buffalo Police Department Station "WMJ" and three radio cars in Monroe County were radio equipped operating from the Rochester Police Department's Station "WPDR".
(1933 Annual Reports)

It was noted in the 1936 annual report that the Trooper Radio Station "WPGC" was operating at 1658 kilocycles and Trooper J. Fred Johns was designated chief operator, later assisted by Corporal John J. Smith.

In 1939, WYSQ, the New York State Police Portable Emergency Transmitter operating at 1658 Kilocycles was first put in use at the First Army maneuvers at Camp Pine (now Camp Drum) near Watertown, New York during August 1939. The transmitter was installed in a twenty-four foot long house type trailer. It was a completely self-contained mobile command post with all communication features capable of accommodating four people for a considerable period of time. The forward half was utilized as living quarters with a convertible couch folding into a bed. There were folding tables attached to the walls, a small kitchenette with a sink, a two-burner Coleman gasoline plate and small ice chest. A kerosene pot-stove with blower provided heat, a 10 gallon water tank with hand pump for water and various drawers and cupboards completed the quarters.

The rear section included radio, telephone and teletype communications operating in a short square "U" position supported by steel drawers and file cabinets. A large trunk in the rear contained a gasoline driven motor generator capable of supplying all equipment and lights. A heavy-duty truck equipped with extra materials and tools for repairs hauled the trailer. Storage lockers along the sides could be used as seats to accommodate fifteen men for transport. The truck was equipped with overdrive and had a top speed of 50 miles per hour.
(1940 NYSP Annual Reports)

During 1941, radio continued to play an important role in communications. Instant contact with the mobile units provided almost instant response to incidents and emergencies. Station WPGC continued in use with transmitter and maintenance provided by the GE Company. Local radio station WOKO continued to provide 10 minutes free time nightly for the transmission of information of general interest to the public. The success of the radio resulted in the installation of transmitting towers throughout the state. The experimentation of the two-way radio was initiated with the construction of eight link 50-watt automobile transmitters. During 1942, a complete two-way radio system on ultra high frequency was completed and placed in service for thirty-seven trooper units on Long Island. Each unit had an effective range of 25 miles.

WHAM RADIO – ROCHESTER, NEW YORK
On October 30, 1934, Radio Station "WHAM", Rochester, N.Y. played the first broadcast of true cases from the files of the New York State Police. The first broadcast was at 10:00 PM and was a ½ hour dramatization of the 1927 murders of Troopers Robert Roy and Arnold Rasmussen near Caneadea, N.Y. Wilmont Wagner, who shot the troopers, was captured, convicted and sent to the electric chair. The program was the first in a planned weekly series presenting real cases from the Troop "A", Batavia, N.Y. files.

Wayne Shoemaker, "WHAM" Broadcast Director visited other barracks in search of new material. Major John Warner and Captain Winfield Robinson edited all scripts. The ½ hour long Thursday evening programs were very popular with programming continuing until about 1941.

On December 22, 1934, Major John Warner played the Schumann Concerto on a nationwide radio network in his first such broadcast. Warner explained that it was a return compliment in behalf of the state police for the interest Station "WHAM" had shown in the troopers work. "WHAM" had carried a series of entertainment programs based on the exploits of the state police. Warner's program was broadcast over the blue network of the NBC system.
(Batavia Daily News)

On February 4, 1938, a libel suit was filed against WHAM radio at the Supreme Court, Canandaigua, New York based on a broadcast in 1936 of real trooper cases. Stephen Rogers, age 33 of Geneva, N.Y., a wrestler was the plaintiff in the $20,000.libel suit. His basis was a broadcast in which the arrest of "Buck Mason" on a charge of chicken theft was re-enacted. He claimed that one of the names he wrestled under was Buck Mason and as a result of the program broadcast, he was identified as the subject of the arrest and had been publicly ridiculed to the extent that it prevented him from gaining employment. His attorney Joseph J. Spillane said that Rogers had been arrested for chicken theft in Wayne County, pled guilty and served ninety days in the Onondaga County Penitentiary. It was contended that the defendants had no right to use his name or alias in a manner that would identify him as the subject of the radio drama. A disposition could not be determined.

CHAPTER THIRTY-NINE
DIVING OPERATIONS

During 1934, a single Morse Shallow Water Diving Apparatus was purchased and put to use at Troop "G", Troy, New York. It consisted of a helmet, air hose, air pump, wading dress and weighted belt. The apparatus made it possible to descend to 50 foot depths and was found to be extremely valuable in the recovery of drowned bodies, lost and stolen property and discarded evidence.

In 1935, a second diving apparatus was purchased. Twenty-five troopers were trained in its use and were available for short notice response.

On April 5, 1937 the efforts of Senator Joe R. Hanley and Assemblyman Harold O. Ostertag resulted in the purchase of a third diving apparatus for assignment to Troop "A". The equipment now consisted of a heavy flat bottom boat with a four cylinder gasoline powered outboard motor hauled on a specially built trailer, a diving helmet, divers gloves, weighted diving belt, a set of submarine telephones and one hundred feet of air hose and rope for safety lines. Sergeant Charles Z. McDonald of the Castile Station had been trained to use the apparatus with its first Western New York use being at Silver Lake, near Perry, N.Y.
(Batavia Daily News – 1937)

CHAPTER FORTY
BLOODHOUNDS

Troopers first utilized bloodhounds in 1934.

Troop "A" was assigned three bloodhounds in the fall of 1937. They were named Olga, Bess and Molly with Trooper Albert R. Perry of the Letchworth, N.Y. outpost volunteering as trainer and handler.

The 1937 Annual Reports noted for the first time the keeping and use of bloodhounds. Several dogs were reported kept around the state and have been found to be invaluable in locating lost or wanted persons.

The bloodhound is lamblike in its gentleness although he does look sad eyed and ferocious. The dogs are taught not to bay when following a scent. That would give a trailed criminal advance notice of their approach or could frighten a lost child. The dogs always track while on a leash and seldom are more than two used on the same case, usually a male and female. They follow body scent and if conditions allow, can on some occasions follow a scent that is four or five days old. There is no smoking when on the trail, because a few whiffs would dull the dog's senses. The scent of a human is stronger than that of any animal with no two people have exactly the same odor.

The State Police at Hawthorne, N.Y. successfully operated the first training school for bloodhounds with Trooper William Horton the instructor, assisted by Trooper Robert Thomson. The dogs start to learn the trade when they are about 18 months old. Until then, they enjoy a normal puppy-hood. Training starts when the dog is taken out into a sizeable field and allowed to sniff a piece of liver in the assistant trainer's hand. This gives the canine the idea that the assistant is a good man to keep his eye on during the proceedings. The assistant runs about 50 feet away while the dog strains at the leash thinking about the liver. He is then allowed to run after the assistant and is given the meat. This procedure is repeated and the distance lengthened at every try. A garment belonging to the assistant is used to teach the dog to follow a given scent. As the dog sniffs, the assistant sprints away and hides. The dog puzzled by the disappearance of the liver gets the idea to follow the scent. He strains at the leash until he finds the assistant. Since the wind may blow the scent to one side of the actual trail, the dog is not expected to stay on the trail, just to go in the right direction. The assistant, to show the trainer when the dog is going in the right direction, lays a paper trail. The dog is now learning how to trail with the assistant completely out of sight. No fooling around is allowed. The dog soon learns not to mix business with pleasure. When the dog locates the assistant, a big fuss is made over the dog and he is rewarded with apiece of liver. This type of training usually takes six months before a dog is put into duty.

CHAPTER FORTY-ONE
NEW BUREAU OF THE NEW YORK STATE POLICE REFERRED TO AS THE SCOTLAND YARD UNIT – 1935

Over the years, many prosecutors, coroners and government officials involved in the criminal investigative system had suggested a unit of specially skilled, trained investigators to assist local police agencies in crime detection.

On May 4,1935, the New York State Legislature enacted a law establishing the Bureau of Criminal Investigation within the Division of State Police for the purpose of investigating and detecting felonies within the state. The law directed that investigations be unified and coordinated, as opposed to the practice of having the county district attorney direct investigations. Politically elected district attorney's were usually untrained and inexperienced in the field of criminal investigation although their expertise in evidence procurement was invaluable. Major John Warner, Superintendent of the New York State Police was directed to provide for each of the seven troops to have an investigative bureau with a supervisor in charge of all investigative work. The supervisor's position was full time.

He was responsible for directing the work of various experts who were retained on a consulting basis, and determine theories that were to be followed through evaluation of evidence and other clues. Bureau personnel were selected from among already trained and experienced members of the state police who had shown exceptional ability as investigators coupled with the ability to direct others in the conduct of inquiries. Each troop commander nominated the bureau supervisor.

It was decided that it would be better to have seven units spread throughout the state instead of concentration in one Central Bureau at Albany, N.Y. This setup would provide flexible systems overcoming the delays and difficulties of having to travel from one central point to the investigative scene. By being so spread, a more prompt response to calls for its service was possible.

Like the Federal Secret Service operatives, Superintendent Warner directed that troopers assigned to the unit remain unknown, at least for the present, identified only by numbers. The time would come when; they would be compelled to testify in court at, which times their identity, would become known. On May 21,1935, Eugene Hoyt, age 29 with three years army experience and a trooper since 1928 was selected to supervise the bureau in Troop "A" by Captain Winfield W. Robinson. Hoyt was last assigned at Friendship, N.Y. and would maintain an office at the Batavia barracks. Eleven troopers were selected to serve in the bureau. They continued their patrol duties, when investigations did not require their time.

Troop "A" First Bureau Detail

Montagu Andrews	Andrew F.Bily
Charles E. Cobb	Michael L. Fort
Donald S. Girven	Oscar Lazeroff
Percy K. Leitner	Clarence J. Pasto
William T. Silage	Vernon R. Voight
Earl R. Wilkinson	

Trooper Andrews was the designated troop photograph and fingerprint expert.

On August 29, 1935, Batavia Police Chief G. Forest Brown requested the assistance of the bureau in a murder investigation. This was the first time the bureau had been called for assistance by an outside agency.

On August 16, 1935, Mrs. Rose Barone Ricotta, age 27 had been shot and killed by her husband, Anthony which had been witnessed by their daughter, eight year old Mary Ricotta. Patrolman Sam Baudanza, first on the scene secured the scene and took the revolver from Ricotta's hand. Anthony, represented by Attorney Louis W.Gerace denied any recollection of what happened stating he had never seen the revolver before. Experts determined that two notes found in the home purporting a suicide pact were not authentic.

On September 25, 1935, one of the first recorded arrests from fingerprint identification in Troop "A" resulted in Clifford L. Sprague, age 27, 11 Maple Street, Batavia, N.Y. being charged with burglary. A photograph of a fingerprint taken by Trooper Monty Andrews from a window at the burglary of the John Barrett gasoline station, Pearl Street Road, Batavia, N.Y. on April 27, 1935 matched Sprague' leading to the arrest. Sprague and Arthur J. Ray, 46 Washington Street, Batavia, N.Y. were charged by Corporal Earl Wilkerson and Trooper Percy Leitner for burglary at the Stafford Country Club. A comparison of fingerprints from Sprague and that photographed at the Barrett burglary matched resulting in the charge. He was arrested and identified his accomplice, as George A. Barbeau; age

23, 260 Ross Street. A stolen radio was recovered from a Jackson Street store operated by James O'Donnell who paid $5.00 for it.

(Batavia Daily News)

BUREAU ASSIGNMENTS AS OF JULY 1936

On 1 Jul 1936, reorganization of the bureau was completed with 90 men permanently assigned. Eugene Hoyt was promoted to Lieutenant and Sergeant Harry DeHollander assigned to the bureau. Corporal Girven was detached and assigned to the Westfield Precinct.

BUREAU ASSIGNMENTS AS OF NOVEMBER 1939

Eugene Hoyt	Harry DeHollander
Harold L. DeBrine	Harold Kemp
Edward J. Doody	Oscar Lazeroff
Earl Wilkinson	Paul J. Mellody
Vernon R. Voight	Albert S. Horton
George S. Wood	Norman H. Lippert
Frank A. Easton	Michael L. Fort
William J. Szymanski	Montagu Andrews

Clarence Pasto who also served as chief clerk.

HIGH PROFILE INVESTIGATIONS

In 1939, investigators were assigned to the Greater New York and Upstate New York areas to conduct an investigation into allegations that employees of the Bureau of Motor Vehicles were accepting fees for approval of driver's licenses during road tests. Twenty-two indictments resulted in Brooklyn and Manhattan.

Also during 1939, thirty investigators were assigned to investigate frauds perpetrated between dishonest State Insurance Fund employees and assureds. One hundred ten (110) indictments resulted with ten (10) auditors being arrested, but only four (4) being convicted. Twenty-two auditors were removed from office with $1,303,646.00 recovered.

(NYSP Annual Reports)

CHAPTER FORTY-TWO
SCIENTIFIC LABORATORY

At the suggestion of district attorneys and local coroners, a central crime laboratory was established through 1935 legislation as an aid to investigation, through the use of scientific and technical methods. The Superintendent of State Police was empowered to employ within appropriations, necessary experts, scientists, technicians and other persons to aid in the detection and apprehension and preparation of evidence connected with criminal violations.

The first State Police Director and scientific laboratory advisor was Dr. Bradley H. Kirschberg of Schenectedy, N.Y., a noted research and forensic chemist. Initial scientific equipment included a ballistic and photomicrograph apparatus, distillation units, magnifiers, helixometers, microscopes, comparators and many other devices to study bullets, shells, chemicals, handwriting, etc.

A list of over one hundred experienced experts, scientists and technicians was compiled across the state who agreed to render their services on a part time, per diem basis, as needed.

The First New York State Police Laboratory was located at 128-130 Church Street, Schenectedy, N.Y. The lab occupied the entire third floor consisting of five rooms
(1935 NYSP Annual Reports)

The laboratory was formally opened on May 21, 1936.

On June 1, 1936, approval was given through the Works Progress Administration to hire qualified laboratory assistants. The staff consisted of two chemists, a photographer, an artist, an electrician, a clerk, a laborer & three typist-stenographers. They were employed for seven hours, five days weekly with one typist working until 9:00pm

Duties of the lab

1. Analyze and examine evidence

2. Assist at crime scenes

3. Assist prosecutors in evidence preparation

4. Testify as needed

5. Prepare & edit monthly scientific bulletins

6. Lecture at the state police school

(1936 NYSP Annual Reports)

In 1937, a spectroscope, spectrograph, spherometer and refractor were purchased. The addition of this equipment brought the lab to a level equal to the best in the country. A research library was maintained and data updated through lab experimentation and testing.

A collection of tire patterns, headlamp lenses, automobile paints and the study of hairs, fibers and residues were kept for comparison of crime scene evidence. A ballistics unit maintained records that could determine chemical composition of ammunition. A standardized autopsy form was published and provided to coroners that could be used in the presenting of information in homicide cases. A monthly scientific bulletin was published and provided to state personnel as well as other law enforcement agencies, prosecutors and various university libraries.

Detection of Deception
Over a two-year period, Dr. Kirschberg studied the detection of deception through physical and psychological methods at Fordham University. The method advocated was that of galvanic skin reflexes with the use of a psycho galvanometer and recorder, later registered under the name "Pathometer". In 1938, these machines were purchased and used in both fieldwork and research by the lab. Professor Allen Hicks of the Albany State College for Teachers along with forty students volunteered to assist in a two-year research project using the Pathometer. It was also used with pathological liars and drug addicts. Should the results be used as evidence, it was of the mind set that the machine was not 100%

correct, was exceedingly sensitive and its use was limited by law. Its use however was helpful in clarifying complicated issues upon examining witnesses.

On May 28, 1941, Laboratory Director Dr. Bradley H. Kirschberg died of a heart attack. Trooper William E. Kirwan Jr., his laboratory assistant was appointed to replace him. Performance evaluations indicated Kirwan was qualified to supervise the lab and its employees. Kirwan resigned his position as a trooper to become its director, a civilian position. Kirwan went on to become Superintendent of State Police some years later.

During 1942 with war conditions came additional scrutiny. A portable x-ray machine and fluoroscope were used to examine exhibits pertaining to instances of sabotage and subversive activities, as well as field examination of explosives, bombs and suspected packages. All trooper investigators were required to attend classes at the laboratory to learn of its capabilities and how to secure and submit evidence.

Dr. Kirschberg received a Chemist Degree from Columbia University and later, the University of Krackow, Austria (Poland). He worked at the Klisch Laboratories for two years, then the US Department of Health detailed with the New York City Police Department. In 1912, he became the City of Schenectady Chemist until 1918, when he enlisted in the US Army during WW I. After the war, he became a consultant and did research work pertaining to chemistry and biology in relation to criminal activity. He was selected to establish the New York State Police Laboratory in 1935.

(NYSP Annual Reports)

CHAPTER FORTY-THREE
TRAFFIC ENFORCEMENT

The invention and increased production of the automobile soon replaced the horse, as the prime means of transportation. Prior to advent of the trooper, the motorist who left the safety of the city limits was required to rely on his own strengths to protect himself. There was a certain element that was a nuisance to decent motorists endangering their lives and rendering the highway unsafe. With the coming of the state police and their efforts, this nuisance rapidly disappeared.

Prior to state police existence, passage of automobile laws were greeted with broad smiles, as it was a statewide joke that no one enforced these laws. Laws to save lives were urgently needed, but as soon as they were passed, they were forgotten. Each year indicated a steady increase in highway deaths.

One of the first laws enforced by troopers was that of dangerous and glaring lights, the primary cause of serious nighttime accidents. These violations eventually disappeared due to strict enforcement. An increase in the enforcement of all laws by troopers made the highway user a better driver by making them more cautious and aware.

On November 10, 1919, Troopers Milton Ferry, George Tetley and Valentine arrested nineteen motorists at Pembroke, N.Y. charging them with having glaring headlights. A plain lens and bulb of improper electric power were in use. All paid a $5.00 fine before Pembroke Justice Charles L. Mallory.

In 1920, there were 571,000 registered automobiles in the state.

It was noted in 1921 that the great increase in automobiles and related traffic problems brought new responsibility to the troopers on patrol. A large number of people could now be brought together at a specific location in a short period of time.

Effective January 1, 1922, auto license plates issued in the state were provided with a distinctive number that corresponded to the county where it was issued. This system made it easier to identify and locate stolen automobiles. An example for plates issued in Wayne County would be numbered from 544-901 to 553-400.

The enforcement of Highway Laws became the trooper's greatest problem in 1922. 11,000 miles of improved highways carried the states automobile traffic with many areas highly congested. Considering the amount of people transported daily in the high-powered machines, fairly good highway protection resulted with only 2000 motor vehicle related deaths. Two thirds of the fatal accidents took place within a city limit. A great deal of highway safety improvement was brought about by troopers on traffic duty through instruction and explanation of traffic laws to motorists. The automobile was now recognized as a necessity of modern life.

In 1922, there were 1,035,000 registered automobiles in the state and in 1923, this number increased to 1,242,851.

In 1926, 102 troopers were assigned to enforcement of the Motor Vehicle Laws. Each trooper was provided an automobile or motorcycle and patrolled all the primary highways of the state.

In 1928, Long Island Parks & Parkways were opened to the public for the first time. Fourteen additional men were authorized and assigned exclusively to this detail. They were tasked with patrolling the parks and parkways, regulating traffic and the orderly parking of cars. That first year had 1,453,000 visitors in 438,000 automobiles. Troopers patrolled 88,987 miles, made 73 highway arrests and issued 150 warnings. With the opening of Jones Beach in 1929, it was estimated that an additional one million visitors would come to Long Island with a total state police presence of 48 troopers assigned. As parkways were extended and new roads built, the amount of visitors and automobile increased. It was estimated that 12 million people visited Long Island in 1937 traveling in 500,000 automobiles.

The tremendous increase in the number of automobiles in the state gave rise to an enormous increase of motor vehicle accidents and other related problems. One hundred twelve troopers on motorcycles were assigned exclusively to patrol all principal arteries with instructions to assist motorists in every way and at the same time to rigidly enforce the traffic laws, particularly reckless driving. Patrol troopers provided valuable information to the New York State Traffic Commission resulting in policies promoting greater highway safety.

TRAFFIC BUREAU
In 1937, the state police took part in a nation wide program to reduce highway accidents. In the belief that enforcement of traffic laws and traffic regulation was a specialized police service, the state police created a traffic bureau. It was composed of carefully trained troopers detailed to engage in systematic patrol of the heavily traveled highways with the idea of reducing accidents.

On May 14, 1937, Traffic Bureau's were formed in each troop. The first Troop "A" traffic supervisor was Sergeant Joseph Brandstetter.

Troopers under the traffic supervisors command and assigned to highway traffic patrol duty only. No other duties were assigned except in an emergency.

A study of accident locations and times they occurred was conducted resulting in a high concentration of patrol duty in these areas. Each troop kept an accident spot map filed by location. With this data, it was possible to determine effects of selective patrol enforcement and make monthly comparisons.

Strict attention was to be paid to highway violations and laws strictly enforced. It was determined that traffic bureau vehicles painted a distinctive color would not only have a Psychological effect on drivers, but would be a constant reminder that patrols were present. Many of the automobiles were painted white and lettered in black "STATE POLICE - TRAFFIC BUREAU – SAFETY PATROL". It was determined that these distinctively marked cars resulted in a reduction in speed and accidents within the areas they were used. Within each troop, certain troopers were assigned to investigate causes of accidents; particularly fatal ones occurring on heavily traveled highways. The Bureau of Criminal Investigation investigated fatal accidents in conjunction with the trooper. If any criminal negligence was found, arrests under the Penal Law were made.

The traffic bureau also made surveys to eliminate hazards and advise on the retention or installation of traffic control signs and signals. As time passed, it became apparent that traffic enforcement was a specialized police service that was critically essential in traffic safety. During the period of June 1 to December 28, 1937, Troop "A" recorded 113 fatal accidents in its eleven county area that resulted in 129 persons killed. The cause of theses accidents was determined to be carelessness and disregard for the rights of other users of the highway.

Trooper Howard Blanding recalled an investigation that resulted in one of the first convictions under the new criminal negligence with a motor vehicle law.

A drunken driver hit a car head on near the Village of Eden that contained a family returning from a Christmas shopping trip in Buffalo, N.Y. Two children were killed and other passengers seriously injured. The driver responsible had been drinking and was charged with criminal negligence. Attorney & State Senator Walter Mahoney who tried every trick possible to avoid having the defendant appear in court represented him. On more than one occasion, twenty-five witnesses had been subpoenaed to appear in court with the defendant being absent due to illness or some other excuse. The judge finally ordered Blanding to take Coroner Dr. DeDominicis to Rochester, N.Y. where the defendant was allegedly hospitalized and bring him back to Buffalo for trial. The defendant was located at a hospital, given a hasty physical examination by the Medical Examiner who ordered him to get dressed. He was taken to Buffalo and put in jail where he could be readily available for trial. He was convicted and sentenced to five years in prison. This was one of the first convictions in the state under the new law.
(1937 NYSP Annual Reports)

CHAPTER FORTY-FOUR
TRUCK WEIGHING

With the birth of the automobile dawned the era of highway improvement. Motorists demanded smooth, well engineered highways, which brought about the expenditure of millions in highway improvement. The main points confronting highway engineers at the time was the elimination of dust to road users and highway surface wear. Due to congestion and increased rates by the various railroad companies, commerce moved to transporting commodities by truck. This demand increased the production of bigger and better trucks capable of more and heavier loads.

The roadways beneath these heavy loads were ground to powder or ploughed into deep ruts in just a few months. Complaints to the State Legislature resulted in the passage of a bill permitting a maximum weight of 800 pounds per inch of tire. Sponsored by Senator Mortimer Y. Ferris, the law also provided that specific measurements be met. A maximum width of 8 feet and height of 12 feet 6 inches were established. Highway Commissioner Frederick Stewart Greene gave troopers the task of enforcing the new law.

It was useless to stop trucks unless their weight could be proven by use of a nearby scale. The 1920 invention of the loadometer permitted a truck to be weighed wherever it was stopped. The loadometer worked on the principle of a combined auto jack, scale and register. The jack not only lifted the truck, but also registered the weight on the register. Lifting the truck completely off the ground would give the trucks total weight.

The original truck weighing detail consisted of a four-man crew with each crew consisting of two troopers and two Highway Department employees. The army provided four used, repainted ambulances to carry the new loadometers. The legend Traffic Law Enforcement - New York State Department of Highways and State Police" was painted on the side of the truck.

On July 14, 1920, Sergeant Rudolph Panzlau, Troopers O"Neil and Murphy were assigned to the truck weighing detail. They worked in co-operation with the State Department of Highways using a machine which weighed trucks called the loadometer. All trucks were stopped that did not meet requirements and were warned to properly equip their trucks or arrests and fines would follow. Maximum loads for trucks were 25,000 pounds. Trucks could only be eight feet wide and 12 ½ feet high. They could not carry more than 800 pounds to inch of tire width. The machine was built especially to weigh trucks and was used in each troop for one week at a time, then sent to another troop. It was first used in Troop "A" at Rochester, N.Y., then on Route 5 between Leroy and Caledonia, N.Y. and again, between Batavia and Buffalo, N.Y.
(Trooper Magazine – 1922)

In 1934, special squads under the direction of headquarters were initiated for the enforcement of laws relating to trucks and buses, particularly overloads. Equipment and a specially designated truck were operated in conjunction with patrols from each troop. A total of 7,716 trucks were checked with 912 charged with being overloaded and 1265 other violations cited. 230 buses were checked with only 20 equipment violations noted.

As an aid to the motoring public, 1934 Legislation was passed requiring trucks and buses to carry emergency lighting to be used in the event of breakdown or lighting failure while moving.

On August 6, 1934, Harry Dutchy of Barker, N.Y. was fined $3.00 when he pled guilty in Batavia City Court to having over twenty tons of sand on his truck. This was six tons more than the law allowed.
(Batavia Daily News)

Attention was continued with enforcement toward overloaded trucks being first on the agenda because of the heavy damage caused to the states highways. It was noted that the attitude of truck drivers had improved toward this enforcement with only 266 overload violations found from 10,517 trucks checked. The enforcement of inadequate brakes was stepped up with the purchase of nine decelerometers distributed among the six troops to test automobile, bus, truck and pleasure cars.

(1935 NYSP Annual Reports)

In January 1937, New York State Legislation went into effect limiting the hours of operation for truck drivers. Known as the ten-hour law, it was enacted because too many truck drivers stayed at the wheel until exhausted resulting in accidents. The law provided that a truck driver could not drive more than 10 hours in any period of 14 hours. The driver was considered on duty, when he reported to his terminal for duty and was not off duty until he left his truck. Rest periods and meals taken were allowed to take up the four-hour allowance. At the end of fourteen hours, the driver had to be relieved or off duty. The driver could not remain in the truck during his off time, which effectively did away with the use of bunks in trucks provided to many long distance haulers. A driving record was required to be maintained by each driver providing location and time left; destination and time arrived with rest times noted. Truckers lobbied that the law was unfair in that required rest stops were not practical and perishables had to be delivered as quickly as possible. The law had not yet been enforced, when methods of evasion to avoid arrest were being discussed which included a second set of driver records and identifying a second driver, as a hitchhiker.
(Batavia Daily News Jan 1937)

Until 1939, the state police only had one loadometer truck equipped with loadometer scales, brake testing decelometers and associated equipment that operated intermittently throughout the state. In the year 1939, 25,862 trucks and buses were inspected resulting in 1,372 arrests for faulty equipment. A second truck was procured to continue effective commercial vehicle enforcement.
(1939 NYSP Annual Reports)

During July 1943, Technical Sergeant David Soule, 38, Tribes Hill, N.Y. in charge of a truck-weighing machine that was transported throughout the state, was arrested and charged with bribery. It was alleged that between September 3 and September 25, 1942, Soule's accepted $1,500.00 in bribes from Earl C. Stacks, a C & E Trucking Official, Rhinebeck, N.Y. and Robert Holmes of Hudson, N.Y. to permit the operation of overloaded trucks on state highways. He was found guilty after trial on October 15, 1943 and sentenced to a term of 5 to 10 years in Sing-Sing Prison. Stacks was found guilty of bribery and sentenced to a 2 ½ to 5 years suspended sentence.

CHAPTER FORTY-FIVE
RE-ORGANIZATION

In 1943, Republican Thomas E. Dewey was the newly elected Governor of New York State. He was known for his tenacious crime fighting campaign against organized crime while serving for many years, as District Attorney for New York City. Dewey initiated an investigation of the State Police Troop Captains and Officers by hiring trained, unbiased investigators. These investigators observed the State Police activities and the actions of those in charge for several weeks. Their reports, when submitted, convinced Dewey that the department was badly in need of overhauling. There had been no change in authority in 25 years with almost all decision making made by long term, original officers who were comfortable within their troops where they reigned supreme. Troop commanders had the authority to transfer without notice, discipline without a hearing and terminate employment if they saw fit.

In April 1943, Major Warner, a democratic holdover initiated a series of transfers amongst long serving troop commanders and other high ranking officers. In a prepared statement, Warner said "that it was for the good of the service." Many law enforcement official's felt that Warner's actions were at the direction of Dewey's administration resulting from reports of the governor's investigation. Some felt it was the first step in a program aimed at shuffling state police personnel with a view of making the Bureau of Criminal Investigation (BCI) predominant over the uniform division. It was said that Governor Dewey also used plainclothes BCI men to investigate candidates for appointment to state posts. Whatever the reason, those that were affected by the transfers had only 36 hours to report to their new duty assignments.

Captain Dan Fox, Troop "C", Sidney, N.Y. prominently mentioned, as a replacement for Warner was given 36 hours to report to Malone, N.Y. Several reasons were given for this transfer. In April 1943, Trooper Matthew Haskins in civilian clothes was arrested by BCI men at a Sullivan County cigar store charged with disorderly conduct in frequenting a gambling establishment. He stated he was there on special assignment for Captain Fox pleading not guilty to the charge. The arrest climaxed a three-year bitter controversy between Captain Fox and BCI Inspector Ernest Maynard, head of the Troop "C" BCI unit. Haskins was acquitted after trial on May 26, 1943. He was suspended in June 1943, appealed the decision, and was re-instated. The Supreme Court determined that there was no provision in the rules and regulations authorizing suspension of a member by the superintendent. Other investigations determined a trooper in Delaware County was working in a real estate business, as a side business without authorization. The mayor of Norwich, N.Y., a close friend of Captain Fox had given him 10 shares of oil stock contrary to regulations on accepting gratuities and several slot machines were discovered in Sullivan County. It was alleged Captain Fox had violated rules and regulations and was not cognizant of criminal activity under his domain which led to his re-assignment.

Almost every high- ranking official submitted retirement papers at the end of 1943. The method used forcing the unplanned retirements was through re-assignment, demotion in rank, accusations of misconduct and a transfer many miles from their homes. Among those retiring was Deputy Superintendent George P. Dutton, Captain James Flynn, Troop "L", Babylon, N.Y., Captain Winfield W. Robinson, Troop "A", Batavia, N.Y., Captain Stanley Beagle, Executive Officer, Albany, N.Y., Chief Inspector Albert Moore, Albany, N.Y., Captain Stephen McGrath, Troop "G", Captain John Keeley, Troop "D", and Captain Dan Fox, Troop "B." All were original camp men. Dewey believed the efficiency of the state police, as an organization, had suffered by the stagnation of the corporal, sergeant and lieutenants on promotional lists. The practice of keeping captains in one troop command for many years instead of transferring them also was detrimental in the governor's opinion. It was felt that the retirements would pave the way for promotions of younger men, which was the primary objective of the re-organization.

In August 1943, Major John A. Warner resigned, as superintendent taking a position, as a Lieutenant Colonel in the US Army. It was said he did not particularly care for the methods employed in re-assigning officers during the re-organization, as all were personal friends. It was felt that this hastened his retirement. Captain John A. Gaffney of Troop "K" was appointed to replace him. An investigation by Warner prior to retirement found evidence of state police bribery and corruption by trucking company officials. In 1943, Technical Sergeant David Soule in charge of the statewide truck weighing scales was charged with accepting a $1,500.00 bribe. He was found guilty after trial and sentenced to 5 to 10 years in Sing-Sing Prison.

Superintendent Gaffney made the following promotions and assignments to replace the many retirees. Joseph B. Lynch, Captain, Troop "A", Herschel A. Gay, Captain, Troop "C", John P. Ronan, Captain,

Troop "D" & John J. King, Captain, Troop "L". He also decreed that all news releases regarding felony investigations would be made through his office and not on a local level. This lasted one week after a tremendous uproar from newspaper editors across the state.

(Batavia Daily News)

1931 SP AIRCRAFT - TREMAINE HUHGES

FIRST WHITE TROOP CARS - 1937

GENESEE CO
FAIR GROUNDS

1940 COMMUNICATIONS TRAILER-GENESEE CO. FAIRGROUNDS

1941 PATROL CAR

1932-E. WILKINSON - L.MELLODY-J.LONG-F.EASTON-DICKSON

1939 ACCIDENT INVESTIGATION

1929 ACCIDENT INVESTIGATION

1940-ALBERT PERRY/BOB MERRING/ DOGS OLGA - BESSIE

1938 LACHNICHT-McGAUGHEY-PERRY

TROOP D ROUGH RIDERS - 1920S

1940 - CAPTAIN DAN FOX -SPOTTED HORSE TROOP

BOOK V – ENFORCING THE LAW

CHAPTER FORTY-SIX
MURDERS IN WESTERN NEW YORK

The 1929 Penal Law described Murder as the killing of a human being that was not excusable or justifiable. The penalty for Murder in the 1st Degree was punishable by death. Murder in the 2nd Degree was punishable by a term of not less than 20 years with a maximum of the offender's life in prison.

ROCHESTER MURDER - 1920
On July 8, 1920, troopers at Batavia, N.Y. were notified by The Rochester, New York Police Department to be on the look out for a Mike Totesco wanted for murder. During an argument, he shot and killed a James Osborn, then fled the city. The next day while on patrol in Morganville, N.Y., Sergeant John Keeley and Trooper Edward Rimmer observed an individual fitting the description given. Unable to satisfy their inquiries, he was taken to the Batavia Barracks for further investigation. Detective Sergeant of the Rochester Police arrived, identified the man as Totesco, and arrested him. He was returned to Rochester, N.Y. where he confessed to the crime.
(State Trooper Magazine - August 1920)

RETSOF MURDER – 1921
On January 15, 1921, 27 year old Albert Torcello shot and instantly killed Retsof "Bad Man" Miginni Aldobrando, known as a bully in the salt mines. The two were part of a card game and had been drinking. An argument resulted in threats by Aldobrando to kill Torcello. While walking toward home, Torcello being threatened with death pulled out a gun and shot Aldobrando in the heart, neck and leg. He died almost instantly. Fleeing the scene, he caught a ride to Leroy, N.Y., then a bus to Batavia where he spent some time. It was learned that Aldobrando was an alleged leader of a blackmailing group and his death brought a sigh of relief to the community. Witnesses indicated that during the quarrel, Aldobrando went for his gun, but was beaten to the draw by Torcello. He was arrested and held for further proceedings. On July 11, 1921, the case was presented to a Livingston County Grand Jury found no cause for action. Torcello was discharged from custody.

STANLEY LUCZAK MURDER – 1922
On March 9, 1922, 37 year old Bethany, N.Y. farmer Stanley Luczak was shot to death in view of his wife, Helen and five children, a brother, Vincent and his wife visiting from Buffalo, N.Y., and farmhands Matthew Mackos and Joseph Szczepay. All were visiting in the house, when the children saw two men looking in through a window. Stanley grabbed a shotgun and speaking in Polish, yelled for them to go away. An attempt was made by them to push a door in without success. Witness Joseph Szczepay said, he observed a party of five men with three men meeting Stanley in the yard and two waiting in a car with its engine running just out of sight of the Luczak house. Stanley went into the yard followed by his family and hired help and immediately was fired upon falling dead on a tree stump. He had been struck in the left leg, right side, the head and heart with a fifth bullet striking the shotgun Luczak had in his hands. The members of the household fled into the house with a shot fired through the door after them. Sometime after the men drove away, Szczepay walked to a neighbor's home and called for the troopers. Luczak had purchased the farm in about 1918 from Batavia, N.Y. butcher Walter Gaczewski.

Sergeant Walter Croadsdale and Trooper Edward Rynkowski (interpreter) responded to the Telegraph Road farm without knowing that a murder had occurred until they arrived. The crime scene was secured while waiting for the arrival of Dr. Stanley B. Hare, acting for County Coroner Ward Manchester.

The troopers located .45 caliber shell casings, and later a pair of repaired gauntlet driving gloves at the scene. It was also determined that the automobile used was a Ford Touring car with side curtains and that it fled toward Batavia N.Y. after the shooting. When Doctor Hare completed an examination of the body, the troopers placed the body in the back of a truck and took it to the H.E.Turner & Co., Mortuary, Batavia, N.Y. where an autopsy was performed.

District Attorney Kelly was notified and took charge of the investigation. He retained detectives from the Whaley-Doyle Detective Agency; Rochester, N.Y. assisted by Sheriff Elliott and Trooper Charles Burnett & Corporal Burton to conduct the investigation. Vincent Luczak was shown the found gloves and said that he recalled a women at a Buffalo, N.Y. boarding house repairing a similar pair that had three damaged fingers for a man named John Sobiskoda. The gloves did indeed show repair to three fingers. Investigation also revealed that Sobiskoda owned a Ford Touring car. On March 12, John Sobiskoda, aged 32, 59 Military Road, Buffalo, N.Y. was arrested and intently grilled by Detective Whaley, Sheriff Elliott and Buffalo Police Department Detectives Edwards and Nowak. He admitted that he had been forcing his attentions toward Edna Luczak, wife of Vincent for some time. It was intended that Vincent be killed so Sobiskoda could pursue his affections toward Edna. As it turned out, they had been having a clandestine affair for some time. Edna Luczak was arrested as an accessory to murder. It was she who told Sobiskoda of the plans to travel to Stanley Luczak's farm on March 13. The other alleged members of the murder group were arrested at Buffalo, N.Y. They were Ludwig Amorzewicz, age 30, Buffalo City Line, John Furtunski, age 20 and Alexander Andrukowski, age 22 all admitted members of a gang of professional bootleggers that were a part of the Sobiskoda plot to murder Vincent Luczak. Police found that the Amorzewicz farm was a main distillery for making illegal whiskey. Seized were a still and six barrels of mash. Indicted by a Genesee County Grand Jury, they were arraigned before Supreme Court Justice Wesley C. Dudley, pled not guilty with a trial date of June 5 assigned. Attorney Matthew W. Bennett of Buffalo, N.Y. represented Sobiskoda and Edna Luczak represented by Harold E. Odd, also of Buffalo.

On March 14, when confronted by Edna, Sobiskoda broke down and confessed to the murder. He said that he had hired Joseph Angraginski, alias Joseph Gordon, 146 Pearl Street, Buffalo, N.Y. to kill Vincent Luczak. He implicated Edna stating that she had promised to provide $600.00 to pay for the slaying and it was she that engineered the plot. He stated that it was he and Gordon that went to the house. He had purchased two automatic pistols for $30.00 at Buffalo, N.Y. He said it was Gordon that looked into the window and that when the children screamed, they both hid in a depression behind a stump in the front lawn. When he drew his pistol, he dropped a driving glove he had taken off to better grip the pistol. Stanley Luczak came out of the house walking toward the stump carrying a shotgun. Gordon fired a shot into the ground with Stanley shooting the shotgun at them. They both opened fire with their pistols and fled the scene. Shot from Stanley's shotgun blast struck Sobiskoda penetrating his clothing, but not penetrating the skin. He said that the three bootleggers had no part in the crime. They were released to the custody of buffalo police to face charges for bootlegging. Angaganski fled the area after the arrest of Sobiskoda.

Sobiskoda was found guilty of murder and sentenced to death, however the sentence was later commuted to life in prison. On April 19, 1923, the verdict was reversed and Sobiskoda was released.

(The procedure at the time was that all serious crimes reported were turned over to the District Attorney who hired private detectives, usually retired city police detectives to investigate the crime for prosecution. The New York State Police Bureau of Criminal Investigation was formed in 1935 and has since conducted investigations, as reported to them.)

LINDEN MURDERS

Linden was a small farming community in the 1920s consisting of about 100 residents living on small spread out, family operated farms. It had a general store, a post office, railroad station a mill and blacksmith shop. Located in the low rolling hills of southern Genesee County, it was a close-knit community with everyone knowing one another. They helped each other as needed, were aware of a neighbors habits and who their friends and relatives were. Many residents gathered at the Morse general store after evening chores to listen to the radio and discuss activities of the day.

FRANCINE (FRANC) KIMBALL

The linden murders began October 16, 1922 when 73-year-old spinster, Francine Kimball was killed in her home. Charles Speed, her nearest neighbor went to the house at about 8:00AM on the 17th finding the house locked and no one about. He returned an hour later and still finding no one home, became alarmed. He told his wife who called Mrs. Kimball's best friend, Miss Grace Smith who along with Mrs. Robert McWithey, went to the home, but a search of outbuildings and the home failed to locate her. They then called Justice Maurice Nelan who went to the location also conducting a search to no avail. They found the telephone line had been cut and contacted the State Police. Corporal Oscar White and Trooper C.L. Ornstedt were notified at about noon and scoured the entire property in vain. Making a final search of the cellar, Corporal White lit a dark area with his flashlight and saw the body stuffed under a fruit cellar shelf covered with an old door. Here head had been smashed in with a heavy object. The time of her death was established to be about 6:00PM on the 16th. Percy Fleming, a Linden resident had seen her in the yard at 5:30PM, as he passed her home. It was found that her cows had not been milked which she did faithfully at 6:00PM daily. Sheriff Elliott, District Attorney Kelly and Captain Robinson were notified with Coroner Ward Manchester responding to the scene. William Doyle of the Doyle Detective Agency, Rochester, N.Y. was retained to conduct the investigation. Mrs. Kimball's two elderly brothers had been away picking apples at the time of the murder. Police could find no clues to help identify the killer. State trooper grilled everyone that lived within a mile of the crime scene. The Batavia Daily News offered a $100.00 reward for information leading to the arrest of the perpetrator. On October 21st, Carl Meyers, a cousin of the dead woman, found a sharp, pointed rock with dried blood and gray hair imbedded on it. It was found in the cellar of the crime scene and it was determined to have been the murder weapon. It was theorized that who ever the killer was had been acquainted with the house. After the murder, the killer locked all windows and doors, then left from a front door locking it upon departing. On October 23rd, the County of Genesee Board of Supervisors posted a reward of $1000.00 for information leading to an arrest. Captain Robinson on November 4th said that he would maintain a core of troopers in the area, but that not even the smallest clue had been obtained towards solving of the crime. As time passed, so did the investigation with any and all leads coming to a dead end. The murder never was solved. It must be presumed that because of the passing of time, the killer or killers have themselves, since passed away.

THOMAS WHALEY – HATTIE. WHALEY – MABEL MORSE

Seventeen months later, March 11, 1924, three more Linden residents were brutally slain, again in the early evening. Mrs. Mabel Morse, age 51, proprietor of the local general store went to the nearby Whaley home for milk. When she failed to return; her store clerk, Myron Smith and Milton Kettle went to the Whaley home looking for her.

They saw smoke seeping from the home; found the doors locked and forced entry into the house, putting out the fire in a first floor bedroom. When the smoke cleared, they found three bodies in a pile covered with kerosene soaked rag rugs and paper. Thomas Whaley, age 65, an Erie Railroad employee had been shot in the neck. His wife, Hattie, age 56, had a single gunshot wound in her head. Mrs. Morse had been clubbed to death with a pickaxe handle found nearby. Two bullets and empty cartridges (32 caliber) were found in the house. As word spread in the hamlet, women gathered to comfort each other and farmers bolted their doors and armed themselves out of fear. Troopers were called immediately with Captain Robinson, Lieutenant George, Troopers George White, Sam Dunlap, Michael Fleming, Joe Brandstetter, George Donnelly, Trixie Lemay and Richard Gibbons responding to the scene. Sheriff Ware and District Attorney Waterman also arrived at the location. An autopsy confirmed that Mrs. Whaley had been shot once through the neck, Mr. Whaley several times through the neck and Mrs. Morse bludgeoned with the pickaxe handle. Mr. Morse immediately posted a reward of $1000.00 with the County Supervisors posting a $5000.00 reward. Buffalo Police Captain Joseph Whitwell, Chief of the Bertillon Bureau, a noted fingerprint expert was retained and went to the scene. Fingerprints taken at the scene were of no value, because they had been damaged by water from putting out the fire. Some felt the murders were the result of a robbery, as the purses had been emptied and watches were missing. Others thought it was maniac that had traveled along the railroad line. As the investigation proceeded, police became more convinced that the murderer was a local resident and concentrated their efforts on that theory. No one was allowed to leave the area unless first checked by police. As word spread, thrill seekers from Batavia, Buffalo and Rochester poured into the area impeding the investigation by causing traffic jams. Local people were interviewed and re-interviewed with no solid leads developed. Captain Robinson had a trooper presence in Linden at all times with one trooper assigned to the hamlet available for immediate duty and two others on horse patrol around the perimeter. One suggestion was to take pictures of the murdered victim's eyes and you find pictures of the person who committed the murder. It was no joke and was reported in a national weekly review to have been used in several important criminal investigations. Again, as in the Kimball murder, time passed with the crimes never being solved. Four victims from the same hamlet brutally killed and an attempt to burn their bodies were known to be the most gruesome crimes of the time.

SAM STOTT – 1925

During December 1924, Sam Stott, an Erie Railroad brakeman, residing at Hornell, New York assaulted the male companion of his former spouse, Margaret Stott with an iron pipe near Birdsall, New York. Before leaving, Stott snarled, "that's what will happen to any man that gets too interested in you." We are divorced she advised, but he is still insanely jealous of me. Allegany County Sheriff Deforrest Bennett obtained an assault warrant for Stott's arrest. Sheriff Bennett along with Steuben County Sheriff Bertram Page and Hornell Police Chief Robert Peters went to the Stott house to execute the warrant, but were told by his current wife, Esta Saxton Stott that he had gone out. An all night vigil on December 2, 1924 was in vain, as Stott never came home. The sheriff's were of the opinion that Stott may have thought he killed the man he struck with the pipe and had fled the area.

In April 1925, Sheriff Page visited the Stott home finding it vacant. Although neatly kept, all the clothing, both male and female was gone. Friends and co-workers of Esta were interviewed and it was found that she had gotten a call from Sam to pack up and meet him, as they were moving. Later the same day, the Hornell police received a report that Frank Murphy, a painter failed to show up for work. A check of his apartment indicated he left in a hurry leaving food on a stove ready to cook with the heat on. It was also determined that Murphy had been one of Sam's best friends and had been seen in the company of Esta since Sam's disappearance. Not knowing if Esta and Murphy had run away together or if there was foul play, the Sheriff placed a missing persons ad in the Hornell Evening Tribune. A response was received from a woman whose husband was a friend of Sam's. She said that a letter had been received from Sam with a Cuban stamp and postmark. He wanted to know if it was safe to come home to his job and wife. She wrote him back telling him that the man he assaulted with the pipe recovered and that he was only wanted on assault charge. She further told him that Esta seemed to very happy and was going around a lot with Frank Murphy.

Sheriff Page was convinced that Stott had murdered his wife and Murphy, but pleadings with the district attorney and state police fell on deaf ears for lack of solid evidence.

In the next few months, letters were received by the family of Esta indicating travel and her failing health all written by Sam. In November 1925, a cable was received indicating Esta had died in a Philippine hospital and was buried at Manila. Sheriff Page cabled Philippine officials for confirmation of the demise and burial receiving a response that there were no records found.

Throughout the year 1926 and the end of 1927, when he retired, Page worked diligently on the case. When he left office, he turned over reams of information of the case to the State Police with an appeal to keep it open. Over the years, Page spent his own money and time trying to solve the case. Finally in the summer 1943, Sam Stott erred by sending a letter to an old friend in Hornell that was given to Former Sheriff Page. He told of his life since leaving Hornell and his new life in Kansas City, but gave no address. Page gave the letter to State Police Inspector Eugene Hoyt who wired all necessary information to Kansas City authorities. He was located using the alias Sam Scott and arrested and declared "thank god it is over". When queried about the remark, he stated " I killed my wife Esta and Frank Murphy", and buried their bodies along a country road outside Hornell. He waived extradition and was returned by train with Inspector Hoyt.

On October 9, 1943, Stott made a detailed confession upon his return to Hornell. This is an edited version of his confession: On April 5, 1925, Esta had met him as requested being driven there by Frank Murphy. He asked Frank to drive them to Alfred Station to get a train to which he agreed. While on the Hornell-Almond Road near the Morris Bridge, Stott accused Murphy of stealing his wife. Murphy stopped the car, reached for a jack handle under the seat and swung it at Stott. He ducked the blow, pulled out a .38 caliber revolver firing once, missing Murphy, but striking Esta in the back seat. A second shot was fired hitting Murphy in the head. Both were dead. He broke into a nearby Erie Railroad tool shed stealing a pick and shovel. He then drove to Pennsylvania Hill where he stripped and burned Murphy's clothing before burying him in a shallow grave along side the road. He then returned to the scene of the shooting where he had already hidden Esta's body and buried her fully clothed. He hid the car in a thicket along the Canacadea Creek until the next morning, when he drove to Dayton, Ohio where he sold the car. He had then traveled throughout the mid and far west, persuading travelers to post his letter from abroad. The day he confessed and with his help, state police with the aid of a Steuben County Highway Department power shovel dug for three days in attempt to locate the bodies to no avail. The Almond road was now a three lane concrete state highway that involved much soil distribution changing the look of the area.

Without a corpus delecti, authorities could not charge Stott with murder regardless of his confession. Acting District Attorney John W. Hollis succeeded in obtaining indictments for kidnapping, assault 1st degree and grand larceny 2nd degree. A jury in Bath, New York acquitted him of kidnapping, but on May 4, 1944 before Judge Arthur King, he was found guilty of assault and grand larceny. On May 24, 1944, Judge King sentenced him to a term of 2 ½ to 4 years in Attica Prison.
(Human Detective Cases Magazine-November 1944)

FRED L. NEBRASS –PEMBROKE MURDER –1925
On May 7, 1925, Fred L. Nebrass, age 45, residing on the Main Road (first farm west of the Genesee-Erie County Line) about 1 ½ miles west of Pembroke, N.Y. was shot and killed by his hired man, Otto Timmerman, aged 60. State Police Corporal Charles Stanton and Trooper Paul Mellody conducted the investigation arresting Timmerman who was found sleeping in a hayloft. Dr. Cyrus Pringle of Akron, N.Y. tended to Nebrass who died soon after. Timmerman had done chores on the farm for his board. Nebrass refused to give Timmerman a ride to Akron, because he had been drinking. Timmerman found a Harrington & Richardson .38 Calibre pistol that Nebrass kept in his truck, walked into the

kitchen of the house and shot Nebrass with one shot. Witnesses present were Freda Nebrass and Mrs. Augustus Heims who were sitting at the table during the shooting. They wrestled the gun from Timmerman before he fled from the scene. Nebrass had owned and operated a rendering plant at William Street and City Line, Buffalo, New York, which was sold to the city for use as a garbage incinerator. He then bought the country estate that was an Erie County agricultural showpiece. No disposition could be found.

ALPONZE PAOLUCCI – 1927
On November 12, 1927, Alphonze Paolucci residing at Alabama, N.Y. was responsible for the death of Georgette Bostolini, his 31-year-old housekeeper who resided with him. He stated that he held a razor in his hand and tried to frighten her into telling him where she had hidden $100.00 that he believed she stole from him. He said that she fell across the razor cutting her arm and then fell through a glass panel in the kitchen door.

Mrs. Eva Towne had witnessed Paolucci carrying the body of Georgette from the kitchen through a yard and throwing her over a fence into a field. She then saw him leave hurriedly carrying a bag. Georgette had been killed by deep slashes to the throat and inner left arm.

An investigation was conducted by District Attorney Darch accompanied by Trooper Clarence Molinaro, a member of the New York Troopers since March 1927. Molinaro spoke fluent Italian and was able to conduct interviews of witnesses and the Paolucci brothers, Armito and Dominic. It was found that after the killing, Alponze Paolucci traveled by train to Vandergrift, Pennsylvania where a cousin resided. One of the brothers provided Molinaro with a letter of introduction as Mr. Molinaro from Oakfield, N.Y.

Molinaro traveled to Vandergrift and introduced himself to the cousin, Louis Paolucci who in turn took him to a boarding house at Edri, Pennsylvania 35 miles away, where Alphonze was located. Trooper Molinaro accompanied by Pennsylvania Troopers entered the boarding house where Paolucci was taken into custody under gunpoint. Trooper Molinaro and Sheriff Legg returned him to Genesee County through extradition.

On February 7, 1928, Paolucci pled guilty to a lesser charge of Murder in the 2nd Degree and was sentenced by Supreme Court Justice Sanford T. Church to from 20 years to life at Auburn Prison. (Batavia Daily News)

STAFFORD COUNTRY CLUB MURDER - 1927
On August 18, 1927, troopers were sent to the Stafford Country Club to investigate the murder of Fred Knoblach, an employee. The assailant was identified as another country club employee, Chester Ball who fled the scene on foot. The most intense manhunt in county history resulted in the search for Ball with a $1000.00 reward posted. On August 22, 1927, Troopers William Cannon and George W. Donnelly captured Ball in a field outside the Village of Leroy, N.Y. without resistance. Information leading to the arrest was provided by Leroy youth Ernest Hutchinson who received the $1000.00 reward. Ball was in such a weakened state, that troopers stopped at a Leroy, N.Y. restaurant to provide for him before taking him to Batavia, N.Y. and interviewed by Sheriff George H. Legg and District Attorney William A. Darch. He was arraigned before Justice Pamphilion and charges read. Knoblach was so terribly lacerated, that death resulted from loss of blood. Ball admitted to being in a terrible fight with Knoblach that morning. With his dying breath, Knoblach identified Ball, as his killer. Ball pled guilty to a charge of Murder 2nd Degree and was sentenced to a term of not less than twenty years in state prison.

PHELPS HOTEL OWNER SHOT - 1929
On March 11, 1929, George P. Mott, age 67, proprietor of the Phelps Hotel, Phelps, N.Y. was reported near death and his housekeeper, Emily Walzer, age 45, under guard at her room charged with shooting Mott. Guests hearing a single shot observed Mrs. Walzer with the pistol in her hand and Mott lying on the floor. The shot had pierced the roof of his mouth and lodged at the base of the brain. She stated that Mott had attempted to gain entry to her room, but she refused. He then took a crow bar and shattered the bedroom door. Frightened, she took a revolver from a drawer and shot him. On March 28, 1929, an Ontario County Grand Jury found no cause for action. Walzer was released from custody.

OAKFIELD SKELETON - 1929
On October, 29, 1929, Oakfield, N.Y. town employee Alfred Kingdon while operating a scoop shovel unearthed a murder victim. While working at the property owned by G. Sherwin Haxton southwest of the village, a human skull toppled down a bank with the gravel. Under the direction of Coroner Dr. August Stein, the entire skeleton was unearthed. Inspection determined it to be that of a young man being struck in the head with a hatchet or other sharp instrument killed him. It was determined the body had been buried from nine months up to two years. It was believed the body was that of Lee Hall, a Batavia resident reported missing in 1926. This murder was never solved.

ELBA WOMAN KILLED - 1929
On November 25, 1929, Theresa Schulz, age 26, Edgerton Road, Elba, N.Y. was brought to St. Jerome's Hospital, Batavia, N.Y. where she died, as a result of a gunshot wound to the left side. Elmer Schultz, her husband was initially charged, however was exonerated of all blame; when it was determined that she was accidentally shot by their four-year old son, Elmer Jr.

EAST BLOOMFIELD FARMER KILLED - 1929
On December 16, 1929, Edward Sowards, age 21 was being sought for the murder of Hiram S. Bailey, an East Bloomfield, N.Y. farmer. Bailey was shot to death in his bathroom and his son; Duane tied up to a barn post. Sowards had boasted that there was a $5,000.00 reward posted for him in Cleveland, Ohio. A beat up funeral wreath was found tied to the front stairs and a murder mystery novel with open pages found on a table. Sowards was arrested for Murder 1st Degree and convicted of the crime in March 1930. He was sentenced to serve a term of not less than 20 years to life at hard labor in Auburn Prison.

PROTECTION FARMER MURDERED - 1929
On December 16, 1929, George Anger, age 42, a Protection, N.Y. farmer was struck over the head with an iron bar resulting in his death. Harold E. Miller, a neighboring farmhand was arrested for the crime. Anger was intoxicated and was angry, because his dog wouldn't perform tricks. He kicked the dog resulting in an argument with Miller that erupted into a fight with Anger being struck with the pipe. No disposition could be found.

WILLIAM WELCH KILLING - 1931
On June 28, 1931, Jesse Welch was drunk and had neglected his chores on the family farm located on the State Street Road, Batavia, N.Y. While in the barn, his brothers, Burt, William and George came to the farm, berated him for being late with the chores and gave him an unmerciful beating. They threw him into a watering through, then dragged him to the farmhouse where he was given five minutes to put on dry clothes and finish his chores. There was further arguing between Jesse and William at the house. Jesse got into a fight with William at this point resulting in his death. Jesse was charged with manslaughter on the complaint of his brother, Burt and arrested by Troopers Frank Easton and John Long. Hobart L. Hines, a Buffalo attorney volunteered to represent Jesse free of charge. Jesse testified that the brothers had beaten him on previous occasions and that when William came to the house, he

feared he was going to be beaten again. At a trial, before Justice Tyrrell, Jesse's case was dismissed on the merits.

SANDY CREEK SLAYING - 1933
On June 10, 1933, Frances McCallister, age 36, proprietor of a gas station at Sandy Creek north of Holley, N.Y. was slain by a single shot, when he jumped on the running board of a car to remind the driver he hadn't paid for seven gallons of gasoline put in the car. John W. Irving, 23, of Albion, an employee ran after the car, as McCallister tumbled from the running board managing to jump onto the rear bumper. He rode there about ¼ mile before the fugitives; two men and two girls discovered him. The man in the back seat broke the rear window with his pistol butt and started shooting at Irving. He was hit in the shoulder and fell to the highway. He obtained a license number, but it was later learned the car had been stolen from Niagara Falls, N.Y. Acting on a tip, Sergeant Harry Adams, Niagara Falls Police Lieutenant John J. Dietz and Orleans County Under Sheriff Herbert T. Clarke arrested Lorne Lally, age 18 and Angelo Presicci, age 21 of Niagara Falls, N.Y. and Sophie Cgerowinski age 17 and Dolores Kolodziej, age 18 of Buffalo, N.Y. Lally admitted to being the shooter. No disposition could be found.

TONAWANDA INDIAN CHIEF JAILED - 1933
On November 4, 1933, Lyman Poodry, age 47, a Tonawanda Indian Chief was sentenced to a serve a term of 2 to 5 years in Atlanta Prison after pleading guilty to manslaughter. Corporal Arthur Rich and Trooper Frank Shutt arrested him on July 22 after his car struck and killed nine-year-old Nancy Salustri on the Bloomingdale Road, Akron, and N.Y. A companion, Eva Casseri, age 12 was also struck suffering a fractured broken left leg and bruises. Poodry was the first prisoner in the area to receive a prison sentence on a plea of guilty involving killing a person with an automobile.

GROVELAND MAN CHOKED TO DEATH - 1933
On December 18, 1933, farmhand George Van Orsdale was choked to death while at the William Martin farm on the Groveland Road near Geneseo, N.Y. Arrested were three brothers, Charles Feathers, age 34, Groveland, N.Y., William Feathers, age 26 and Arthur Feathers, age 31, Conesus, N.Y. Re-kindling an old quarrel, the Feather brothers appeared at the Martin farm where they accosted Van Orsdale. Martin went to his aid, but was himself set upon. He went into the house to call for help and when he returned, Van Orsdale lay dead. He had been choked to death. Lieutenant Gerald Vaine arrested the brothers. No disposition could be found.

ORLEANS COUNTY SHOOTING - 1935
On August 5, 1935, 66 year old Walter Bonsall, operator of a boat livery on the Oak Orchard Creek north of Albion, N.Y. was charged with Murder 1st Degree for the fatal shooting of Peter H. Roach, 77, Buffalo, N.Y. Roach died instantly from gunshot wounds to the left side and neck. Investigation by Sergeant Harry Adams, Troopers Ralph Gibson and Harold Verplank. It was determined that Roach was shot by accident, when he went to the aid of the intended victim, Warren Patterson, a neighbor of Bonsall's during a quarrel. On December 11, 1935, Bonsall was found guilty of Murder 2nd Degree after trial. Orleans County Court Judge Bertrum E. Harcourt sentenced him to not less than 25 years but not more than 30 years in Attica State Prison.

FARMER'S HELD IN KILLINGS - 1935
During December 1935, William E. Norton, 48, of Moss Brook, N.Y. was charged before Friendship Justice M.Carey Drake with the slaying of Lewis S. Baker, 56. Sergeant Harold DeBrine said Baker was killed by a shotgun charge as he approached Norton's home. DeBrine laid the shooting to a long-standing feud. No disposition could be found.

Hazekian W. Goodwin, 55, of Humphrey, N.Y. declared he shot his friend, Earl Johnson, 31, in self-defense during an argument at his home. The men had been drinking and came to blows over the disappearance of $55.00. Goodwin picked up a shotgun and fatally wounded Johnson. Both were held for action of the Grand Jury.

LOTEMPIO – YATES - PANEPENTO MURDERS – 1936 - 37
On June 27, 1936, Frank A. LoTempio, 38, 24 Trumbull Parkway, Batavia, N.Y. was murdered gangland style while attending a wedding reception of a cousin, Frank LoTempio & Caroline Rizzo at Buffalo, N.Y. He was entering a car owned by his brother, Russell, when a dark sedan sped down Seventh Street with guns blazing. Eight shots hit LoTempio killing him instantly. He had just helped his wife, the former Josephine Mancuso and his sister, Mrs. Alfred Panepento into the car, when he was killed. No one else was injured. The car used had been purchased new using a fictitious name and was found abandoned a short distance away

LoTempio along with his brother, Russell were prosperous gamblers and bookmakers that enjoyed a good reputation in always meeting their obligations. For many years, they organized and ran the Savoy Athletic & Social Club and operated a bookmaking operation in the club rooms located in the Kraft Building on Liberty Street, Batavia, N.Y. They then opened the "Cocoanut Grove" nightclub on the second floor of the Kraft Building. The Cocoanut Grove was then relocated about three miles east of Batavia on the Main Road and eventually closed due to lack of business. Roulette and card games were played, but the main business was in betting on horse races. Operations were relocated to Ellicott Square in a building they owned at 305 Ellicott Street, Batavia, N.Y.

On October 30, 1936, gangland killers attempted to kill Russell LoTempio, 33, a Batavia bookmaker by planting a bomb in a car driven by William Yates, 35, 66 Swan Street, Batavia, N.Y. The bomb exploded under the floorboards, as they were leaving Medina, N.Y. Yates escaped with cuts and bruises, but Russell suffered injuries requiring the amputation of his left foot above the ankle. (Samuel Yates, 38, Batavia, N.Y., a cousin to William was shot to death while attending a wake on August 26 at Buffalo, N.Y.) Since his brother's death, police placed a tight lid on book making operations so the business was moved to Medina, N.Y. Lieutenant Eugene Hoyt assigned troopers to guard them around the clock.

It was believed the bomb was placed near the exhaust system on the left side of the car igniting an attached fuse, when it became hot. Police believed a rival bookmaker who unsuccessfully declared himself a business partner killed Frank LoTempio and Sam Yates was killed, because he talked too much about the LoTempio murder. Russell traveled a circuit, as a professional big time gambler working as a roulette dealer and high stakes player. He returned to Batavia after contracting Tuberculosis, which halted his activities. He had been married to a nurse from Saranac Lake who died of tuberculosis. They had one child that died at infancy.

On August 14, 1937, gangsters came to Batavia, N.Y. with guns blazing killing Alfred Panepinto, 35, Niagara Falls, N.Y. and wounding Samuel Sce, 27, 106 South Swan Street, Batavia, N.Y. Panepinto had been living with his brother, Anthony at 339 Jackson Street for several months prior to his demise. The gunmen appeared in the doorway of LoTempio's Pool Room, 305 Ellicott Street at about 12:20 AM and fired shotgun and revolver blasts into the room where several men were playing cards. Panepinto, holding a pair of sixes, was shot in the back of the neck dying instantly. Sce was hit in the back by a shotgun slug recovering from his injuries.

Police theorized the slaying was connected to the previous murders of Frank LoTempio and attempted murder of his brother, Russell. Batavia Assistant Police Chief Thomas Donoghue was talking with Patrolman Edward Hinkson near the corner of Ellicott and Goade Park, when the shots were fired.

They ran to the scene with guns drawn just as other occupants of the pool hall were fleeing out the front door. At gunpoint, all were ordered back into the building and searched. They were all questioned, but because the gunmen remained out in the dark, could not make an identification of the killers. Those present at the time of the shooting were Joseph LoTempio, a brother to Frank and Russell, Philip Pastore, Paul Colombo, Deputy Sheriff Samuel Disalvo, Charles Cino, Samuel Mirando, James Pifalo, Floyd Aramino, Andrew Liberto, Samuel Conti, Alfred Strollo and Michael Cecere.

Sergeant Harry DeHollander and Corporal George Wood were assigned to work with Batavia Police on the murder investigation. There had been several such slayings in Western New York that had never been solved. Refusal of witnesses to talk was the norm. They either refused to talk or if they did, would reveal only as much information, as they knew the police already had. Troopers located the automobile used in the murder in the eastern end of Genesee County the day after the shooting. It had been purchased used, under a fictitious name. The car was secured at the Batavia Barracks. These cases remain unsolved.

TORCH MURDER - 1936
On December 16, 1936, Harold J. Smith, 32, West Bloomfield, N.Y. farmhand was held in connection with the torch death of his friend, Lewis E. Rose, 28, found lying on the roadside near East Avon with his clothing ablaze. Smith gave a story that Rose had fallen out of his automobile and that when he lit a match to see if he was ok, his greasy clothes caught fire. Other motorist's traveling the road put out the burning clothes and took Rose for medical treatment. He died at Strong Hospital, Rochester, N.Y. Smith was held on a charge of Murder 1st Degree. On April 14, 1937, a Livingston County Grand Jury returned a no bill. Smith was released from custody.

CATTARAUGUS INDIAN MURDERED - 1937
An all day murder investigation was conducted on January 10, 1937 on the Cattaraugus Indian reservation by Lieutenant Eugene Hoyt and Sergeant Harry DeHollander resulting in the arrest of Archie White, 57 charged with murder. The victim was identified as Simon Hemlock, age 47, a neighbor of Whites with the crime witnessed by another neighbor, 53-year-old George Seneca. The three were at Whites home drinking alcohol with the conversation turning to firearms and marksmanship ability. White took a shotgun off the wall at which time Seneca left to return home. As he exited, he heard a shotgun blast, but did not return. White apparently went to bed. When he got up in the morning, he found Hemlocks body in the same chair that he was sitting in the night before with his right hand blown off and a gaping hole in his side. White then walked to Seneca's home and told him Hemlock was dead. They notified Reverend David Owl who called for the troopers. White stated that he had no recollection of the shooting. He was turned over to federal authorities for prosecution in federal court.
(Batavia Daily News – 1/11/37)

MEDINA WIFE MURDERED - 1937
On October 12, 1937, Daniel Green, 27 of Medina, N.Y. was charged with the murder of his estranged wife, Eunice, age 35. Jealousy was deemed the motive, as Daniel believed his wife was stepping out with other men. A chance meeting at the corner of Gwinn and Park Streets in the village led to an argument. Green, using a three-inch long paring knife stabbed Eunice eight times in the chest piercing the heart. She was found lying in a pool of blood by her sisters, Mrs. William Board and Mrs. Ray Parker who had just dropped her off so she could speak with her husband. Sergeant Charles Burnett, Sheriff Herbert Clark and Medina Fireman Leo Renello found Green hiding in a truck early the next morning. He confessed to the murder, was charged before Justice Frederic Skinner and held for grand

jury action. On November 24, 1937, Green was found guilty of Murder 2nd Degree and was sentenced to a term of 20 years to life at Attica Prison.

OAKFIELD BARBER SLAIN - 1937

The bullet riddled body of Joseph "Hank" Ottaviano, 24, Garibaldi Avenue, Oakfield, N.Y. was found on the morning of December 31, 1937 by his brother Louis. He had heard what he thought was backfiring at about 4:00AM, but fell back to sleep. He found his brother dead, while on the way to work. He immediately notified Constable George Lesso who in turn called Inspector Eugene Hoyt who went to the scene. Five bullet holes were found in the car. Joseph was killed from a close range shot to the temple. Skid marks at the scene indicated gunmen had squeezed Joseph's car to a halt. He was never known to be in trouble and was well liked by everyone. He had worked as a Western Union messenger, saved his money and went to Barber's School. He then opened "Hank's Barbershop" on Oakfield's Main Street. It was believed that Joseph, a lady's man was killed for some personal troubles, possibly jealousy inspired by his attentions to a girl.

NORTH ROSE MURDER - 1938

During January 1938, an argument over the refusal of a father to share his monthly $12.00 old age pension check with his son was the motive for murder at North Rose, N.Y. Seventy-three year old James Bassett was shot with a 12 gauge shotgun and his house set on fire in an effort to destroy the evidence. Trooper Michael Fort, Clayton Bailey, Corporal Paul Mellody and Sergeant Clifford Lee took Chester Leroy Bassett, 34, into custody. Chester said he needed $6.00 of the money to pay for a visit to his estranged wife in Michigan. The father refused and in a drunken rage, Chester shot him in the head from about fourteen feet away. He then poured kerosene on the body and set it on fire. He fled the scene and got as far as Erie, Pa. where he turned himself in to police. Taken into custody by troopers, he admitted to the crime. No disposition could be found.

PENN YAN MURDER – 1939

On September 25, 1939, the battered body of 13-year-old high school girl Evelyn Reed was found on a wooded knoll two miles south of Branchport, N.Y. Evelyn, an only child of Mr. and Mrs. Sidney Reed of Indian Pines, Penn Yan, N.Y., vanished a week earlier. (September 19, 1939) She was on her way home from school with books under her arm, to bake a cake in celebration of her mother's birthday.

CCC volunteer searchers Lester Ramsey and Walter Cleslewicz searching one hundred feet west of the Branch port- Hammondsport road on the Peter Lounsbury farm found her. Her books were found nearby hidden under brush.

An investigation by Coroners Dr. Rudolph Shafer of Corning, N.Y. and James Sanford of Bath, N.Y. determined that Evelyn died of shock and a cerebral hemorrhage the result of a sharp instrument penetrating her skull. Evidence at the scene indicated a struggle based on injuries to her hands and arms.

Less than an hour after the body was found, State Police Sergeant Harry DeHollander and Trooper Michael Fort arrested twenty-six year old Norman James Wheelock at his Prattsburg, N.Y. place of employment, charging him with first-degree murder. Wheelock, a lineman for the Prattsburg Telephone Company owned by his father became a suspect several days earlier on observations of witnesses placing him at or near the crime scene.

Wheelock, whose identity was not immediately revealed because of the highly incensed area residents, was taken to Batavia, N.Y. for questioning by Sgt. DeHollander, Trooper Scott, Corporals Wilkerson and Mellody. While at Batavia, he made the following admission. "He saw the Reed girl walking along Elm Street and offered her a ride home which she accepted. He then drove south through the Village of Branchport and pulled off of the road into a wooded area. He pulled her out of the light truck about one hundred feet into the woods where he assaulted her. He struck her several times with his fists. When she screamed and tried to run away, he stabbed her with a screwdriver. He thought she was dead so he returned to his truck, retrieved her books and hid them under some weeds. He then drove back to Prattsburg eighteen miles away."

On November 9, 1939, a trial was held at Hornell, N.Y. before Justice Nathan D. Lapman of Geneva, N.Y. After only 2 ½ hours of deliberation, the jury found him guilty of Murder in the First Degree. The entire process from arrest to sentence took 47 days. Attorneys Alton Whightman of Bath, N.Y. and W. Earle Costello of Corning, N.Y represented Wheelock. District Attorney George A. King of Corning, N.Y. prosecuted. Defense attorneys pled for a disposition of insanity in the slaying to no avail. On August 1, 1940 Wheelock met his maker by way of the electric chair at Ossining State Prison.

Evelyn Reed was buried in Pulteney, N.Y. Her closest friends were honorary pallbearers and included Betsy and Carol Wineguard, Janice McElligott, Marilyn Bassage, Joyce Wheeler, Phyllis Rector, Ruth Pinneo, Dorothy Chauncey and Polly Whitaker. Active bearers were Stanley Riffle, Russell Tindall, Bruce Rushmore, Howard Turnbull, David Cole and George Hultse.

LYNDONVILLE CHILDREN SLAIN - 1939
On December 12, 1939, Trooper J.B. McMahon responded to the report of a fire at the George Dunham farm located on the Creek Road, between Waterport and Lyndonville, N.Y. where he discovered murders had been committed. Investigation by Corporal Albert Horton and Frank Easton revealed Pearl Dunham had hit her four daughters on the head with the blunt end of an axe, slashed their wrists with a razor and poured kerosene on them setting them on fire. She then retired to her room slashing her wrists in an apparent suicide attempt. Dead at the scene were Ruth Dunham, age 15, and Carol Dunham, age 4 dead from crushed skulls. Frances, age 9 died the next day of a crushed skull. Shirley, age 8 and Mrs. Dunham, age 45 were taken to Medina Hospital where they recovered. Shirley suffered a bruise to the head, body burns and blood loss from a slashed artery. Mrs. Dunham had been under a doctor's care for a nervous disorder. Hiram Squires and J.E. Plummer, neighbors noticed smoke coming from the Dunham house. They smashed in the front door and discovered the bodies. Mrs. Dunham recovering from her injuries was committed to Matteawan State Hospital, Beacon, N.Y. where on January 4, 1940 she took her own life by hanging.

BROCKPORT MAN MURDERED
On September 15, 1940, Paul Wolfe, 35, Brockport, N.Y. was killed during a Holley barroom argument over Hitlerism. Inspector Eugene Hoyt and Corporal Earl Wilkinson investigating found that Wolfe, a supporter of Germany's Adolph Hitler, got into a heated argument with Anthony D'Amico of Fancher, N.Y. and William Bartlett of Clarendon, N.Y. The three exited the bar and while outside, it was alleged Wolfe took a punch at D'Amico. Blows were struck with Wolfe being left in a daze or unconscious on the sidewalk. An autopsy indicated that he died from a violent blow to the jaw causing a brain injury. D'Amico was charged with Manslaughter and Bartlett held, as a material witness. Wolfe had been employed at Duffy Mott, Holley, N.Y. On November 6, 1940, an Orleans County Grand Jury returned a verdict of no cause for action. D'Amico was released from custody.

LITTLE GENESEE GIRL SLAIN

On May 21, 1943, Frank Smith, 48, RFD 1, Bolivar, N.Y. was arrested for Murder 1ˢᵗ Degree. He was arraigned before Justice M. Cary Drake of Friendship, N.Y. who ordered him held for grand Jury review. The body of Thelma Snyder, age 9 of Little Genesee, N.Y. was found in a farm thicket two months after she was reported missing. She had been brutally murdered with an axe. Troopers working round the clock on the case were Harold Debrine, Charles Stanton, Stanley Smith, George Wood and Claude Stephens. Suspicion fell on Smith, when he showed no interest in being part of a search for Thelma. Every person in the community was engaged in combing and searching fields, woods and streams. Smith admitted that he had lured Thelma into a wooded area under the pretext of looking for foxes. He had earlier watched her walk with her father, Gerald Snyder to a bus stop. After Gerald boarded the bus for Olean, Smith lured Thelma into the woods. There, he assaulted and killed her with a blow from the head of an axe. He secreted the body returning to his wood chopping chores. Lifelong Little Genesee resident Edgar Sherman recalled Smith as an oddball farm hand who lived like a hermit and drove a team of horses with wagon for transportation. Smith had befriended Thelma as they went for walks together in the woods. He recalled Thelma's body being found in a stand of evergreen trees off of State Highway 17 toward Ceres. He didn't think Smith was given the electric chair, rather a lifelong Attica Prison sentence requested by Mrs. Snyder so Smith could think about his deed.

TROOP A

Case # 444V

Class

RETURN THIS PAPER

COMPLAINT REPORT

Complainant___Mrs. Elwin Chaddock___ Street or R. F. D.___

age___Linden___ Township___Bethany___

nty___ Telephone___Attica, 3 F. 2.___

plaint Rec'd at___Barracks___ By___Sergt. Serve___

e___3/11/24___ Time___7-45 P.M.___ Assignment___Tprs. Gibbons & Donnelly___

STOLEN AUTOMOBILE DATA

ke___ Engine No.___ License No.___

del___ Style___ Factory No.___

y Color___ Wheels, kind and color___

cial Equipment, marks or injuries to aid identification___

below complete details of complaint; correct names of suspects or witnesses; accurate descriptions of persons or property missing:

COMPLAINT   burning

Phoned from her home and stated that Thomas Whaley house, in Village burning of Linden and that there was blood seen in house, requested Tprs,

7-50.P.M. Tprs. Gibbons & Donnelly left on the above complaint,

8-40.P.M. Cpl. Fleming left barracks for Liut. George home and from there with Lieut. for Linden,

8-45.P.M. Phoned the above complaint to the Capt. at his home, Captain requested Cpl. Brandstetter to come for him with car,

8-50.P.M. Tpr. Gibbons phoned from Linden and reports three people murdered, and to notify Dist. Attry and Coroner,

8-55.P.M. Captain and Cpl. Brandstetter left barracks for Linden,

9-05. Tried to locate Dist. Atty. Waterman and was unable too, His Sister Mrs. Grace Garnier who lives at the Dist. Atty. home said that he had left with Sheriff for Linden,

9-10.P.M. Tried to locate Coroner Ward B Manchester and Mrs. Manchester stated that he had left for Linden,

3/12/24
12-30. AM
Lieut. George phoned from Linden and reported that Mr. & Mrs. Thomas Waley and Mrs. George Morris of Linden had been murdered to night between six and seven P.M. and to notify Buffalo and Rochester Police Dpt, s also Cpl. Benway and Tpr. Decker, to look over all suspect may have blood on their clothes, if found hold and notify,

12-35 A.M. Phoned Rochester Police Dpt, the above.

12-45 A.M. Phoned Buffalo Police Dpt, the above.

12-55 A.M. Phoned Tpr. Decker at Caledonia the above, he stated that would get out at once,

1-00.A.M. Phoned Cpl. Benway at Clarence the above and he stated that

$5,000
REWARD!

Murder!

TWO WOMEN AND ONE MAN BRUTALLY MURDERED.

On the afternoon of March 11th, 1924, at the hamlet Linden, on the Erie Rail-road, in the Town of Bethany, Genesee County, N. Y., between the hours of 5:30 and 7 o'clock, Thomas Whaley, Hattie Whaley his wife, and Mrs. Mabel Morse, the wife of George Morse of Linden, New York, were murdered in the home of Thomas Whaley by an unknown person or persons. Mr. and Mrs. Whaley were both shot to death and Mrs. Morse was beaten to death. The pocketbooks of the victims were found rifled in the house.

Mrs. Morse wore a large open faced gold wrist watch with a gold chain bracelet attached. This is gone. Search all pawn shops for wrist watch.

Mr. Whaley's watch is also missing. It is a silver watch, heavy hunting case, Elgin movement No. 5,540,631, 15-jewel watch, size 18. Case badly worn, as it had been carried by Mr. Whaley for 30 years.

The bodies of the victims were all dragged into a bedroom and covered with rugs and set on fire after being saturated with kerosene oil.

The County of Genesee offers a reward of $5,000 for information leading to the arrest and conviction of the person or persons guilty of the murder of Thomas Whaley, Mrs. Thomas Whaley and Mrs. Mabel Morse.

Address all communications to

HENRY W. WARE, Sheriff of Genesee County, Batavia. N. Y.

CHAPTER FORTY-SEVEN
COCK FIGHTING

For many years, the cock fighting gentry of Western New York had matched wits with troopers in the pursuit of their sport, and more often than not, the troopers won. The planning of a raid was usually the duty of a lieutenant. It may have appeared that a cock- fighting raid was simply a matter of getting a tip, gathering a raiding party and driving to the scene, but in reality, it was like a military maneuver pitting the trooper's skills with the cock fighters. Cock- fights were usually held during the late evening or at night and advertised by word of mouth

Heavy steel spurs were attached to the legs of the fighting-cocks. Two birds would be placed in a 12 foot square pit enclosed by boards about two feet high with bark or sawdust on the fighting surface to give them good footing. Over the pit would be a cluster of bulbs lighting the affair. The birds would fight until only one survived. Burlap bags would be found hanging from pegs in an adjacent room, each holding a bird for fighting. An attached tag giving the owners initials and the weight of the fighter inside the bag identified birds. Most birds weighed between 5 and 5 ½ pounds. A dormitory for the birds was located adjacent to an enclosed area that served as a training arena. The birds valued at $100.00 each, were trained wearing pads in place of the spurs and had no fat on their body. Confiscated birds were killed and given to public institutions, but it wasn't known if they were eaten or not.

On the night of a raid, the lieutenant would gather a group of 25 to 30 troopers from outlying posts that would meet at a designated rural location. This method was used, because the cock- fighters would have "spotters" keeping an eye on the Batavia and Precinct Barracks for any unusual activity. Only one state car was used with the personal cars of the lieutenant and sergeants utilized with raiders wearing overcoats and soft hats. This was done, because spotters cruised near the area of the cockfights looking for the fur caps and sheepskin coats usually worn by the troopers. Back roads were taken to a second designated location where the raiding party met plain-clothes troopers who had been watching the fight location and reported on it's progress. Again using back streets, the troopers would surround the location to prevent escape while a group led by the lieutenant would enter through the front door. One trooper was left with the cars, as the trooper's tires had been slashed during previous raids. There would be a flurry of activity, as participants tried to escape, but to no avail. A local Justice would be brought to the location usually with no complaint, since he received $3.50 for each case heard. Participants usually gave phony names that were not checked on. Troopers would fill out all the necessary paperwork on location while waiting the Justice's arrival. A normal crowd at a fighting event would be in excess of 100 participants wagering on the outcome of the fight. Listed are examples of raids on the cockfighting industry.

OGDEN COCK FIGHTS
On May 30, 1922 a raid on a farm near the Red Onion Road, Ogden, N.Y. led by Sergeant Panzlau resulted in the arrest of 132 men for cock fighting and 83 gamecocks seized. The location was a natural amphitheatre in a wooded area near stop #5 of the Rochester, Lockport and Buffalo trolley line. It was the largest ever held in the area and was equal to a mini fair with tents set up for sale of refreshments. A shot fired by troopers to get the crowds attention ricocheted striking Leon Frances DeValder in the hip. He was taken by automobile to Lee Hospital for treatment. Gates Justice Charles McDowell was driven to the scene and an on site court established. All posted bail totaling $2,760.00 for their appearance before Justice J.L. Humphreys, Spencerport, N.Y.

DURRINGER HOTEL, FORKS, N.Y.

On June 8, 1922, raiders led by Lieutenant Walter Croadsdale visited the Durringer Hotel, Forks, N.Y. arresting 57 patrons and seizing 28 live and dead birds. All were charged with participating in cock fighting, immediately arraigned before Sloan Justice Peter Inda, entered pleas of guilty with each being fined $10.00. An elaborate pit with banked seats and lighting near the hotel was said to have cost $15,000.00 to construct.

BROCKPORT, N.Y.

On January 9, 1931, Lieutenant Gerald Vaine led a raiding party of 25 troopers to the Burch Livery Stable barns at Brockport, N.Y. where cock- fights were in progress. All 29 participants were arrested with nineteen fighting birds confiscated. Judge Homer Benedict was brought to the location, court held and each participant fined $10.00.

DUNKIRK, N.Y.

On January 9, 1932, Lieutenant Lawrence Nelson and Sergeant Charles Stanton raided a vacant house on the Roberts Road, Dunkirk, N.Y. where cockfights were in progress. Howard Douglas, the promoter was fined $50.00 by Justice John F. Green. Thirty-five men and women spectators paid $10.00 fines and the birds seized.

GROVELAND, N.Y.

On April 17, 1937, raiding troopers led by Lieutenant Gerald Vaine arrested 89 spectators, confiscated 35 fighting birds and broke up fixed crap game at Hampton, a Wadsworth Estate farm. Troopers turned back a wild rush for freedom with nightsticks. All present were charged with witnessing a cockfight, a misdemeanor under the law prohibiting cruelty to animals, were fined $10.00 by Groveland Justice Craig Ross and released. The birds were given to a welfare organization for soup, as they were too tough to be eaten. The Wadsworth mansion had burned several years earlier and Thomas Servis who was charged as a spectator operated the farm. A crap game was in progress with troopers finding a pair of loaded dice. Their owner having won a substantial sum, now exposed, paid most of the fines with his winnings.

NUNDA, N.Y.

On July 1, 1940, Troopers led by Lieutenant Gerald Vaine and Sergeants William Ireland and John Krick confiscated 163 birds and arrested 67 owners near Nunda, N.Y. in a raid of one of the biggest gamecock fights in the state. Entrants were from throughout the state and it was to determine the state champion. The open arena was in a wooded area on what was known as the Arthur Brink farm. The owners pleading guilty before Justice Albert Conrad were fined $10.00 each and released. Rochester Humane Society members Harry and Rudolph Panzlau (a former trooper) also were part of the raiding party.

CHAPTER FORTY-EIGHT
PROHIBITION 1919 TO 1933

Temperance may be defined as: Moderation in all things healthful; total abstinence from all things harmful. (Greek Philosopher Xenphon – 440 B.C.)

Prohibition, the 18th Amendment or Volstead Act, as it was known, passed in January 1919 and was a measure designed to reduce drinking by eliminating businesses that manufactured, distributed and sold alcoholic beverages.

The prohibition era had a sense of lawlessness since consumption was not eliminated, only an attempt to curb production. Organized crime took over the manufacture and distribution of almost all illicit alcohol produced during the 1920's and early 1930's. Stills and speakeasies popped up in every center of population. Over-zealous police and federal agents violated civil rights when searching for and destroying paraphernalia of alcohol. While most Americans respected the law, the shine of "dry" began to wear off. As the great depression set in, prohibition was seen as an affront to personal liberty pushed on the nation by religious moralists. Alcohol was also seen as a source of revenue for the local, state and national governments. On February 20, 1933, Congress passed an amendment repealing prohibition.

MULLAN GAGE ACT – NEW YORKS PROHIBITION LAW
In April 1921, the New York State Legislature passed the Mullan-Gage Bill into law. It was closely patterned after the Federal Volstead Act giving authority to law enforcement in the enforcement of prohibition. It was short lived, as many newly elected legislators had campaigned on the repeal or modification of the law. On June 1, 1923, the law was repealed in total.

TROOPERS ENFORCEMENT OF PROHIBITION LAWS
Created in 1917, the new state constabulary was responsible for the enforcement of all laws. Due to an increase in automobile accidents caused by drivers with inadequate, glaring or no headlights, the increased enforcement of headlamp laws resulted in many residual arrests for violation of the newly enacted prohibition laws. Troopers found bootleggers intentionally drove without lights in an attempt to evade police. Violators were initially arrested on federal charges and turned over to federal authorities. With the enactment of New York's Mullan-Gage Act, violators were charged under state law and processed through the local judicial system.

There were daily instances of arrests by troopers for prohibition & liquor law violations. Alcohol was being produced in bathtubs for home use and sale to a friend or two. Stills were established in rural wooded areas, barns and back rooms all across the country for large-scale production and distribution. Alcohol legally produced in Canada brought premium prices and was smuggled across the border by whatever means were available. The following will acquaint the reader with various methods used to avoid detection and the type of arrests that were made.

On December 23, 1919, Victor Fisher, proprietor of the Hotel Victoria, 452 West Main Street, Rochester, N.Y. traveled to Buffalo, N.Y. where he purchased two ten-gallon kegs of wine and a two-gallon keg of whiskey. While returning, he was stopped by Troopers George Tetley and Henry Smith near Batavia, N.Y. for not having working headlights on his automobile. The illegal alcohol was observed in the rear seat. He was charged with having liquor in dry territory under the state tax law. He posted bail before Justice Henry Ware for appearance at a later date.

On May 12, 1920, seventy-two quarts of whiskey smuggled from Canada and a touring car came into possession of Trooper Edwin Evans at Youngstown, N.Y. As Evans approached a car parked with no lights, it suddenly sped away. He gave chase for several miles with the pursued vehicle running off of the road. Two occupants of the car were seen fleeing on foot to evade arrest. The car and contents were confiscated.

On May 18, 1920, Troopers Henry Wagner and Harry White seized a truck carrying 720 quarts of whiskey valued at $7,000.00 near Caledonia, N.Y. The occupants, brothers Anthony and Philip Panfona of Buffalo, N.Y. were charged with not having headlights on the vehicle and illegal possession of a pistol. They were released on $250.00 bail. Federal authorities were notified for further prosecution under the prohibition law.

On May 25, 1920, Troopers C. Leo Lunney and Corporal Gerald Sullivan, acting on a tip that whiskey was being made at a house on the Darien-Corfu Townline Road, investigated and found Thomas B. Natoli busily engaged in making liquor. The still located in a woodshed had a twenty-gallon capacity. Found in his kitchen were two barrels of whiskey mash and four barrels of wine mash. Natoli was charged with operating an illegal still and avoiding taxes. He was arraigned in federal court.

Sergeant George Tarbox and Trooper McDougall chased a Hudson car bearing Michigan license plates for many miles before it ran off the road into a shallow section of Chautauqua Lake. The driver leaped from the car and disappeared in the dark. The car was pulled from the lake and found to contain two barrels containing 100 gallons of whiskey. The car and barrels were turned over to Federal Authorities. The car was auctioned in front of the federal building in Rochester, N.Y., selling for $1,100.00.

On January 18, 1921, Troopers Gerald Sullivan and Parks arrested Liberante Purna, proprietor of the West Shore Hotel on South Street and James Ross who operated a restaurant on the north side of John Laduca's building, Main Street, Oakfield, N.Y. Both were charged with maintaining a public nuisance and selling hard cider to the public. Pleading guilty before Justice Olmsted, each paid a fine of $25.00. Also arrested was Carmino Feliccione for having a concealed stiletto and revolver. He paid a $50.00 fine.

On May 5, 1921, a raiding party executed a search warrant at a hotel owned by Ralph W. Brown of Tonawanda, N.Y. Troopers Armon P. Gunnison and Joseph E. Holcomb had lived at the hotel and over several weeks had observed the illegal activity of an organized gang of bootleggers working between Canada and the United States. The bootleggers smuggled illegal liquor hidden in bags by using the Niagara River route for entry. High-powered motorboats traveled around the south end of Grand Island with the contraband stored at Brown's Hotel. Troopers found 240 quarts of gin, 360 quarts of whiskey, as well as champagne, brandy and wine valued at $50,000.00. Two cars and two trucks under guard carried the confiscated alcohol to the Batavia Barracks where it was secured until turned over to federal authorities.

On May 10, 1921, a raid of the Central Hotel, Angola, N.Y. resulted in fourteen-barrels of liquor being confiscated and bartender Jack Florani arrested for selling alcohol. Bail was posted for a later appearance. At the Oak Café, Akron, N.Y., troopers confiscated moonshine, wine and cider and arrested proprietor Sebastian Mazza. He was charged with maintaining a public nuisance and pled guilty before Justice Frank Crego paying a fine of $25.00.

On May 20, 1921, the Rice Hotel, West Brighton, N.Y. was said to be wide open and sold alcohol to a trooper. A raid produced a seizure of $50,000.00 of fine whiskeys hidden in false walls and buried in a room-sized pit in the back yard. Owner Henry Rice and bartender William McHugh were released on bail after arrest. On June 4, 1921, Monroe County Judge Willis K. Gillette ordered $40,000.00 worth of the liquor returned to George Finnerty, the owner of the alcohol. He had rented a room from Rice where he kept the liquor stored in the locked room. Judge Gillette found the search to be illegal, as the room rented to Finnerty was not subject to search. On May 28, 1921, the Livingston House, Avon, N.Y. was raided with 50 quarts of scotch and cognac confiscated. Owner John Bohen and bartender Thomas Reynolds posted $500.00 bail after arrest. The Clyde Hotel, Clyde, N.Y. was raided with $300.00 in whiskey and cider seized. Owner D.E. Heinzman posted $500.00 bail after arrest.

On June 9, 1921, a Genesee county Court Jury found Thomas Natole, owner of the Oakfield Hotel guilty of alcohol sales. This was the first conviction for a liquor related arrest in the county under the states new excise law. The next day, his wife Mary Natole pled guilty to an identical charge from an unrelated incident. Sentencing was postponed until all similar cases were disposed of. On June 10, 1921, Corfu Hotel owner John F. Smith was the first to be tried under the Mullan-Gage Act, the states new dry enforcement law that repealed the excise law through inclusion.

On July 11, 1921, troopers for the third time raided a resort on the Leroy-Caledonia Road (Route 5), Limerock, N.Y. owned by Mrs. Frances Deleo where they seized illegal wine and cider. She was charged with selling intoxicants. Twenty-five male patrons were charged with Disorderly Conduct. Justice R. C. Cullings was summoned to the location and a session of midnight court was held. Six men were discharged, ten were fined ranging from $1.00 to $5.00, five received suspended sentences and four had their cases postponed.

On July 25, 1921, a raid at Jerry Crick's resort on the York Road, Caledonia, N.Y. resulted in the seizure of two barrels of cider and sixty bottles of home brew and wine. Crick pled guilty before Caledonia Justice Tennant to liquor law violations. Nine patrons were arrested for Disorderly Conduct and paid fines ranging from $5.00 to $10.00. They were identified as Samuel Bowden, George Smith, Steve Grecor, Richard Anderson, Adam Smith and William Smith of Mumford, James Baird and Edward A. Lee of Caledonia and Edward Jakse of Bergen.

On July 27, 1921, the Monroe County Sheriff's Department raided the Russell Hotel at Webster, N.Y. arresting proprietor Mary DeField for prohibition law violations. Six barrels of cider and a quart of whiskey were found and confiscated. It was learned that troopers when in the area stayed at the hotel. Patrons expressed regret that the troopers were absent when the raid occurred.

MOONSHINE
On March 19, 1923, the properties of the United State Gypsum Company (USGC), Oakfield, N.Y. located at the intersection of Duck Pond & Hutton Roads was raided by troopers where a large amount of mash and three working stills were confiscated. The location was a clump of houses resided in by about twenty-five USGC miners and their family's who in turn had about ten boarders each. It was described as a thickly populated settlement where the men would fight, drink, gamble and work at intervals. Sergeant Gerald Sullivan and five troopers along with H.B. Croswell and B.B. Norton, USGC property officials, led the raid.

OAK HILL COUNTRY CLUB
On August 5, 1924, the former Spring Brook Hotel owned by the Oak Hill Country Club of Rochester, N.Y. and used as a private rooming and boarding house for their employees was raided and proprietor Samuel Vigaretti arrested. He was found guilty of conducting a Public Nuisance before East Rochester Justice Hatch, was fined $50.00 and released. Eight residents pled guilty to Disorderly Conduct, were fined $10.00 each and released. Two barrels of cider, a bottle of alcohol and a bottle of wine were seized and destroyed. On August 7, Vigaretti appeared before Pittsford Justice William Murray claiming his roomers had been intimidated by the trooper's rough talk and flashing of their pistols during the raid. He did not feel the trial before Justice hatch was fair. Warrants were issued for Sergeant's Michael Serve, Michael Fleming and Troopers George Donnelly, Henry Rogers, Percy Leitner and Thomas Longo. Troopers said it was an act of revenge by Vigaretti for an earlier raid at the hotel. All charges were ultimately dismissed.

On May 27, 1925, Cherry Creek, N.Y. farmer William Hall was arrested for making moonshine whiskey. Troopers reported that it was one of the largest stills ever found. Confiscated were four barrels of moonshine whiskey that was found in the farmhouse. Brewing equipment and 1,600 bottles of beer were seized.

On August 15, 1925, troopers and federal dry agents raided the "Bucket of Blood" saloon in Holley, N.Y. seizing four barrels of cider, thirty gallons of wine, twenty-five cases of beer and a quantity of wine. Nick Ferrari of Rochester, N.Y. was charged and turned over to federal authorities.

On November 11, 1930, federal agents along with Trooper Samuel Vint and Lyman Fortner raided a distillery on South Pearl Street Road, Oakfield, N.Y. They arrested Santo DeFazio, age 26 and Samuel Grimaldi, age 29 of Batavia, N.Y. for the Possession and Manufacture of Alcohol. Both were turned over to federal authorities. Two mash tubs with a 30,000-gallon capacity, a 1500-gallon still and a 500-gallon still were found on the premises. Thirty gallons of alcohol was seized that tested to be 185 proof. The stills were destroyed.

On June 4, 1931, Troopers John Bihn and Irving Librock stationed at Hamburg captured an outboard motorboat and twenty-six cases of Canadian Ale. The troopers came upon twenty cases of ale hidden on the beach at Woodlawn, N.Y. They remained on watch and were rewarded when a motorboat approached from the direction of Canada. Three men aboard began unloading an additional six cases of ale. Charged with smuggling were Nicholas Stark, Cedric Haines and John Held all of Woodlawn.

On June 20, 1931, Corporal Albert Horton Trooper Eugene Hoyt patrolling near Albion, N.Y. seized twelve thousand bottles of Canadian Ale and a truck valued at $7,000.00. All were turned over to federal authorities for prosecution.

Troopers Harold Debrine and Anthony Bily arrested William P. Ryan, age 55, proprietor of the Palaco Billiard Parlor, 104 Main Street, Wellsville, N.Y. on February 9, 1932. He was charged with Possession and Sale of Alcohol and possession of two slot machines. The slot machines were destroyed and monies found in them given to the town's poor fund.

On February 23, 1933, Trooper Percy Leitner and Raymond Regan arrested Thomas Kelly, age 42 and William Roach, age 23, Buffalo, N.Y. residents after an eight-mile chase. They were part of a smuggling operation that brought choice alcohol into the United States from Canada by airplane two or three times weekly. A plane would land in a farm field located on the Richley Road, Darien, N.Y., which was owned by Gerald Crouse. Two men who transferred fifteen to sixteen burlap bags full of alcohol from the plane to the waiting automobile met the plane. The troopers acting on a tip that a plane had landed observed the plane rapidly departing and a car entering the road from the farm field. A chase ensued that ended on the Broadway Road several miles west of Darien Center, N.Y. The alcohol was found in the back seat. The two bootleggers advised that they had no knowledge of the pilot or the smuggling operation. They said they were hired to meet the plane and pick up the packages. They were turned over to federal authorities charged with smuggling.

On February 26, 1940, Troopers Harry DeHollander, Albert Horton and William Szymanski conducted a raid on the Tinkham Road, Darien, N.Y. arresting Alex Cruiscike, Cheektowaga, N.Y. and destroyed a 500-gallon still. Cruscike, alias Stanley Strauss, was charged with Possession of an Unregistered Still and Non-Payment of Alcohol Tax. He was held under $2500.00 bail for appearance in federal court.

On August 23, 1940, Troopers Donald Girven, Frank Hackett and Francis Quadlander stopped a car driven by Patsy Scorgo, 42, Rochester, N.Y. on a back road in Byron, N.Y. Smelling alcohol, a search of the vehicle found nineteen five-gallon cans of alcohol. This led to the finding of a still in a barn located on the Newell Farm on the Coward Road. Arrested on location were Alphonse Torre, age 61 and Giuseppi Lacagnino, age 40 of Rochester, N.Y. A 400-gallon still and 3,675 gallons of working mash were destroyed. The trio was turned over to federal authorities.

During prohibition, troopers only had benefit of the New York State Prohibition Laws fashioned after Federal Law from 1921 to 1923, when it was repealed. Troopers continued to make arrests under the federal law. In these instances, those arrested and their booty were turned over to Federal Agents for prosecution. Under federal law, a first offense for almost any prohibition violation was a fine of up to $1000.00 and up to a six-month jail term. A second offense was punishable by a fine of up to $5000.00 and up to a five-year prison term. The confiscated alcohol was destroyed and any vehicle used to transport the illegal goods was seized and sold at auction.

The following are original memorandums issued by Captain Robinson regarding prohibition enforcement.

May 7, 1928.

Memorandum:—

1. The attention of the Lieutenants and Sergeants is again called to the orders of Major Warner against the troopers taking a position on the road late at night and stopping all automobiles which come along, looking for booze.

2. If you have read Monday morning's newspapers you will see what happened to the two coast guard officers who stationed themselves on the Lewiston Hill, in fatigue clothes, and shot the man from Niagara Falls. If these officers had been troopers, they not only would have lost their positions but would have had to stand trial for manslaughter, furnishing attorneys at their own personal expense.

3. There will be no night work in this troop, which requires the stopping of automobiles on the road, unless there is actually present on the spot with the patrol, a Lieutenant or a Sergeant, preferably both Lieutenant and Sergeant.

4. If such night work actually is necessary, the men will be in full uniform and take their stand under a street or road light where they can be plainly seen and their uniform distinguished. If no street or road light is at the spot, they will back their automobile into the ditch in such a position that the headlights will be thrown on the troopers and their uniforms.

5. The use of plain clothes, fatigue clothes or any disguise is absolutly prohibited.

6. If such an affair as that mentioned in the second paragraph above evers happens in Troop "A", the Lieutenant in charge of the division and the Sergeant in charge of the district will both be held responsible not the Captain.

Captain.

PROHIBITION RAID - LATE 20S - ORLEANS COUNTY

CONFISCATED FIGHTING COCKS - TPR H. ASHE ON RT.

BOOK VI – ACCIDENTS AND DISASTERS

CHAPTER FORTY-NINE
FATAL AUTOMOBILE ACCIDENTS

AVON, N.Y.

On September 2, 1924, Michael Curry, 1025 West Avenue, Buffalo, N.Y. was instantly killed, when he struck the hub of the wheel on a car driven by William Yale of Rochester, N.Y. while traveling south on the Avon-Lakeville Road. Trooper Otto Bahr who investigated said Curry lost control after slamming on the brakes when passing Yale. Trying to avoid a head on collision, he ran into the Yale car, then flipped onto its top pinning its occupants in the wreckage.

ALDEN, N.Y.

On September 3, 1924, William Maleck, age 18, 78 St. Joseph Avenue, Buffalo, N.Y. was killed instantly, when his motorcycle crashed into the side of a freight train at the Erie Railroad crossing on Main Street, Alden, N.Y. Witnesses observed Maleck traveling at a high rate of speed as he neared the tracks just prior to the accident. There were no gates at the crossing, but a bell sounded the alarm of the approaching train.

BERGEN, N.Y.

On June 1925, Troopers Fortner and Macy went to the scene of an accident on Rochester-Batavia Road directly in front of Mott's Tavern, Bergen, N.Y. that resulted in a triple fatal. Killed were Charles Bubes, age 30, Charles Kopezynski, age 25 and the driver, Fisher Balser, age 25 all of Rochester, N.Y. The 1925 Cadillac car left the road striking a large maple tree broadside. The bark was stripped from the tree with the car lying in a ditch, a mass of tangled metal with only the motor and radiator intact.

BASOM, N.Y.

In July 1925, 59 year-old Basom, N.Y. resident Warren W. Winslow was struck and killed while walking along the Allegany Road near the Judd Road. A car driven by Claude Perfitt of Albion, N.Y. struck him from behind throwing him to the pavement where he suffered a fractured skull.

BATAVIA, N.Y.

On October 14, 1926, a Studebaker Touring car driven by Mrs. Harris Tillon lost control at the railroad overpass on the Bergen-Batavia road, turned completely and rolled over coming to rest on its side in a ditch. There were six women in the car traveling from East Aurora to Rochester, N.Y. to attend a church conference. Dead were Miss Iva Woodruff, age 28 and Mrs. Martin Schang, age 49 of East Aurora, N.Y. Mrs. Adelbert Schumann, age 49 suffered a fractured skull, Mrs. R.L. Willis, age 55 suffered severe arm and facial lacerations while Mrs. Tillon and Mrs. Albert Booth were uninjured.

PEMBROKE, N.Y.

In July 1929, Troopers Chester Acer & Davis investigated a fatal accident on the Batavia Road, Pembroke, N.Y. two-miles east of Pembroke in front of the Gustave J. Moesch refreshment stand. Charles Vale and his wife were both killed, when struck head on by a car driven by L.R. McNellan of New York City. Witnesses observed Vale making a turn into the refreshment stand directly in the path of the McNellan car. Both died instantly.

CRITTENDEN, N.Y.

On May 26, 1930, five persons in a 1924 Ford sedan were killed when their car crashed into the side of a locomotive of the North Shore Limited, a fast New York Central passenger train at the Alden-Crittenden crossing grade. Dead were Elmer Christner, 20 of Brick House Corners, Samuel Miller, 17, of Fargo, Mamie Miller, 21, Ransom Road, Clarence and sisters Kate, 27 and Eleanor, 20 of

Napanee, Indiana. Troopers Albert Perry and Arthur Rich made an investigation and reported the flasher signal was working properly. Train engineer Tracy Stebbins of Rochester, N.Y. said the, car traveling south struck the locomotive near the rear step and was dragged 120 feet along the track. The group were believed to be on their way to a Mennonite service in Alden, N.Y.

CORFU, N.Y.
On September 20, 1930, eleven year old Robert H. Strang, Corfu, N.Y. was instantly killed when struck by a car driven by Elmer Z. Voelker, 40 North Lyon Street, Batavia, N.Y. Troopers Sam Vint and Judson Peck said the accident happened on the Pearl Street Road two miles east of Corfu, N.Y. The Strang boy was crossing the road to go to a neighbor's for milk and had run into the path of the car. Other drivers who had witnessed the accident confirmed this account.

JAVA, N.Y.
On December 9, 1931, a truck loaded with livestock hurtled down the Route 78 east hill of Java Center crashing into the side of an Attica & Arcade train that stood on a grade crossing. Two men were killed and one injured. Dead were George A. Bauer, 42, Perry, N.Y. and Bert Abbott, 55, Silver Springs, N.Y. Earl Morgan, 40, Silver Springs, N.Y. was taken to Mercy Hospital with a fractured skull, internal injuries and severe facial lacerations. Troopers Edward Doody and Richard Brecht who investigated said that it appeared the brakes had failed on the overloaded truck. The accident was witnessed by John Bambic of Java Center who observed two of the trains cars lift off the tracks from the impact. He said chickens that were part of the load were hurled over the four-car train. Joseph S. Almeter of North Java was stopped, when the truck came racing past him smashing into the train. The truck was a total wreck with the dead and injured wedged in the wreckage. Casualties among the animals included three cows, three calves and half dozen chickens. The train crew was made up of Arcade, N.Y. residents Gus Berwanger, conductor, Earl Dean, engineman, Vern Wagner, fireman and Trainmen Morris Hopkins and Reuben Roblee.

BATAVIA, N.Y.
On January 24, 1932, a 1925 Chrysler driven by Arthur Northrup, 42, West Rush, N.Y., left the road knocking down four gasoline pumps, turned over onto its top and burst into flame. A body burned beyond recognition was identified through a key tag, as Roy "Barney" Ditzel, 46, proprietor of a gasoline station a mile east of Corfu, N.Y. Troopers William McNaughton and Clarence Pasto investigating determined Northrup was traveling east on the Genesee Road at a high rate of speed, when it left the road. Ditzel was a passenger in the car. Harold Heath, operator of the gasoline station where the accident occurred said the car was on fire before it came to a stop. Northrup was able to crawl from the wreckage with his clothing on fire. Mrs. Heath using rags quickly extinguished the flames. Northrup was hospitalized and could not recall clearly what had happened.

CALEDONIA, N.Y.
On July 5, 1934, Charles W. Jerome, 23, 168 Victoria Street, Buffalo, N.Y. and his three month old son, William died the result of a head on accident that occurred on West Main Street, Caledonia, N.Y. Trooper John Rowe and Caledonia Police Chief Silas Smith (a former trooper) investigating determined that Jerome had apparently fallen asleep, crossed the center line striking a tractor trailer truck driven by Chester Shaner of New Castle, Pa. The force of the impact totally wrecked the ford touring car with the trailer overturned on the roadway.

CLARENCE, N.Y.
On March 18, 1935, retired Clarence, N.Y. undertaker Fred Miller was being given first aid by a motorist that had knocked him down when a speeding car struck Miller decapitating him. The death car never stopped. Adrian Ross and Arthur Stapelton were on their way home to Akron, N.Y. when they struck Miller who was walking in the center of the road. Lights from oncoming prevented Ross,

the driver from seeing Miller. Troopers Frank Lachnicht and Kaye Crosby said the accident occurred at the near the top of the Clarence Hill on State Route 5. A teletype message was flashed for the death car with it not being located.

AKRON, N.Y.

On December 5, 1937, Troopers Kenneth Weidenborner and Lynn Wheeler investigated a fatal head-on accident near the Grant Pole, Akron, N.Y. that resulted in the death of Albion, N.Y. nurse Edna Blear, age 51 from a fractured skull. She was a passenger in a car driven by Edward Schultz of Hertel Avenue, Buffalo, N.Y. when it collided head on with a car driven by Robert Fountain, age 19 also of Buffalo. As the dying woman was being lifted, a rescuer lit a match and the gasoline-soaked car burst into flame. Her dress caught on fire, but was quickly extinguished.

OTHER TRAGEDIES

TRAIN WRECK

On October 21, 1920, a tremendous explosion awakened the entire city of Batavia, N.Y. A New York Central freight train with a long string of cars exploded near the Harvester Avenue crossing. Captain Robinson, Corporal Michael Serve and Troopers Miller, Ellis and Bankraatz rushed to the scene, secured the area and aided railroad men. The locomotive had exploded killing the engineer, William J. Cobb and fireman Frank Volkwein, both of Buffalo, N.Y. and student fireman Frederick Eckrich, Rochester, N.Y. The fifty-ton boiler was blasted off the tracks with pieces found over ½ mile away. The main boiler tore up ties and tracks 100 feet ahead of the blast. The front plate of the engine was thrown for more than 100 yards with the engine cab shooting straight up in the air bringing down telegraph poles and wires. The cause appeared to have been the sudden injection of cold water into the boiler of the engine, which was almost dry.
(State Trooper Magazine 1920)

BLACK DIAMOND EXPRESS DERAILMENT

On may 13, 1922 at 10:35 am, near Leroy, N.Y., the Lehigh Valley railroads famous Black Diamond Express Train struck an automobile driven by Thomas R. Brodie, a local farmer, who was attempting to cross the tracks in front of the fast moving passenger train. The accident occurred just west of the north Leroy Station resulting in Brodie being killed and the derailing of five cars. Trooper Edward C. Herbold in nearby Leroy, N.Y. hearing the loud noise caused by the crash rushed to the scene where he organized and directed rescue work. He was later awarded a medal of distinguished service for his efforts. The five derailed cars went over a forty-foot embankment just west of Oatka Creek. The Brodie car was hurled fifty feet in front of the train killing Brodie instantly. Doctors Cole, Graney and Ganiard of Leroy rushed to the scene, as well as Doctors Horace Laseur and F.D Carr of Batavia, N.Y. Hundreds of cars rushed to the scene and were pressed into service taking injured to Batavia Hospitals. Reverend Dean P.J. Enright of St. Peter's Church, Leroy, N.Y. administered last rites to the dead and seriously injured at the scene.

Fatally injured were identified as:
Thomas R. Brodie, Leroy, N.Y.
F.E. Clay, salesman, Portland, Maine
E.E. Croser, Clifton Springs, N.Y.
Mrs. Arthur C. Deroire, Geneva, N.Y.
Mrs. Russell O. Buchfield, 121 Depew, Buffalo, N.Y.

Treated at Batavia Hospital (Western NY residents only)
C.L. Saccomanns, 206 Swan, Buffalo, NY
Frank & Mary Rastaettar, 63 Furman Street, Buffalo, N.Y.
John P. Burke, 319 Prospect, Buffalo, N.Y.
Mrs. C. Ortina, 200 Aetna Bldg, Rochester, N.Y.
Charles Schenk, 460 Franklin, Tonawanda, N.Y.
Cyrus Field, 936 Depot, Niagara Falls, N.Y.

Treated at St. Jerome's Hospital, Batavia, N.Y.
Mrs. Felix O'Rourke, 40 Garden, Seneca Falls, N.Y.
Donata Chiafaro, 196 Oliver, North Tonawanda, N.Y.
Mrs. Rosabella Tracy, 57 William, Geneva, N.Y.
Francis Weiner, Niagara Falls, N.Y.
John Humphrey, Buffalo, N.Y.

Carlos Seward, a Leroy Justice of the Peace was following behind Brodie just prior to the accident. He said Brodie had slowed for a freight train traveling west and proceeded across the tracks, when it cleared. He believed Brodie had seen the oncoming train but misjudged its speed, which was at about 65 mile per hour. The accident resulted in five dead, twenty-four seriously injured and a multitude of minor injuries.
(Batavia Daily News)

FRED PARKER BARN FIRE
On September 10, 1933, a barn located on the Fred B. Parker farm, East Main Street, Batavia, N.Y., just out of the city limits, was burned to the ground. Fifteen troopers from the nearby barracks went immediately to the scene saving the residence from destruction. Melissa Perky, Marcia LeSeur and Emma Glossner who were at the farm led thirteen horses from the barn to safety. Batavia City firemen refused to answer the call based on city policy not to leave the city limits. Troopers felt that a chemical truck would have been of great value in saving a portion of the barn. Captain Robinson suggested the towns purchase such a truck to be kept at the barracks which could be sent out immediately manned by troopers. A few days later, the following editorial appeared in the Batavia Daily News: "Troopers have volunteered to give the necessary service required to make a rural fire truck useful in the towns within the county. This was a way to remedy the problem of jurisdiction. It however didn't remove the element of stupidity from the iron clad rule which prevented the Batavia Fire Department from going just outside the city limits to help a neighbor in distress."

SOUTHERN TIER FLOODS
Starting July 7, 1935 and continuing for several days, heavy rains caused the worst flooding that had existed in the state since 1865. Bridges and roads were washed out along the Mohawk River, with heavy damage caused in the western, central and southern parts of the state. Hornell, Hammondsport, Marathon, Watkins Glen, Elmira, Norwich, Binghamton, Whitney Point along with many other smaller villages were practically cut off from all communications until July 11. When the flood finally subsided, it took until July 27 for conditions to get back to near normal. Troopers were on duty almost 24 hours a day preventing looting, re- routing traffic and aiding in the giving of food, clothing and medical attention to the many flood victims. Thirty people lost their lives as a result of the flood with troopers recovering seventeen bodies and rescuing 470 other flood victims by removing them from danger areas. Troop "A" had 25 men on duty in the Hornell, N.Y. area and 8 in the Penn Yan, N.Y. area.
(1935 annual reports)

PAVILION AIRPLANE CRASH

On April 1, 1936, an American Airlines plane en-route from Newark, New Jersey to Buffalo, N.Y. with mail, burst into flame and crashed during a raging snowstorm. The crash scene was in a hillside pasture on the Ralph Shepherd farm located on the York Road about two miles east of Pavilion, N.Y. Dead at the scene were pilot Sanford L. Underwood, 34, 129 Hamilton Drive, Snyder, N.Y. and assistant flight superintendent William L. Garrett, 38, Newark, N.J. Witnesses saw the plane flying low over the village with it's tail on fire. An explosion was heard before it hit the ground. Shepherd and his hired man, John Chamberlain were first on the scene. Underwood was dead at the scene while Garrett lived for a few minutes before dying. Troopers John Long, Judson Peck, George White and Donald Girven were sent to the scene. Investigation indicated that there was no fire until the plane hit the ground rupturing the gasoline tanks that exploded and burned. The sparks flying from the sputtering of engine exhausts may have given the appearance of the plane being on fire according to investigators. It was determined that the pilot had turned around in an attempt to get out of the raging storm when the crash occurred.

COWLESVILLE PLANE CRASH

On October 27, 1937, Mrs. Austin J. Feuchtwanger, 53, her son, Austin Feuchtwanger Jr., 26, Riverside, Connecticut and Pilot Richard Babcock, 24, Canton, Massachussets were killed instantly when their privately owned plane plunged straight down into a pasture one mile south of Cowlesville, N.Y. The Feuchtwangers were flying to Buffalo, N.Y. during a light rain and fog to meet Courier Express publisher William J. Conners Jr. Witnesses William Slonka and Stephen Witek heard the roar of the engine and observed the planes lights dip and plunge downward. Troopers Kenneth Weidenborner, Joseph Gormley, Richard Brecht, Sam Vint and Percy Leitner responded to the scene. The crash scene was about a half mile from the road on the Albert Merlau farm located on Bullis Road. The victims were crushed in a three-foot deep hole created from the crash. It was surmised that the pilot had lost his bearings in the fog and was seeking a place to land when the crash occurred.

TRAIN CRUSHES CAR – FOUR KILLED

On August 19, 1943, four youths returning home from the Genesee County Fair were killed instantly, when their car collided with a speeding New York Central train on the Wortendyke Road, Batavia, N.Y. Dead at the scene were Patricia Ann Schreder, 17, Attica, N.Y., Shirley Jean Ryan, 19, North Alexander, N.Y., Richard C. Crane, 25, Dakota Street and the driver, Gerald E. Bush, 20, Wohlers Street, Buffalo, N.Y. Trooper Percy K. Leitner said the car struck the locomotive near the cab. The front of the car was torn off and wreckage and dead strewn for 100 feet along the railroad bed. All died form fractured skulls.

WAYLAND TRAIN WRECK

On August 30, 1943, a serious train wreck occurred just south of the Village of Wayland, Steuben County, New York. The Lackawanna Limited struck the left side of a freight engine tearing up 300 feet of track and leaving a twisted mass of wreckage scattered along the right of way. A steam jacket torn from the freight engine allowed escaping steam to enter some of the passenger coaches causing agony and death. Twenty-eight passengers and crewmembers were killed and 117 passengers injured.

Twenty-three troopers arrived at the scene along with members of the Steuben and Livingston County Sheriff's Deputies. Dead were removed to local funeral homes in Wayland, Dansville, Bath, Hornell and Corning. It took several days before all dead and injured were identified.
(1943 NYSP Annual Reports)

BOOK VII – HUMAN INTEREST

CHAPTER FIFTY
NEW YORK STATE TROOPER FIRSTS

Trooper Elmer B. Crowell made the first ever arrest by the newly formed constabulary, when he arrested an intoxicated soldier at the Genesee County Fairgrounds on the morning of September 19, 1917. The soldier was locked up over night in the Batavia City Jail and turned over to military authorities in the morning.

The first felony arrest and indictment in Genesee County occurred on 19 November 1917, when Troopers James L. Bortz and Harlow A. Doane arrested Teresa Castellitti at the Rome Hotel, Batavia, N.Y. for violating the liquor tax law. The indictment read as follows:

Defendant did while employed at the Rome Hotel unlawfully sell and deliver to James L. Bortz one glass of ginger brandy containing one gill of brandy without having obtained and posted a liquor tax certificate as required by law.

Signed by James R. Kelly, District Attorney

(Indictment Records –1910 to 1920, on file & made available by the Genesee County Clerk's Office)

Troopers were the first police agency to carry firearms outside of the uniform.

Major Chandler first introduced Herring Bone parking in 1917 at state fair, Syracuse, New York.

The first trooper appointment was John Hopkins who was born in Ireland. He was one of the first members of Troop "A", promoted to Corporal in 1921 & transferred to Troop "C". He was later promoted to Sergeant working and residing in the Ellenville, N.Y. area. He retired in 1943.

On November 1, 1921, the First New York State School for Police was opened at the YMCA at Troy, N.Y. Troopers from Troop "A" Batavia, N.Y. that attended that first session were: F/Sgt. William George, Troopers Edward Herbold, Harold Becker, Michael Fleming and Homer Harrison.

On September 15, 1931, the newly installed state police tele-type system was put into operation statewide. The original sending and receiving equipment linked only a few stations initially.

In 1931, a newly installed aviation unit was formed, but abandoned in 1932, when the pilot, Tremaine Hughes and Passenger Theophilus Gaines were killed in the planes crash near Cazenovia, N.Y.

In 1935, the scientific laboratory was created in the loft of a building at Schenectedy, N.Y.

In 1935, legislation created the Bureau of Criminal Investigation that was a separate detective bureau within the State Police to investigate serious and complicated crimes.

In 1935, bloodhounds were acquired and used in search for evidence, lost persons and fleeing criminals.

In 1936, state police formed a diving unit for recovery of drowning victims and stolen or lost property.

Until 1937, open troop cars were driven with some horse patrols still in use. The open cars were replaced with sedans that also introduced the all white patrol cars. Sidecar motorcycles were abandoned in favor of single unit motorcycles.

In 1943, the last horse patrol was utilized.

CHAPTER FIFTY-ONE
HUMOR

VICTOR, A DOG – 6/05/20
Life with the state troopers is the only life for Victor, a setter dog who has become attached to Troop "A". The dog enlisted without permission of his guardian who, after endeavoring to keep the dog home, permitted Victor to join the troopers. Victor ran away from home, following the rider in gray garb to the barracks where it calmly took up quarters. Taken back several times by the troopers. The dog returned to the barracks so his owner decided to let him stay. Victor follows every trooper into the store near the barracks and begs for treats, as he has an unusually sweet tooth. Pop, candy and ice cream are rapidly devoured.

TRAMP ARREST – 5/21/21
Troopers arrested a tramp and took him to the barracks near dinnertime. When the dinner call went out, all the troopers went to the dining room and the mans dinner, the same as that fed to the troopers was brought out on a tray. No guard being present, he finished his dinner, got up, stretched and leisurely walked out the door. He went into the garage, made inquiries for work and was directed to the Batavia Car Works on Clinton Street where he applied and was hired. Although his absence was immediately noticed, the troopers decided that any man with that amount of nerve and good intention should go free.

TROOPERS DUPED - 11/21
A band of bootleggers not only got through with a load of "hooch", but also drove away with a load seized by troopers. The bootleggers were driving a truck with the liquor openly displayed. On the seat with the driver were two men handcuffed together. The driver said he was a federal agent, had caught the pair and was taking the alcohol in for storage. The troopers then asked if he would take in a load of booze confiscated by them. He agreed. It wasn't until sometime later that the ruse was discovered, when the troopers went to check on the status of their seizure.

MARATHON MAN
Sergeant Edward Rimmer earned his pay on November 6, 1924, when he ran for over two miles along Clinton Street in pursuit of a runaway Rochester, N.Y. youth. The boy escaped by hiding in a wooded area. His companion, Angelo Paris was caught by Dayton J. Carmichael of the Triangle service station at the corner of East Main and Clinton Street. Paris was returned to his parents.

LOST BUGGY – 11/30/25
Brothers Frank and Walter Votery of Bethany, N.Y. were charged with public intoxication and jailed, when unable to post bail. According to troopers, they started out from Batavia for a buggy ride with "moonshine on the road, in the buggy and in the Votery's." While traveling along Bank Street Road, they fell out of the buggy. The horse continued on its way. Local residents notified troopers when the

intoxicated brothers began making inquiries in the area seeking their lost horse and buggy. Troopers Harvey Gregg and Donald Guerin made the arrests and later located the lost horse and buggy.

LOVE OF DOG – 07/01/28
Matteo Recchio, age 35, 37 Hutchins Street, Batavia, N.Y. had gone for an evening drive with his wife and small dog. He stopped across the road from the Crandall Hotel to make repairs to a punctured tire. Mrs. Recchio decided to take a stroll while waiting repair of the tire. When she exited, she slammed the door behind her crushing the dog to death that was about to exit with her. Matteo Recchio was so upset; he took out a penknife and stabbed holes in the tire, then started chasing his wife threatening her with the knife. Oliver O. Crandall observing the event interceded and was also chased by Recchio. Troopers Clarence Cudabec and Samuel Vint arrested Recchio for Assault 3rd Degree and took him before Justice E. Harry Miller who released him on $15.00 bail.

HUNTER HAD A RABBIT, DOG HAD A PHEASANT – 01/13/29
Thomas Ross, age 44, 156 Vine Street, Batavia, N.Y. was discharged after a jury trial for a Conservation Law violation. Troopers patrolling near Godfrey's Pond heard a shot being fired and hurried in the direction from where it came. They observed a dog owned by Ross carrying a pheasant in its mouth evidently retrieving it for his owner. Confronted with the evidence, Ross pulled a rabbit from his hunting pouch declaring he had just shot it supported by the fact it's heart was still beating. Troopers examined the pheasant and the rabbit and found that number 5 shot had been used to shoot both which was the same, as was in Ross's possession. During trial, the troopers admitted they heard only one shot. Ross was found not guilty. After the case was over, one of the jurors pointed to the dog and said: "There is the guilty party in this case. The troopers should have arrested the dog."

MOTHERLY TROOPERS
A woman was telling this story to a friend while returning from the state fair. The sweetest kid was lost by the stands today. She cried like everything so I took her over to a trooper. I couldn't get her to stop crying, but you know what he did? He took her in his arms and said he was just going for an ice cream cone and would she care to join him. He asked if she preferred vanilla or chocolate, and before they got to the dairy building, she told him her name and address. Them cops are so motherly. What we'd like to know is who pays for the ice cream cones and how many are bought a day. Being taxpayers, we Syracusian's are interested. (Syracuse Post Newspaper- 9/9/30)

STOLEN CHICKENS
State troopers discovered that some of the tasty chicken they had been eating recently had been stolen from local farms. Trooper Theodore Lewis acting on a tip investigated and arrested Elmer Orr, age 35 of Groveland, N.Y. Orr and his brother in law, Leonard Wells of Darien, N.Y. were charged with stealing twenty 100 bags of beans from the Lester Gubb farm, Elba, N.Y. Orr also admitted stealing chickens from the Warren W. Hawley farm of Bank Street Road, Batavia, N.Y. and two live calves from the farm of George B. Collins, Elba, N.Y. and Harry Forward farm, Pembroke, N.Y. The chickens were sold to Batavia markets that supplied the barracks with foodstuffs.
(Olean Times Union - 1933)

PHEASANT HUNTER – 11/17/34
It was reported that two troopers stopped an elderly man, because he was carrying a hen pheasant near Batavia. When queried, he produced two additional pheasants from his hunting coat. When asked if he shot any others, he indicated that he had three more birds back in the woods. He was permitted to go into the woods alone and retrieve them, but never came back. The troopers never saw him again. "Can you imagine a trooper letting someone caught with three illegal pheasants getting away that easy." Troopers denied the incident ever occurred.

TROOPERS IN SKIRTS

A wolf in sheep's clothing has no greater deceptive powers than the state troopers in skirts. Five Buffalo youths were charged with robbery and assault in connection with attacks on "spooners" who parked on Howard Road, a "lovers lane" near Athol Springs, N.Y. Imagine the surprise of Anthony Nappo and Vita Maniscalo, aged 20 of Buffalo, N.Y., when they yanked the door open of a parked car and were grabbed by the scuff of the neck, one of them a girl who was nestled in the arms of Sergeant Harold Debrine. Arrested at their homes were brothers Ralph Sorrentino, 18, Joseph Sorrentino, 16 and Frank Jacobi, aged 19. All were held for Grand Jury action. The wives of Troopers Frank Easton, Michael Fort and William Szymanski furnished costumes and make up to transform them into eye appealing girls. With Lieutenant Eugene Hoyt, Sergeants Harry DeHollander and Debrine as their escorts, the girls went to "lovers lane" in three automobiles. Easton was rated as the most alluring as it was his head on Debrine's shoulder when the youths opened the door. He wore a hat with a waving plume and a red flowing scarf around the neckline of his evening gown. There had been several complaints from young couples that had been robbed of small amounts of money with one girl assaulted at the Howard Road location.

CHAPTER FIFTY-TWO
A DAY WITH A TROOPER – OCTOBER 14, 1933

Written by Bud Hutton, Buffalo Times staff writer.

A sparse gray line weaves through the daily lives of New York States thirteen million citizens. From the lights of the city, through the winter cold of the hills and backwoods, the line stretches, contracts, shifts here and there. Murder! Call the state troopers. Crime! Call the state troopers. Advice to the lovelorn! Call the state troopers. Thus the gray line, the New York State Police Department moves through each day, the trusted thread on which the tillers of the soil and the punchers of clocks shape their ends.

In the area surrounding Buffalo, N.Y. contains 100 square miles. At Wanakah barracks, a cheery place on the shore of Lake Erie, there are 12 units in that thin gray line that reaches from wind swept Lake Champlain to Long Island's sandy shore, from the borders of New England to the surfed fringe of Lake Erie. There is crime to be checked. There are neighborhood quarrels to arbitrate. There is murder and then again, there is Mrs. Jones' dog having puppies. Events of minor or major import, all part of the checkered backdrop before which those men in gray daily stage their show. Thus, the spinning of the gray thread.

By the old clock on the wall of the Wanakah barracks, it is 8:40AM. Behind the desk, where a teletype writer jangles out its story of commands and warnings, sits a tall, thin figure, intent on assigning his 11 men that the 100 square mile be patrolled. A trooper works near him, checking an automobile license plate number. The door opens, enters Sergeant William Ireland, 14 years in the department. A day with a trooper? Come on, clamber into a roadster, shift gears and out on the highway we go. The hum of the radio hums in the cars tonneau. We've got to make the outside tour say's the husky, square shouldered Sgt. Ireland. It is Cold. The sergeant's knuckles are eventually chilled white. He drives on. The outside tour. Since 5, 6 and 7 o'clock this morning, ten others have been making their

135

rounds, one corporal and nine troopers. There are 300 halls of public assembly to be inspected; there are seven airports and a shifting total of pilots whose licenses must be examined. There are poolrooms and dance halls; there are lonely squatters and one million people.

We pass three squalid huts. Not many years ago a complaint was made to the substation that a mother and father were mistreating their horse on a farm near here. Troopers investigated. Dead in the yard was a horse. Its hind legs had been chopped off. They went to the farmhouse. On the kitchen floor sat the seven youngsters and their father and mother. All were eating fresh horsemeat. Troopers changed that meat diet from their own pockets. And now another loop in the threads pattern is spun. Here in Alden is a long, low touring car. Two troopers are in it. "Hyah fellows." "Morning sarge." Anything doing? No, how about you? Looks like we got those potato thieves. Since the last arrest, there hasn't been a robbery of a potato patch. We move to the sub-station. A radio hums here. One begins to understand that while the thread is thin and sparsely woven, there are other weaves that join on the loom. The radio is one. The sergeant signs a "check blotter" in the station and we again are rushing down the highway.

Here not far from the scene of the petty potato thefts, is a gray somber house. Two men sat in the kitchen of that house one March night this year. Between them was a bottle. One was a Hungarian farmhand. The other his employer. Next door waited a woman. They drank, troopers said. In the morning, neighbors found the employer dead with nine stab wounds in his body. The farmhand was not around. The woman said he had been at a farm near Salamanca during the past three weeks. Now the loom that carries the gray thread shuttles faster. Quietly they investigate. A talkative farmwife in Salamanca gives them details. The farmhand has been here. He has gotten letters from Alden. They find him, but no letters. They talk to the dead man's wife. She is confused in her story. The farmhand from his jail cell, further muddles the original tale, they concentrate. Now the loom moves swiftly. The two are confronted with each other's stories. There are more denials; more investigation. At length, the gray line announces the employee has confessed to the murder of his employer for $59.00. The woman is held on an "aiding and abetting charge". The loom slows down. The pattern has been spun again.

We move on. Cars parked at the highway's edge must be inspected. Then in contrast to murder is Sgt. Ireland's next duty of the day. An owner of a dance hall near Springfield, a sometime farmer, has been stalling off the sergeant's demand that the fire underwriter's inspect the place and he has to be convinced. Everyone, the gas station attendant who services our car will tell you, knows the troopers. Everyone is their friend. On these rural crimes, sergeant, who is of aid to the troopers? Well the rural mailman and most all residents of the section themselves. They all want to help. Here is a gabled house with lofty windows. Two years ago, "Red", a trooper waited on the front porch here for a man who had been wearing a gun while drunk. In the tree above, hidden by the foliage sat the man. "Red" waited for him to come home. It was dangerous to allow an armed man about the neighborhood. Ten, eleven and finally midnight, "Red" waited. So did the man. "Red" stayed awake, the man didn't. Fifteen minutes later, the quarry tumbled from the tree asleep. He was disarmed and put to bed. There have been a hundred murder hunts, chases (the troopers call them shags) after bootleggers. But they have been told and retold. And now we enter Silver Creek. On the outskirts, 160 miles have passed. Scarlet and gold spill over the autumnal countryside. A policeman flags us to a stop. Did you hear, Nugent got his over near Sheridan? About a quarter to one. The sergeant is silent. Details: Trooper Jerome Nugent is dying in a Dunkirk Hospital. This morning, he was alive, part of the autumn landscape. We return to the barracks. Duty goes on. A shroud has fallen over the spinning of the patterns. Yet the loom clanks on. The gray thread must weave unbroken.

CHAPTER FIFTY-THREE
ADMIRAL BYRD'S LAND CRUISER

During the 1934 Antarctic Expedition led by Admiral Richard Byrd, Dr. Thomas C. Poultier, Scientific Director of the Research Foundation of Armour Institute of Technology was second in command. He visualized the need for a self-contained exploration unit that could be used in all snow-covered terrains at the South Poles. Through corporate and private funding, a monster machine called the "Snow Cruiser" was built in 1939 by the Pullman Standard Car Manufacturing Company of Chicago, Illinois at a cost of $150,000.00.

The monstrous machine was 55 feet long, 20 feet wide and 15 feet high weighing approximately 75,000 pounds. Power was supplied by two 150 HP diesel motors, each directly connected to a traction type generator. A 75 HP traction motor was affixed to each wheel and power could be directed to any wheel or combination of the four. Each wheel was equipped with a hydraulic lift making it possible to raise any one or any combination of the 10-foot, rubber-tired wheels a height of four feet. It could turn around within its own length, move sideways at a 25-degree angle or climb a 37 % grade. It had a cruising range of 5000 miles with a maximum speed of 30 MPH. Enough space was available to carry a years supply of food and water for a crew of five, two spare tires, 2,500 gallons of diesel fuel and 1000 gallons of gasoline for a five passenger, ski mounted cabin plane moored on top of the deck. It was painted red with orange, black and silver stripes so it could be easily seen from a distance.

The cruiser, driven by Dr. Poultier, left Chicago on October 26, 1937 en-route to Boston, Massachusetts where it was to be loaded on the ship "North Star" for it's trip to Antarctica. The cruiser named "Penguin I" was plagued with problems on it's overland trip. In Columbia City, Indiana, a truck sideswiped it knocking off a wheel hub. At Ft. Wayne, Indiana, a fuel pump developed problems. Six miles later, it struck a bridge and plunged eight feet into a creek. It was stuck for three days. A couple of days later, two new electric motors had to be installed. On November 7, 1939, the cruiser entered New York State on Route 20 at Westfield, N.Y. Travel security was provided by Lieutenant Lawrence Nelson and eight troopers. An overnight stop was made in Hamburg, N.Y. where minor repairs were made and the cruiser refueled. On November 8, a wheel locked causing the cruiser to a halt at Texaco Town (Pavilion) where it remained overnight for repairs. The progress and problems of the cruiser had been headline news for several days. This unexpected delay provided an opportunity for Western New Yorkers to observe the monster first hand. While there, Superintendent Eber Palmer of the Batavia Blind School brought 125 students to the location. They were permitted to grasp its size through their sense of touch. Many local citizens took advantage of the situation with busloads of students being brought in from area schools. Nothing had ever caught the interest of Western New Yorkers, as the red monster crippled at Texaco Town. The thousand's that came were in awe of its size. Repairs were made and the cruiser rumbled off reaching Lafayette, N.Y. where it spent the next night. Reaching its Boston destination on November 13th, the cruiser was loaded aboard ship and two months later, unloaded on the Great Ice Barrier where the Antarctic begins. The overland trip took 17 days to complete.

The journey from Chicago to Boston proved to be a nightmare for police. It's shear size caused many problems. It had difficulty making sharp turns, sometime taking hours to make a single turn. Steep hills taxed its power to the maximum, on some occasions, requiring a pull from local Department of Transportation trucks. Roads were closed, traffic re-routed and barriers erected when it ran off the road or needed timely repairs.

While being offloaded, the ramp partially collapsed under its weight crashing into the bay ice. In spite of its huge wheels, inadequate traction proved damaging to any movement. After a week, it was freed from the ice. It was found the cruiser had better traction and moved best while in reverse. The cruiser's longest trip of 92 miles was driven completely in reverse. Byrd's expedition extended into 1941, but with World War II pressing, Congress would not approve funding to continue. The cruiser was left behind at Antarctica in an underground ice garage. In the late 1940s another expedition found the vehicle and discovered it needed only air in the tires and some minor servicing to make it operational. It was again rediscovered in 1962, still perfectly preserved. As of 1985 there has been speculation as to its location. Antarctic ice is in constant motion and the ice shelf the cruiser was on is constantly moving out to sea. The vehicle is either buried under many feet of ice or it is resting on the bottom of the Southern Ocean.

CHAPTER FIFTY-FOUR
DOMESTIC TROOPERS

On January 29, 1936, Rochester, N.Y. newspaper Times-Union reporter Albert Moss spent a day with the troopers filing this report.

Do you know that the New York State's gray riders, trooper's, are real home fellows. That is, they know how to make beds, sew buttons on their clothes and mend socks. That's all in the life of a trooper.

Times-Union reporter Albert Moss called on Sergeant Harold Kemp at the Pittsford Substation to get the low down on how a state trooper spends his time at home. The substation is the attractive home of the Kemp's. The living quarters echoed with laughter of two small children of the couple, Roger, 7 and Eugene, 5. They are quite proud of their soft-spoken (and who is not as stern as he looks) dad. Asked if they were going to be state troopers when they grew up, they quickly informed the interviewer that they intended to be sailors.

One of the rooms of the house is the sergeant's office. In it is a desk on which is a typewriter. Along one side of the room is a shelf of law books. In one corner stand two high-powered rifles, which bring you back to the realization that the most important part of a trooper's life is to protect the community from the lawless. Just to the left of the office is the barracks room. In this room are cots, made up in army fashion. This is the room for troopers who may be assigned to the Pittsford Substation. Usually, there are three other troopers staying in Pittsford. This being vacation time, only one trooper, C. Leo Watkins, is at the station. November 15 to April 15 is furlough period. This is also the period when many of them must report to the State Police Training School in Troy, N.Y. Summer is the busy period in the troopers' work. No school or furloughs are provided during summer months.

The Batavia Barracks is the main station of the troopers in this part of the state. Avon is the precinct station. Outposts are in Churchville, Spencerport and Webster. In the wintertime, patrols from Pittsford and Churchville take over the Spencerport and Webster sections. Troopers Kenneth Hemmer and George Wood are stationed at Churchville. In the winter months, policing (painting and carpenter work) is done in Batavia and Avon.

A trooper gets one night off every two weeks. He leaves his station at 5:30 PM and must return at 7:15AM the following morning on his night off. When the trooper is in the barracks, he must make his own bed and keep his uniform looking trim, as well as pressed. If the trooper is in the barracks, the state pays the bill, but if he on assignment far from the barracks, he must dig down in his pocket. Rules and regulations demand he must look neat at all times.

The trooper must report daily on each and every detail given him. Even settlements of family quarrels are the subject of a written report. These must be typewritten. Duplicates go to Avon and Batavia. They are consolidated at Batavia and forwarded to Albany headquarters. Mrs. Kemp is the cook in the Pittsford station. And do the boys like her cooking? Grins broke over the ruddy faces of the sergeant and Trooper Watkins, when they were asked that question. "Say, in writing this up don't you make it appear we are a lot of softies" remarked the sergeant in a business voice.

CHAPTER FIFTY-FIVE
WORLD WAR II & THE STATE POLICE

After the outbreak of World War II, President Franklin D. Roosevelt declared a national emergency designating the Federal Bureau of Investigation (FBI), as coordinator for internal security. Despite being low in authorized manpower, the state police took an active role in national security. They provided escorts for military convoys, monitored traffic and provided security near military installations and defense facilities, as well as assisting in the transportation of sensitive war materials. The Bureau of Criminal Investigation (BCI) had previously established a list of all potentially dangerous matters of national security interest that served as a reference point for domestic security forces. Troopers were responsible for fingerprinting thousands of workers in essential positions at defense plants. They inspected various public utilities and war plants, conducted investigations on reported sympathizers, aliens, agitators and subversives. Troopers also conducted Civil Defense classes training Auxiliary Police in techniques and methods of handling chemical and incendiary bombs. This was done in addition to their normal, every day duties. By the end of the war, 305 members of the state police were on active military duty. Six members lost their lives while on active duty. In 1942, state police members purchased $181,000.00 in War Bonds.

During early 1942, federal regulations were in place setting a national speed limit of 35 MPH. This was an effort to save on much needed gasoline for the war effort. On an average month, troopers stopped and arrested 207 persons for exceeding the speed limit. There was strict rationing of specific items, such as gasoline, clothing, shoes, certain food items and tires. Automobile owners were allowed only the tires on their car and one spare. Pleasure driving was not permitted.

In Troop "A", 39 members were called or volunteered for active military duty. Of those, only Earl Wilkinson failed to return. He was killed in a military plane crash on May 24, 1942. To fill the void left by those called to duty, the state police for the first time hired female employees to take over clerical duties at troop headquarters. This freed troopers for patrol duty and to conduct criminal investigations. Troopers were also charged with monitoring critical military and utility facilities. The first females hired at Batavia and possibly in the state were Berniece Rudolph (Skelton) (May 17, 1943 to August 3, 1969), Viola Shwingel (Roblee) and Edith Schreiner (Bloom).

TROOP "A" MEMBERS THAT SERVED IN THE MILITARY DURING WW II.

F.P. Adriance	US Army Aviation Student, 22nd College Training Detachment, Canisius College, Buffalo, N.Y.
Elner F. Anderson	US Army - Corporal, Military Intelligence APO 9442, New York, N.Y.
Clayton E. Bailey	US Navy - Chief Specialist, Box 118, FPO, San Francisco, California
Howard C. Blanding	US Coast Guard – Enlisted as a Chief Specialist, Attended the Coast Guard Academy, New London, Connecticut – Commissioned an Ensign, then Lieutenant JG aboard ship. Witnessed the raising of the US flag on Iwo Jima.
John s. Cole	US Army -Sgt., Battery "C", 551st AAA Bn, Camp Butner, North Carolina
Glenn H. Corliss	US Army Air Corp - Pfc., Box 413 Dalhart, Texas
Charles E. Day	US Army - Lieutenant Colonel, MP HQ., APO 887, New York, N.Y.
Florence J. Driscoll	US Army - Corporal, Military Intelligence
W.D. Eastman	US Army - Pvt., 420th Air Base Squadron, Rome Air Depot, Rome, N.Y.
John D. Fennell	US Army - Sergeant, Military Police, N.Y. ,N.Y.
A.C. Fecher	US Army - T/Sgt, HQ Co., 80th Tank Bn., APO 258 North Camp, Polk, Louisianna
Mickey L. Fort	US Navy - Boatswain, Receiving Station, Navy Yard Washington, D.C.
Harold E. Hackett	US Coast Guard -Ensign, Federal Bldg, Wilmington, North Carolina
D.J. Harley	US Army - Corporal, Military Intelligence, N.Y.N.Y.
Ingwald P. Hicker	US Army - Sgt., 1223rd, MP Co., APO 638, N.Y., N.Y.
C.W. Jermy	US Army - 3/1/41 - S/Sgt., HQ Co., 334th Infantry, Camp Howsze, Texas. Awarded States Conspicuous Service Medal for exceptional service. First member of Troop A to enter service in WWII. Holder of Bronze Star, Purple Heart, and received battlefield commission to 2nd lieutenant, then promoted to 1st lieutenant. Served with 334th Infantry, 84th Division.

C.A. Jorgenson	US Army - Pfc, HQ Co., 3rd Bn.,168th Infantry New York, N.Y.
J.B. Kross	US Army - 2nd Lieutenant, 1192 MP Co., N.Y.N.Y.
H.E. Kunow	US Navy - Seaman, Co 240, Training Center, Sampson, N.Y.
Frank A. Lachnicht	US Navy - Chief Boilermaker, Pier 92, West 52nd St., N.Y.,N.Y.
J.W. Lawrence	US Army - Pvt., Co "A", 510th MP Bn., Ft. Sam Houston, Texas
C. L. Linbald	US Coast Guard - Specialist 1st Class, Cadet Training Ship Danmark, New London, Ct.
C.L. Macartney	US Navy Air Corp Cadet, Naval Air Station, Corpus Christi, Texas
B.F. McFarland	US Navy - Chief Specialist, US Naval Training Ctr., Sampson, N.Y.
Arthur D. McCaughey	US Navy - Apprentice Seaman, Co 408, US Naval Training Ctr., Sampson, N.Y.
E.J. McMahon	US Army - Aviation Student, Class 44K, Group E., Squadron 44, SAACC
J.M. McMahon	US Coast Guard - Chief Specialist, Mounted Beach Patrol, Charleston, S.C.
R.H. Merring	US Navy - Boatswain Mate 1st Class,Co.B, 123rd USN - Construction Bn., FPO, San Francisco, Ca
J.F. Neary	US Army - 1st Lieutenant, 4472 MP Detachment Birmingham, Alabama
A.R. Perry	US Army
F.P. Quattlander	US Army Air Corp - 1st Lieutenant, 23rd Photographic Recon. Squadron, 5th Photographic Group, N.Y., N.Y.
Eugene Redden	US Army - Cpl., Military Intelligence, CIC Detachment, APO 9524, N.Y.,N.Y.
R.R. Regan	US Army - Captain, MP Hq., 1st Infantry Div., APO, N.Y., N.Y.
William A. Rimmer	US Army – Drill Instructor, Fort Blanding, Florida
Gerald J. Schusler	US Army Air Corp - 2nd Lieutenant, PO Box 31, Liberal, Kansas

Jacques S. Stickney	US Coast Guard - Chief Specialist, Guard Base, Toledo, Ohio
Sam Vint	US Navy, Seabees, Camp Peary, Virginia
Kenneth E. Weidenborner	US Navy - Chief Specialist, Naval Training Ctr., Farragut, Idaho
Earl R. Wilkinson	US Army Air Corp - Killed in 1942, plane crash in Maine

During June 1943, the Department of Defense toured Western New York with a captured Japanese min-submarine. It had been captured the day after the attack of Pearl Harbor on a coral reef near Hawaii. The officer in charge of the submarine was found on the beach where he had attempted suicide. Two other crewmembers were never found and were presumed dead. The submarines compass malfunctioned throwing the submarine off course. It was to have been used during the attack of the US Fleet at Pearl Harbor. It was 81 feet long, weighed 35 tons having a range of 150 miles. Nitro-glycerin was stored in its nose that would explode, when the submarine rammed its target. The tour was part of a campaign to raise money for the war effort through the sale of War Bonds.

On September 16, 1943, the state police manpower was reduced to 630 men statewide with no hope of an increase. With the manpower at an emergency stage, a request was submitted to the Draft Board for an occupational deferment of all troopers being called by the draft. In earlier years, troopers were exempt from the draft. To meet manpower needs without impeding police service, sub-stations were combined or closed with troopers detailed to cover a larger area. Troopers worked longer hours and their four-week annual vacation was reduced to two-weeks. Gasoline rationing reduced the amount of traffic on the road releasing those troopers assigned to traffic duty to do general police work.

Division Manpower in September 1943.

Troop	Authorized	Actual	On Military Duty
A	122	83	39
B	110	83	27
C	120	90	30
D	130	99	31
G	130	92	38
K	143	97	46
L	110	86	24

CHAPTER FIFTY-SIX
THE GRAY RIDERS ARE COMING

In 17, many years back
Were formed the State Police, in gray and black
Born in time of storm and strife, each one pledged
To give his life
To never swerve, never fear
To serve the country he loved so dear.

Years passed on, and ever on
Till soon their honored place was won
Through ceaseless toil and winning zeal
They became the "troopers", the people's ideal

Many men found the routine rough
Stepped out of the ranks saying, it's too tough
But always others took their place
Honest in purpose with smiling face

And now, with our flag in danger again
We go to fight with might and main
That no one may our freedom take
Rather would we our lives forsake

We will come back, but not all
To answer again the troops roll call
Some will fall bravely on battlefields
The spirit of the trooper never yields

And when we come back from foreign lands
Marching to tune of martial bands
As troopers once more we'll be crime fighters
Honored veterans. The states gray riders.

Written by Trooper Clayton E. Bailey, Troop "A"
Batavia, N.Y. in about 1941-42

Clayton E. Bailey served in the New York State
Police from 1936 to 1966 attaining the rank of Captain.
He was a Chief Petty Officer in the US Navy from
1942 to 1945 earning the nickname "Chief". He resides
at Poughkeepsie, N.Y.

BOOK VIII – BITS & PIECES

CHAPTER FIFTY-SEVEN
TROOP "A" BITS & PIECES – 1917 – 1919

The following are excerpts taken from the Batavia Daily News:

TROOPER INJURED
On October 1,1917, Trooper Harvey Doane, the Troop "A" Blacksmith suffered a broken left wrist and fractured rib, when his horse reared and fell with the rider underneath. He was treated and returned to his home.

QUARANTINE
On October 12, 1917, Troopers were assigned to help the Department of Health in the enforcement of a smallpox quarantine on the Cattaraugus Indian Reservation near Salamanca, N.Y. Forty cases of the disease were found on the reservation with health officials having difficulty in getting the Indians to submit to vaccinations and to remain on the reservation.

RUNAWAY YOUTH
On October 12, 1917,Trooper Henry Coots located Walter S. Miller, an Alexander Road youth who had been missing since September 27th. Trooper Coots and Carl Miller, father of the boy traveled north toward Lockport, N.Y. in Millers automobile. Trooper Coots stopped at various farmhouses along the way interviewing residents. He soon got on the trail and located the boy in Gasport, New York.

DOGS KILLING SHEEP
On December 15, 1917, several troopers were assigned to Mount Morris, N.Y. to round up and dipose of untagged dogs responsible for killing sheep. Thirty dogs were shot and as many farmers were forced to register their dogs. This was the result of several local farmers complaining that the many mongrel dogs were causing great damage to their sheep herds.

TROOPERS VOLUNTEER FOR WAR SERVICE
On May 27, 1918, every member of Troop "A" volunteered to fight overseas for Uncle Sam. A letter was sent to Governor Whitman signed by every member of the troop offering to enlist for military service overseas. The only condition was that the entire troop be taken, as one cavalry unit. The offer was declined.

TROOP ACTIVITY FOR 1918
On January 8, 1919, Captain Willis Linn reported on 1918 activity of the Troop "A". Miles patrolled 175,632 by motorcycle and automobile and 73,000 by horse. Fines collected were $6,244.50. 898 arrests were made with 626 convictions and 790 investigations of reported crimes. Among the laws enforced were the Anti-Loafing Law, Dog Quarantines, Conservation Law, Humane Law and Peddlers Law. Troopers cleaned up an unwholesome condition surrounding Fort Niagara by raiding disorderly places.

STATE POLICE MADE GOOD
Of all the new activities entered upon by the state in the last 20 years, there is not one that has given the people at large a better return for the money expended than the Department of State Police. The work that the State Troopers have done keeping the highways safe for men and vehicles of all

kind is worth many times the total cost of the mounted force without taking into consideration the suppression of crime and the preservation of the peace. It has attracted the favorable notice of the National Highway Protective Association, which keeps a record of automobile accidents.
(Jamestown Journal-January 7, 1919)

STOLEN AUTOMOBILE
On January 29, 1919 during the early morning hours, Trooper Edward Rimmer was returning to Batavia from Buffalo, N.Y., when he observed several men standing around a stopped car without any lights on it. He stopped to investigate and during questioning, he observed one of the men make a motion toward his hip pocket. Rimmer drew his revolver and covered the men. They immediately ran behind the car and off into the woods with Trooper Rimmer firing several shots after them. None were hit. Further investigation revealed the automobile had been stolen several days earlier from Frank Hewitt of Lewiston, New York. Found in the car were a case of dishes stolen from a Clarence, N.Y. freight house, as well as tires and tubes stolen from Hartell Brothers, Forks, New York

ROBBERY ARREST
On February 7, 1919, two discharged soldiers were charged at Geneva, N.Y. for robbing a jewelry store. Investigation further revealed that they possessed two handguns stolen a week earlier from the Trooper Barracks at Batavia, New York. Corporal Henry Coots of Canandaigua, N.Y, conducted the investigation.

ARMOUR, N.Y. ARRESTS
On May 6, 1919, Troopers Halbert DeFreest and Edward Pfeiffer arrested three youths in soldier's uniforms between Springfield, N.Y. and Armour, N.Y. after they crashed a stolen automobile into a farmers hay wagon. Disregarding orders to stop, the officers opened fire on them causing them to lose control. No one was injured. The automobile had been stolen from Charles Spiess, 130 Meech Street, Buffalo, New York.

E. HARRY MILLER
On May 22, 1919, Justice of the Peace Eugene H. Miller, East Pembroke, N.Y. filed a petition releasing two men from the Monroe County Penitentiary where he had sentenced them to six months after they were arrested for breaking into the unoccupied home of Merton Parker of East Pembroke, N. Y. Miller said he was not a lawyer and that three state troopers told him that it was his duty and that he had the jurisdiction to sentence the men. He learned later that since the charges were Burglary, a felony, he could only convene a hearing and or forward the case to grand jury.

MOTORCYCLE CHASE
On June 19, 1919, with bullets flying and motors throbbing at high speed, Troopers Halbert DeFreest and Edward Pfeiffer gave pursuit on a motorcycle to armed thieves in an automobile, recovering about $800.00 worth of stolen tires stolen from Eden, N.Y. As the car approached without lights, the troopers ordered it to stop. Instead it sped away. With DeFreest driving and Pfeiffer in the sidecar they gave chase. As they got closer the occupants leaned out and fired 12 shots. Trooper Pfeiffer fired seven shots at the fleeing car. One of the shots from the automobile struck the transmission of the motorcycle forcing it to coast. One of Pfeiffer's last shots went through the rear mica of the car striking an occupant causing the car to run into a ditch. The occupants fled into woods on foot. A Posse of ten farmers was formed, but due to darkness, the thieves escaped. The next morning, a posse of three hundred farmers searched to no avail. The car stolen from Paul Banker of Buffalo, N.Y. also contained twelve tires, four spark plugs and a boycemeter, as well as a pile of bloody cotton on the seat from the injured occupant.

LICENSE FORGERS
June 20, 1919 - Head of state troopers after license forgers: Troopers have discovered that automobile owners in attempt to avoid paying their yearly license tag fees are forging the numbers on their license plates. Troopers were ordered to be vigilant for these forgers as well as for violators of the anti-glare headlight law. The first statewide conviction of anti-glare law was obtained in Niagara County:

HEELS BEAT WHEELS
On July 8, 1919, Troopers on horseback caught man with auto: Heels beat wheels when Corporal John M. Keely and Trooper Edward Rimmer of Troop "A" on horseback chased and caught a youth who failed to stop the automobile he was driving without 1919 license plate. The troopers were riding their horses on East Main Street near Cedar Street, Batavia, N.Y., when the automobile traveling east passed them displaying a 1918 plate. The driver failed to heed their order to stop and continued on his way. The troopers gave chase on their horses, along with Sergeant Edward Miller who observed the chase and jumped into a troop car to give pursuit. The troopers on horseback caught the youth near the New York Central overhead before Miller got there in the car. Investigation revealed the youth had left the State Mental Institution in Buffalo, N.Y. He was returned to the mental facility with no charges being filed.

MULE RECOVERED
On July 8, 1919, Sergeant Edward Miller and Trooper George Tetley recovered a stolen mule and wagon reported stolen by Thomas O'Brien of West Bloomfield, N.Y. A local youth was arrested, the mule & wagon returned and a fine paid of $15.00 in damages.

NO REAR PLATE
On July 25, 1919, Trooper James J. Bortz of Troop "A" was convicted of not having a rear license plate on his car. Patrolman Timothy Meegan at Buffalo, N.Y. charged him. A suspended sentence was meted out by city court Judge Standart.

AUTOMOBILE-MOTORCYCLE ACCIDENT
On July 29, 1919, while driving his automobile in Pembroke, N.Y., Charles Lakota of Rochester, N.Y. who was driving a motorcycle ran into Sergeant Edward Miller. He was arrested for reckless driving, taken before Justice E. H. Miller and fined $25.00.

ESCAPEE
On July 30, 1919, Troopers George Tetley and Russell Webb arrested an escapee from a convict camp near Akron, N.Y. He was turned over to Erie County Penitentiary Superintendent Robert E. Hunt.

ALLEN CREEK GAMBLERS
On August 26, 1919, Corporal Henry Coots and Trooper John F. Howard caught 16 youths ranging from 18 to 24 years of age, shooting craps on the bank of Allen Creek in Brighton, N.Y. The Troopers in civilian clothes captured the men at the point of two service revolvers. Taken before Justice of the Peace George M. Keller of Brighton, each left $5.00 bail for their appearance in court, but not one appeared to plead his case.
Troopers Magazine -December 1920)

CHAPTER FIFTY-EIGHT
TROOP "A" BITS & PIECES – 1920 –
1929

HARMONY'S HERMIT

During January 1920, Troopers C. Leo Lunney and Everett Giles were patrolling in the Town of Harmony near the Pennsylvania border. The winter weather was bitter cold with snow knee deep on the horses. The blowing, drifting snow forced them off of the road into open fields where Stephen Cook, a local farmer, hailed them.

He lodged a complaint against Frank Hitchcock, a hermit dwelling on the edge of a swamp nearby. He said Hitchcock was a queer acting individual who lived alone and kept to himself. Neighbors put up with his many eccentricities, because they feared threats that he had made. On one occasion, Hitchcock complained about the location of a neighbor's fence. During the night, he took it down and relocated it fifty feet from its previous location. The day before, Hitchcock's horse had become mired in a swamp. The hermit left him there hopelessly bogged down through the night. He had been alive earlier that morning, but neighbors feared to go near him.

Gile's and Lunney found the hermit's cabin built of assorted materials, windowless with a hole cut in one side for a door. The abode's interior reeked and it had hard packed dirt for a floor. They found Hitchcock, a ragged, dirty, bearded man sitting by a small stove dining on boiled skunk that he had cooked in an old tomato can. Despite his appearance, he spoke coherently. When queried, he said his horse was dead. He had put it out of its misery when it became mired in the swamp and he couldn't get it out. He said he hit it in the head with an axe. The troopers found the animal dead of exposure with no marks on its head. Hitchcock was arrested and taken before a Village of Panama Justice of the Peace and committed to six months in the Chautauqua County Jail where he could be observed for possible commitment to an asylum.

(National Journal of Law and Order – April 1922)

VFW – WALSH POST

On February 17, 1920, state troopers organized the Sergeant Francis A. Walsh Post of the Veterans of Foreign Wars. Seventeen names were listed on the original charter. An Amalgamation of the American Veterans of Foreign Service and Army of the Philippines, Cuba and Puerto Rico in Pittsburgh, Pennsylvania organized the Veterans of Foreign Wars of the United States of America. The VFW had a record of 21 years service spent in welfare work for the service and ex- service men and the promoting of loyalty, love of country and comradeship. The motto is " LOYALTY AND FORTIDUDE ". To be eligible, you must have been in the service during a time of war. Any veteran that was eligible could contact Trooper John R. Kearney at the barracks to apply.

(Batavia Daily News)

ESCAPEE CHASE

On June 23, 1920, Robert Goodman, aged 20 of Buffalo, N.Y., a self confessed auto thief made a mad dash for freedom from the custody of Troopers Edward Rimmer and John Holcomb. The sensational chase led through Batavia, N.Y. back alleys and rooftops. Crashing gunfire from the trooper's pistols drew a large crowd to the chase. Goodman was found hiding in a hay pile in the barn of P.H. Williams of 43 State Street.

(Batavia Daily News)

STOLEN SUIT
On July 5, 1920, John Fargo, a Leroy, N.Y. farmer moved to sympathy from a hard luck story given by sixty three year old John Arnold gave him a job on his farm. Two days later, Arnold disappeared and so did Fargo's Sunday suit. Corporal Joseph Colligan and Trooper Edward Rimmer did a search of all roads near the farm with no success, but investigation along the railroad tracks running behind the farm found that Arnold was traveling west along the railroad line. They located a woman who had given breakfast to a man of his description and five miles further; they overtook Arnold striding along resplendent in a new suit of clothes. A kind-hearted Justice of the Peace, overcome by Arnold's destitute condition, gave him a home for two months, rent free, in the county jail. (State Troopers Magazine – August 1920)

HOLLEY POLICEMAN SHOT
On July 13, 1921 at 3:00 am, Holley Patrolman Frank Lockwood surprised three men burglarizing the W.E. Nelligan & Co. of State Street, Holley, N.Y. The burglars shot him twice, once in the right shoulder and again in the chest with the bullet passing out the back. He caught them in the act of loading tires into an automobile. Neighbors hearing shots notified the troopers and an immediate alert went out. The heavily laden automobile was last seen traveling west from the village. Sergeant Herman Gorenflo and Trooper Philip Burkland working in Orleans and Niagara Counties picked up the robbers trail near Lockport, N.Y. The bandits were pursued for ten miles until they abandoned their car and took to the woods. The two troopers battled the bandits in the dark with several exchanges of gunfire taking place. The bandits surrendered and were returned to Holley for arraignment. Patrolman Lockwood was treated at his home recovering from his wounds. The men identified themselves as Thomas Daniels, Frank Murray and Daniel Carson of Syracuse, N.Y.

In September 1922, Lieutenant Governor Wood during ceremonies at the state fair presented a Distinguished Service Medal to Sergeant Gorenflo for the capture of the burglars. Gorenflo was also promoted to the rank of lieutenant and assigned to Malone, N.Y.
(Batavia Daily News – 7-13-21 & 9-15-22)

BURGLARS CAPTURED
On July 27, 1920, Trooper Earl while at Angola, N.Y. was notified that the men's clothing store of Fred C. Mathies, Silver Creek, N.Y. had been burglarized and $4000.00 worth of goods taken. Earl found automobile tracks in the soft mud behind the store, but they were wiped out by other traffic on the main highway. He and Chautauqua County Sheriff's Deputy Eugene Fox searched blindly and after several hours, found a pair of men's stockings lying along a seldom-used road. As they approached what was believed to be a deserted house, they saw activity, when three men fled into a wooded area. Two others persons located in the house were arrested when items from the Silver Creek burglary were found. The three that fled were arrested a short time later. Stolen property that was recovered from many area burglaries was estimated at about $100,000.00. The gang of five was arraigned before Justice William H. Bartlett and confined to the county jail held for the grand jury.
(State Trooper Magazine – August 1920)

MISS DOROTHY HUTCHINS - DAUGHTER OF THE SQUADRON
Superintendent Chandler gave the title of New York State Trooper to Dorothy Hutchins in 1920. She was an accomplished horsewoman, skilled at swimming, pistol and rifle shooting, and played the violin and piano. Major Chandler and Captain Percy Barbour were so impressed with her skills as an all American girl, they offered her the designation as Daughter of the Squadron. She readily accepted the unique honor. A modification of the uniform was made for her and used as a riding habit. She was born at Johnstown, N.Y. Her outdoor skills were learned from her parents, Mr. & Mrs. William Conger Hutchins. She attended Johnstown Public Schools where she studied violin and piano. She

then attended National Cathedral in Washington, D. C. for five years. When World War I broke out, she entered Gloversville Business College where she studied typing and stenography. She was then given a position as assistant secretary to Congressman Crowther in Washington, D.C (December 1920 Journal of Law and Order)

BATAVIA ARREST
On November 15, 1920, John Moyles, aged 33, 3 Buell Street and Roland Rider, aged 28, 37 Otis Street, Batavia, N.Y. were charged with Burglary and Petit Larceny by Corporal Michael Serve and Trooper William Ireland. Moyles and Rider had entered the Erie Railroad shanty at the East Main crossing and took a red lantern. They then went to the Lehigh Valley Railroad bridge overpass placing the red lantern in the middle of the road and concealed themselves. When approaching automobiles stopped because of the perceived danger, the two appeared from where they were hidden. They would approach the cars seeking alcoholic beverage by acting as prohibition agents flashing badges. Willaim Neville, 41 Porter Avenue, Batavia, N.Y. having no alcohol was allowed to proceed. He reported the incident to the trooper barracks. Judge Tyrrell released them for a later court appearance. (Batavia Daily News)

TONAWANDA PLANT
On January 28, 1921, troopers were sent to Tonawanda, N.Y. to assist local police in the protection of workers at the Beaver Board Company plant that had just reopened under a reduction of wages. No serious incidents were reported.

INSPECTIONS
In 1921, members of Troop "A" were ordered to inspect every theatre, dance hall, lodge and clubroom in its jurisdiction under provisions of the states new fire prevention laws. A report of findings was made to the State Education Department.
(State Troopers Magazine – July 1922)

NEW YORK TELEPHONE COMPANY
In 1921, the Department of State Police entered into a co-operative agreement with the New York Telephone Company wherein any person needing the services of a trooper could pick up a phone anywhere in the state and simply say "I WANT A TROOPER". The telephone operator would then notify the closest trooper station and notify telephone customers to watch for a trooper passing through the area. Large cardboard placards were placed at post offices and other public gathering places.

RAILROAD POLICE
On March 10, 1921, legislation was passed transferring authority for the appointment and revocation of licenses of all railroad and steamboat police from the governor to the Superintendent of State Police. The superintendent immediately revoked all old appointments and instituted a policy for new appointees to be carefully investigated. Many unqualified and unfit political appointees were not rehired.

FEARON BILL
A significant piece of legislation was approved, when the Fearon Bill was passed on 26 April 1921. The bill authorized appropriations for an additional 116 troopers to be hired to bring the manpower to 350 men. This bill also provided for the creation of two new Troops, "B" at Malone, N.Y. and "C" at Sidney, N.Y. An additional appropriation provided for a New York State School for Police at Troy, N.Y. The curriculum was evaluated and approved by the New York State Board of Regents. This was the first police school in the nation certified by a state education board resulting in graduates being awarded a state certificate, as a professional policeman.

With the addition of Troops "B" & "C", the Troop "A" area of policing was reduced to the following counties: Niagara, Orleans, Monroe, Erie, Genesee, Livingston, Wyoming, Cattaraugus, Chautauqua, Allegany and Steuben.
(1921 NYSP Annual Reports)

TRAMPS
On April 29, 1921, troopers embarked on a tramp crusade arresting 19 men for vagrancy in one day. This was in response to the unusually high amount of chickens being stolen from local farmers. All were given suspended sentences with the exception of four Negroes who were sentenced to 25 days at the Monroe County Penitentiary.

HIGHWAY TRAFFIC
The greatest problem during 1921 was the enforcement of highway laws. The volume of traffic was enormous with registered vehicles in New York State and from visiting states being able to form a line from New York City to Buffalo, N.Y. through Albany nine times over. This high amount of traffic mostly traveled on 11,000 miles of improved highway caused heavy congestion in many areas. In 1922, there were 1,035,000 automobiles registered in New York State.

TROOPERS DOG KILLED
On October 10, 1921, "Billy", a three month old Belgian police dog was struck and killed by a car in front of the trooper barracks. He gave promise of becoming a valuable member of the troop. He was a favorite with Captain Robinson.

FORMER TROOPER ARRESTED
On December 23, 1921, Arthur Finnerman of Canisteo, N.Y., a Former Trooper at Troop "A" was charged and held for intoxication. It was alleged he was driving an automobile 60 miles an hour when he collided with another vehicle injuring two people.

State Police manpower in 1922 was at 348 statewide.

TROOPER TRANSPORTATION
In 1922, the horse was still the mainstay for travel by the troopers particularly in winter and inclement weather. The State Police Department maintained enough mounts to be available for two thirds of the manpower at all times. In addition to the horses, each troop was assigned 7 or 8 automobiles.

LOCALLY ASSIGNED TROOPERS
1922 legislation made it possible for towns and villages wishing the full time services of troopers to arrange for a permanent facility location with the expense being paid by the community.

MOTORCYCLE'S
In July 1922, five motorcycles were issued to the Troop "A" for use in patrol duty for a total of seven. One was assigned to Chautauqua County, one to Niagara County with the others assigned to specific highways areas. The designated areas were between Batavia and Pembroke, Pembroke and Clarence, Stafford to Caledonia, Caledonia to Rochester and Caledonia to Lima. Orders were given to cycle men to watch the highways for reckless drivers. Under the Highway Law, any driver who exceeded 30 MPH was deemed to be driving in a reckless manner. Troopers were instructed to pay close attention to vehicles not slowing down for children near country schools and not reducing their speeds on blind curves.
(National Journal of Law and Order- July 1922)

In 1923, there were 1,242,851 automobiles registered in New York State.

TROOPERS SUED
In1923, Howard F. Peters of Rochester, N.Y. sought $5,000.00 in damages for malicious prosecution against Troopers Earl Foley and Michael Fleming. The troopers arrested Peters the result of an investigation of an automobile collision with Herbert S. Sweet, the Rochester School Superintendent. The action was dismissed after a hearing.
(The State Trooper Magazine 1923)

GYPSIES
During the spring 1923, Troopers arrested five gypsies at Pembroke, N.Y. on the complaint of Joseph Harris, 647 Elmwood Avenue, Buffalo, N.Y. on charges related to fortune telling. Justice William J. Tyrell levied a total of $70.00 in fines, but when it came to pay the fines, all claimed not to have any money. With a jail sentence looming, money was found secreted in shoes and other non-descript locations. It was noted that there was a group of 200 all traveling easterly in Cadillac, Chandlers or Dodge automobiles.

Trooper James D. Burke found two to three hundred Brazilian gypsies camped near the farm of Mrs. Albert Warsop 1-½ miles east of Alexander, N.Y. Several had been charged with Petit Larceny. They pled guilty before Justice Fred G. Gardner, were assessed a total of $65.00 in fines and followed the courts directions to continue on the move out of the area.

TROOPERS ON BIKES
On June 23, 1923, Captain Winfield Robinson announced that troopers would respond to nearby calls on a bicycle, because they were quicker and less cumbersome than horses. He said that a bicycle was also going to be used on the Rochester-Scottsville road.

SAFE BLOWERS CAUGHT
On November 17, 1923, Troopers Edward Herbold and Walter Richardson on patrol in Stafford, N.Y. arrested Patrick J. Murphy, Edward Smith and Harold C. Martin, all of South Buffalo, N.Y. They were charged with burglary, when over $1,000.00 was found in various locations on their person. A fourth suspect escaped in the dark. Found in a pile of lumber near where the men were arrested was an arsenal of four loaded revolvers, two bottles of nitro-glycerin, detonator fuses and burglars tools. They admitted to dynamiting the safe at shoe manufacturer D.Armstrong & Co., 155 Exchange Street, Rochester, N.Y. that night, where they took $1,000.00 after overpowering two guards and binding them with rope. Evidence found during the arrest linked the three to the murder of Mayme Bigham on November 11, 1924 during the robbery of her Buffalo, N.Y. drugstore. Mrs. Bigham was the former Mamie Morgentern of Attica, N.Y. The trio was turned over to the Buffalo Police Department for prosecution. Others involved were soon arrested with information provided by the trio. On January 16, 1925, Ambrose Geary, age 40, Edward (Silent) Smith, age 30 and Harry Malcolm, age 25 were put to death in the electric chair at Sing Sing Prison. Patrick Murphy, a fourth member was on death row awaiting results from an appeal. James Monks, a fifth member turned "Stoolie" was spared the death sentence for his assistance in the case.

STOLEN CAR RING
On December 10, 1923, Corporal Michael J. Fleming arrested Joseph Clark, Messina, N.Y. for possession of a stolen car. Clark was a member of a gang of car thieves stealing cars from central New York. The cars were taken to a location near Messina, N.Y. where they were shipped into Canada and sold. Clark admitted to stealing six cars during the past month. He provided information that resulted in the arrest of the gang leader and recovery of several stolen cars. While being returned to Batavia by train, he was in the custody of Trooper James Fox, when the train was involved in a wreck. Fox removed the handcuffs from Clark who helped provide life saving assistance at the scene.

Because of his valuable service, troopers recommended clemency of the court. Clark was sentenced to a suspended sentence.

MANPOWER INCREASE
1924 legislation was passed increasing the manpower of each troop from 58 to 78 men with the addition of one lieutenant, three sergeants, four corporals and twelve privates. The law also provided troopers the powers to execute warrants issued by a magistrate anywhere in the state. Division manpower was now at 468.

TROOP "K" BARRACKS DESTROYED
On March 3, 1924, the Troop "K" barracks at White Plains, N.Y. burned to the ground during a severe storm. The men present saved all the horses, a majority of records and part of the surplus equipment. Under the generosity of Captain John Lubbs, 102nd Ammunition Train Armory, White Plains, N.Y., troop headquarters was established in armory offices. The men and horses were quartered at the Hillandale Farm, New Rochelle, N.Y. for a nominal fee.

NIGHT PATROL DUTY
During the summer of 1924, the increase of highway traffic demanded a new approach to the troopers on patrol duty. Every trooper worked traffic duty on Saturdays, Sundays and holidays. A system of night patrols was augmented to assist night travelers and apprehend thieves using the cover of darkness for their getaway. The newly created Department of Motor Vehicles worked closely with the troopers.

GIRL SLASHED
On April 24, 1924, Angelo Bello, Batavia, N.Y. slashed the face of sixteen-year-old Jennie Chellano from ear to mouth with a straight razor while at the Felix Lesniewski grocery store, 219 S. Liberty Street, Batavia, N.Y. Chellano was taken to St. Jerome's Hospital for stitches and was reported in good condition. Bello said he did it because, he was "crazy mad" over her refusal to marry him. Sergeant Michael Serve and Trooper Oscar White who saw him walking through fields near Oakfield, N.Y, arrested Bello. He was charged with Assault 1st Degree.

FREIGHT TRAIN ROBBED
On July 28, 1924, four trains were stopped on the DL&W line near Wayland, N.Y. Semaphore railroad signals were cut by the robbers who stopped the trains by using red flares. Seven cars were broken into while the railroad crew was held at gunpoint. Large crates were loaded into waiting trucks that sped away from the scene.

YOUTHS ALLEGE ASSAULT BY TROOPERS
On July 27, 1924, Sergeant Michael Fleming and Trooper Thomas Longo arrested Oakfield youths Waldo Derwick, Victor Scroger and Theodore Stevens for reckless driving and a catchall section of the penal law for using abusive language. It was alleged that the youths attempted to pass the troopers who refused to give them the road. They finally passed on the right at which time Scroger yelled out " Where the hell do you think your going". They were taken to the barracks where Fleming demanded to know who made the remark. Scroger said that he did where upon Fleming struck him in the face. Longo then punched him in the face. The three pled not guilty and were released for a later appearance. On August 6, 1924, a jury trial with Justice William J. Tyrrell presiding was held. The youths were acquitted after trial.

On August 11, 1924, Batavia City Court Judge LeSeur based on the complaints of Derwick and Scroger, issued assault warrants for Fleming and Longo. Batavia Police Chief Daniel Elliott served the warrants. The charges were presented before a Genesee County Grand Jury who on November 7, 1924, returned a no indictment against the troopers.

PUBLIC BUILDINGS
On September 2, 1925, Lieutenant James Flynn was placed in charge of the inspection of places of public assembly in the eleven county Troop "A" area outside of cities. Any place that could house more than one hundred people was inspected for new safety regulations, which had been passed on July 1st. One taboo was that no dance hall could be located above a garage.

HORSE COMPETITION
On September 21, 1925 – Troop "A" won the coveted Jockey Club breeding bureau challenge cup during competition at the New York State Fair. "Alburg" ridden by Corporal Joseph Brandstetter won first honors and three silver loving cups in the following competitions: best turned out enlisted mans horse, best single horse, best cavalry remount. This was the first year Troop "A" took first place.

RECORD KEEPING
In 1925, Troop "A" started a simplified system of record keeping. First Sergeant Oscar White would receive a complaint and enter it in the blotter. A trooper would be assigned and a report made by him upon completion. Sergeant White then read the report and if important, sent it to Captain Robinson to read. It was then given to Sergeant Samuel Dunlap, the Troop Clerk for distribution to proper channels. Trooper Richard O. Dayton, the Abstract & Arrest Clerk who entered it in the complaint book, made two copies. The original was sent to Albany Headquarters and a copy given to Corporal George F. Tetley, the File Clerk who filed the reports by alphabetical index of names.

SLOT MACHINES
During Thanksgiving 1925, Troopers Benway and Ward arrested Max Hoffman, Leroy Sawyer and Floyd Brawer of Webster, N.Y. for possession of gambling devices. Two slot machines were confiscated from Hoffman's Hotel, one from Sawyers billiard room and one from Brawer's automobile accessory store. A day earlier, two were confiscated from the John T. McGrath restaurant and one at the William's Restaurant in Brockport, N.Y. Both owners were charged. The slot machines were of the type that dispensed a package of mints at each operation.

TROOPER BEATEN
On March 22, 1926, Trooper Homer Harrison was severely beaten near Foti's service station, Frewbsurg, N.Y. while attempting to arrest a man for intoxication. Ernest Babcock of Warren, Pa. tried to free the arrested man by beating the trooper in the head with his fists. Babcock was arraigned before Justice Scott Petersen at Frewsburg and committed to the Chautauqua County Jail.

GUN BATTLE
On August 12, 1926, Corporal James Wolcott and Trooper Theodore Martin were involved in a running gun battle near Westfield, N.Y. with John Gould, age 30 of Buffalo, N.Y. and James McClelland, age 50 of Chicago, Illinois. They were driving an automobile stolen from Doctor Pritchard of Buffalo, N.Y. When the troopers stepped out into the road ordering them to stop, they sped up nearly striking the troopers who gave chase. Shots were fired at the troopers who returned fire striking the automobile several times. The chase continued for about seven miles until the fleeing car drove into a culvert after failing to negotiate a curve. Both men were captured at gunpoint and taken to Mayville, N.Y. where District Attorney Glenn Woodin preferred charges for First Degree Assault. .

HORSE COMPETITION
On September 7, 1926, Troop "A" again took horse competition honors at the New York State Fair. "Alburg" was the grand champion in the open to military classes ridden by Trooper Donald Guerin.

"Arner" ridden by Trooper Harold Wolf won three ribbons, "Alma" ridden by Trooper Samuel Vint won two ribbons and "Arcadia" ridden by Trooper Clarence Dixon won one ribbon.

TROOPERS RENAMED
The year 1927 marked the end of the Department of State Police. Under New York State reorganization legislation effective January 1, 1927, the Department of State Police officially became the Division of State Police under the Executive Branch of Government

PAY INCREASE
On March 29, 1927, legislation approved a trooper's pay raise of $100.00 a year for four years. A new trooper hired at $900.00 would by paid $1300.00 at the end of four years. This was in effect for six years with a six-year trooper receiving $1500.00. The Troop Captains would get a raise of $1000.00 to $3400.00.

MANPOWER
On July 8, 1927, the troop manpower was increased to 95. This increase was due to the increased demand on the department for traffic control and highway enforcement. The Motor Vehicle Bureau previously exercised these duties.

LONG ISLAND DETAIL
During the summer of 1927, the parks on Long Island were opened to the public for the first time. Fifteen troopers were assigned to Long Island Parkway duty. In 1928, the manpower was increased to 48.

PRISON ESCAPEE CAPTURED
On May 26, 1928, Lieutenant Samuel Freeman and Sergeant Charles Burnett acting on a tip arrested twenty-four year old James Sweet, Andover, N.Y. at the home of his mother in McKeene Pennsylvania. Sweet was wanted for escape from the Hutchinson, Kansas reformatory, the stealing of six cars and shooting at Corporal John F. Mersmann, when he went to his home to apprehend him earlier. Sweet was returned to Hutchinson, Kansas.

RANDOLPH, N.Y. ARREST
On May 28,1928, Sergeant Richard Gibbons and Trooper David Mousseau assisted Secret Service Agent Thomas F. Daly in the arrest of Augustus Johnson, an Indian living at Randolph, N.Y. It was the first arrest ever made for violation of the World War 1 Compensation Act. It was alleged that Johnson altered an adjusted service certificate for the purpose of obtaining $70.00 drawn on at Silver Creek, N.Y. bank. The offense was punishable by a fine of $5000.00 and or fifteen years in prison. He was held for Federal Grand Jury presentation.

Division manpower in 1928 was at 593 statewide.

ATTICA SLOTS
On July 20, 1928, Troopers John Rowe and Theodore Lewis conducted three raids in the Village of Attica where they confiscated 5 slot machines and destroyed them. Arrested were Frank H. Fleig, Augustus Zahler and Raymond E. Slack. Zahler was discharged before Justice Stockwell, with Fleig and Slack receiving suspended sentences. $36.25 found in the machines was turned over to the town's poor fund.

CLOSE CALL
On July 31, 1928, Sergeant Leslie Benway saved the life of 12 year old Marie Ditzel, daughter of Paul Ditzel, Batavia, N.Y., when she fell into the Tonawanda Creek while playing, twice disappearing under water.

155

Division manpower in 1929 was at 618 statewide.

IDENTIFICATION BUREAU
Each troop headquarters was equipped with full modern fingerprinting and photographic equipment with a sergeant in charge. Each sergeant received extensive training at the Bureau of Criminal Identification at the New York City Police Department, the New York City Police College and various state prisons. The services would now be available to any district attorney or police department in the state.

INCREMENT PAY
1929 Legislation provided compensation in the form of pay increases for length of service, as an inducement to retain trained, experienced officers. Other legislation reopened an option allowing members of the force who had not joined the retirement system, to do so, and obtain benefits derived from the system.

RANDOLPH BARBER DIES IN CUSTODY
On February 24, 1929, George J. Patterson, age 33, Randolph, N.Y., a local barber was at the Randolph Hotel in an intoxicated condition. He was asked to retire to his rented room at the hotel by proprietor John L. Wade, but refused. He became more highly insulting and boisterous. Wade called for the troopers with Sergeant Richard Gibbons and Corporal David Mousseau responding. Patterson was arrested, but refused to go along hanging on to everything he could, as he was dragged out. At one point, it was alleged that Gibbons struck him on the head with a blackjack causing a gash that bled profusely. The trooper's explanation was that it happened when he struck his head on a plate glass door. He was taken to Salamanca Hospital where Dr. Joseph M. Trotter who treated him gave him a shot of morphine. Early the next morning, Patterson died. In April 1930, Patterson's mother Jennie seeking damages for his death filed a lawsuit. Named in the lawsuit were Gibbons, Mousseau, Wade and Trotter. On April 19, 1930, a Supreme Court Jury at Little Valley, N.Y. found no cause for action.

PRISON RIOTS
Prison riots in July 1929 at Dennemora & Auburn Prisons and again, at Auburn, N.Y. in December 1929, brought the attention to the public of the value of a trained, equipped and disciplined force.

LETCHWORTH PARK
During the summer of 1929, two troopers were assigned full time, for the first time at Letchworth and Allegany State Parks for traffic and crowd control.

Due to the immense statewide increase in automobiles on the highways, 112 troopers on motorcycles were assigned exclusively to traffic control on principal arteries of the state during summer months and high traffic use.

ESCAPEE KILLED
On April 30, 1929 Harry A. Jones, age 30 of Potter, N.Y. was shot and killed during an escape attempt. Jones had been arrested by Troopers Joseph Seeley and John Nesbitt charged with mortgaging property not his own. Justice Orville Randolph committed him to the Yates County Jail in lieu of $500.00 bail. While at the intersection of Main and Chapel Street, Penn Yan, N.Y., Jones bolted for his freedom. Ignoring warning shots from Seeley's revolver, he was shot and killed instantly while climbing a high fence.

GOVERNOR'S BODYGUARD
On May 1, 1929, Lieutenant Gerald D. Vaine was assigned as Governor Alfred E. Smith's bodyguard. His duties required that he reside in the executive mansion and travel extensively with the governor.

He also was assigned protection of Royals Prince of Wales and Queen Marie of Rumania during their separate tours of New York State.

PISTOL COMPETITION

On August 19, 1929, a pistol shoot between teams from the troopers and Buffalo Detective Bureau was held at the 108th Army Regiment Range near Knowlesville, N.Y. The trooper's team was made up of Leo J. Miller, Norman H. Lippert, Edwin B. Chamberlain, Devillo H. Chamberlain and Irving E. Librock. The detective's team was comprised of Raymond E. Berley, Patrolman Richard Jenkins, Renney Nichols and J. Lester Conley. Each shooter fired ten shots at rapid, timed and slow fire from a distance of 25 yards. The Buffalo team with a score of 1303 to 1295 won the match.

FLYING INSTRUCTIONS

On August 15, 1929, Donald Woodward, President of the D.W. Flying School, Leroy, N.Y. offered troopers free flying lessons. These were two, twenty-hour flying courses intended to qualify students for a private pilots license. It is unknown if anyone accepted.

A JOURNAL OF LAW AND ORDER

A State Trooper Bulletin

IT is obvious from the attitude of the press and the general public that the Department of State Police is gaining recognition as a powerful force for law and order in New York State.

This recognition by the people, while it fills us with pride, should not make us completely satisfied with our work, but rather should it stimulate a desire to advance still further and merit an even greater approval of the state.

Our success so far has been based upon three propositions. First, the right type of man; second, a common sense policy; third, instilling in the minds of the public a respect for the trooper.

The proper type of man means a man physically and mentally right, who is a gentleman, and who is honest.

Man has five senses and with these he must make his way in the world, but he has in addition a God-iven attribute which is distinctly his own, and that is his will. THE POWER TO DECIDE FOR HIM-SELF.

The past is gone, all that is left of it is memory or records. The future is not yet here, and cannot be reckoned upon with any degree of certainty. But the present is NOW. It is here.

Since the present only is ours, the great secret of success is to perform each act or duty as carefully and well as though it were to be the last act of life.

The man who commits a crime, who does wrong to his neighbor, who is crooked in a deal, is not happy.

To be descent, honest and straightforward makes one live a pleasant life and enables one to enjoy work, play, and amusements, and (if blessed with good health) all the things that make life worth while.

In these times the enforcement of prohibition opens peculiar opportunities for bribery of officers of the law. Probably not a trooper in this command but has been approached.

It is said that "every man has his price." This may or may not be so. Certainly every man is subject to temptation, but if "every man has his price" then a trooper's price must be so high that no one can reach him.

I think we have no man in our department as it stands today who would accept a bribe, and I hope we never enlist one, but should such a one get in, he will not last long, for the person who gives the bribe can never be trusted. He always tells. He tells it braggingly as an evidence of his own smartness, and a secret known to more than two people is no longer a secret.

"Respect for the troopers" has been a hobby of the superintendent since the beginning. Shakespeare said: "All the world's a stage, and all the men and women merely players." So a good way to study types of people is to think of them in plays we have seen.

A policeman upon the stage is usually a comedian.

sented as a hard-boiled individual with his hat over one eye, a cigar at an angle in his mouth, administering the "third degree" to some poor criminal who has the entire sympathy of the audience.

The element of fear engendered by this last type of officer leads to hate, and hatred of the police will never insure respect for the law.

If a child fears his father constantly, he will soon hate him, and the father's influence over the child is lost.

The State Troopers have by kindliness, by decent living, by common sense, and by honesty brought a proper psychology into police work, and that is respect for themselves as well as respect for the law.

Were an actor today to take the part of a trooper and appear in that character upon the stage, we know that he would not be a signal for laughter but would hold the respect and sympathy of the audience. The drama "Tiger Rose" and the screen picture "The River's End" are examples of this, both of which feature a member of the Royal Canadian Mounted as the hero.

Our policy is not to nag. To be strict, to be fair, to think twice before acting, but when we do act, to act quickly and surely.

The calumny and invective that has been hurled at our men in riot duty has made no impression on us. We have with stood it in a way that has made a great and favorable impression upon the public.

We who call ourselves "soldiers of the law" aim to uphold it among rich and poor alike; we take no sides in disputes of class and rank; we recognize no rights of labor or capital except the common one of justice to both.

We stand for the people of the Empire State—all of them who are law-abiding.

We are interpreters of the law to those who question, upholders of the law to those who seek its protection, and relentless enforcers of the law to those who seek to break it.

GEORGE F. CHANDLER,

CHAPTER FIFTY-NINE
TROOP "A" BITS & PIECES – 1930 –
1939

1930 trooper manpower consisted of 95 officers and men in each troop.

As troopers gained experience conducting criminal investigations and progress was accomplished in the use of newly installed fingerprint and photographic equipment, more and more local authorities were calling on the state police for assistance. These investigations were previously conducted through private investigators, usually retired city police detectives. (Annual Reports – 1930)

ATTICA SPEAKEASY RAID
On December 8, 1930, a raiding party consisting of Sgt. Homer Harrison, Troopers Samuel Vint and Jay R. Carmichael along with Sheriff Grover Ahl raided "Petes Place", an alleged East Main Street, Attica, N.Y. speakeasy confiscating five gallons of moonshine whiskey. Proprietor Peter Tozvary was arrested, taken before Justice of the Peace Robert O. Stockwell where he posted $2000.00 bail for appearance before the grand jury. The raid was conducted under the direction of District Attorney Lynn S. Bentley who had been carrying on an active campaign to dry up Wyoming County. (Batavia Daily News)

JEALOUS SUITOR
On December 22, 1930, Porter Webster, age 23, Alabama, N.Y. was arrested and charged with the critical shooting of Helen Dunn, age 25, Shelby, N.Y. and Walter Bryant, age 23, Spencerport, N.Y. the night before. Webster and the Dunn girl had lived together for four years at the Town of Albion, N.Y. On the night of the shooting, they had an argument with Helen going to her parent's home. That evening, they invited Bryant, a visitor to accompany them to a dance being held at the home of an uncle, Thomas Dunn on the Feeder Road, Shelby, N.Y. While there and dancing with Bryant, a shot was fired through a window striking Helen in the back causing serious damage to her kidney and large bowel. The bullet passed through her body into Bryant's abdomen lodging in his liver. Investigating leads, Sergeants Harold Debrine, Charles Burnett and Corporal Paul Mellody found a 22-caliber rifle at the home of Webster's mother. They then learned that a 1924 Overland Sedan owned by Darwin Townsend, Alabama, N.Y. had been stolen and that Webster had relatives living in Stanards, N.Y. He was located at Stanards, N.Y. and arrested. Orleans County District Attorney William H. Munson lodged first-degree assault charges.

DESERTED BABE
On March 28, 1931, a two-week old baby boy abandoned on the East Pembroke, N.Y. porch of Reverend J.J. Gilhooley was identified through hospital footprint records and the mother arrested. Gilhooley had received a phone call to check his back porch. Doing so, he found the infant wrapped in a blanket from Buffalo General Hospital. Sergeant Edward Rimmer, Troopers Earl Wilkerson, Oscar Lazeroff and Montagu Andrews responded. Trooper Andrews made prints of the infant's feet. A trip to the hospital noted the child was born on March 15, 1931. A nurse at the hospital identified the mother as Miss Ruth Louise Harrison, 180 High Street, Buffalo, N.Y. Harrison was located and arrested on a disorderly person charge.

TROOPERS SAVE DROWNING BOYS
On August 3, 1931, Robert Larson, age 11 and Donald Woelffel, age 12, both of Rosedale Street, Buffalo, N.Y. were paddling a makeshift raft in the conservation pond at the Hamburg Fairgrounds, when it overturned. Cries for help went unheeded by picnickers, but were heard by Troopers William Ireland and Oscar Lazeroff. They rushed to the pond, dove in and swam back carrying the frightened boys.

CHILDREN DIE IN FIRE
On November 27, 1931, Russell Demerest age 5 and Helen Demerest, age 17 months perished in a fire that completely destroyed a small house at Godfrey's Pond outside of Batavia, N.Y. The mother had gone into Batavia with a neighbor leaving the children alone. Working with shovels, Sergeant Michael Serve, Troopers Charles Stanton, George Donnelly and Edward Bund sifted through the ashes finding the body of the boy where the baby's crib had stood. He was burned beyond recognition. It was determined that the boy had picked up the baby in an effort to save her and both died there from the intense fire which fused the two bodies together.

FUGITIVE CAPTURED
On February 16,1932, troopers investigating a cottage burglary followed a five mile snow trail of footprints from Owasco Lake to Dansville, N.Y. that led them to the home of Earl Holbrook. Here they found Holbrook's brother in-law, Herbert M. Peasley, age 22, Niagara Falls, N.Y. Peasley was an escapee from Auburn Prison and was immediately taken into custody by Sergeant Harry Adams. During his short-lived freedom, Peasley had stolen a car leaving it at Corning, N.Y. and had broken into a cottage stealing clothes and tennis shoes. He was turned over to prison authorities.

BEAR KILLS BOY 1932
On October 11, 1932, five year old Peter Ryan, 205 South Main Street, Albion, N.Y. was killed, when his father, Edward consented to the boy's wishes to get a closer look at two bears that were chained to a fence on Route 31 near the Mount Albion Cemetery.

Fred Redshaw and his son Hector from Industry, N.Y. owned the two three hundred pound black bears. They had been purchased several years earlier for $300.00 and were used as an attraction at a gas station owned by Redshaw on Dumplin Hill located on the Scottsville Road near Rochester, N.Y.

Redshaw and his son were returning from Lockport, N.Y. with the two bears, when their truck broke down near the Mount Albion Cemetery. The bears had been on display in front of the Lockport Motion Picture Theatre during the showing of the movie "Bring Em Back Alive". While repairing the truck, the bears were chained to the cemetery fence.

Peter Ryan approached the bears and was standing two to three feet away, when one of the bears lunged at him. His thigh was torn open by the bear's claws, as he was pulled into the bears grasp and held. Edward Ryan, passerby's and the Redshaws finally freed the boy. While enroute to Arnold Gregory Hospital, Albion, N.Y., he died from shock and blood loss.

On October 12, 1932, Andy, as the killer black bear was named was shot and killed under warrant by Lieutenant Gerald Vaine. It's mate, Amos was to be placed into the Rochester Zoo, but when it was found there was no room for her at the zoo, she was also to be killed.
(Batavia Daily News)

BROTHER & SISTER WED
On March 13, 1933, Louis Hudak, age 28 and his sister, Helen Hudak, age 18 were charged under the Domestic Relations Law and fined $50.00 each by Corfu Justice Horace Sumner. Troopers Percy

Leitner and Clarence Pasto charged them, when it was learned that a priest married them 18 months earlier. Having come from Hungary eleven years earlier, they said that such marriages were sanctioned in their home country. They were placed on probation to report to a priest and arrangements made for separate maintenance. The marriage was voided under provisions of the law.

BERGEN WOMAN POISONS HUSBAND
On April 18, 1934, Troopers Earl Wilkinson and Elner Anderson arrested Viola Linney Trost, 33, Bergen, N.Y. charging her with 1st Degree Assault. She admitted to mixing a tablespoon of strychnine sulphate in an aspirin and administering it to her 40-year-old husband, George H. Trost. He became terribly ill, was on the verge of death, but recovered. On June 26, Viola was released from custody and placed on one to two years' probation by County Court Judge Newell Cone after her plea to 2nd Degree Assault. Leniency was recommended because of her complete confession, her desire to make amends and forgiveness of her husband.

SCIO ARSON
On October 22, 1934, police near Scio, N.Y. searched the countryside for 52-year-old Charles Prindle who was heavily armed. It was alleged that he set fire to two barns owned by Mrs. Lucia Wright on the Knight's Creek Road near Scio and fired his rifle at a farmer and troopers. Prindle in an intoxicated condition appeared at the Wright farm and entered a barn where Darrow Rogers was milking with Mrs. Rogers and Clara Prindle, a daughter of Charles present. He called out that he wanted to speak with Mrs. Rogers, but she replied she wanted to have nothing to do with him. He then pointed a 30-30 rifle at her that was knocked out of his grasp by Mr. Rogers, just as it discharged. All fled the barn while Prindle lay on the floor. He came out of the barn firing the rifle at the Wright house with a bullet going through a wall striking a radio across the room. About twenty minutes later, they noticed fire in the barn's hayloft and a second smaller barn across the road was also on fire. Rogers who had his new car in the smaller barn ran to save the car, but was forced back into the house by Prindle who fired a shot. Two horses, a cow and calf perished in the fire. Hay, grain and machinery and the barns loss were valued at $7,000.00. Sergeant Harold DeBrine and Trooper Andrew Fisher were investigating some time later, when Prindle approaching the Wright house, saw the troopers and fired a shot into the house. Gunfire was returned, but Prindle disappeared in the dark. He managed to evade the trooper's intense search by keeping to wooded areas. A week after the arson, he was sighted by Trooper Perry walking in a wooded area of the John Thurston farm in the town of Wirt where he was taken into custody. After intense interrogation, he admitted to setting fire to the Wright barns, but denied shooting at the troopers. He was held for grand jury action. On January 25, 1935, Prindle pled guilty to Arson 2nd Degree and was sentenced to a term of not less than five years or more than ten years in the Attica State Prison.

In 1935, Troop "A" had thirty- three automobiles and over twenty motorcycles, trucks and horses for patrol duty. (Batavia Daily News – 2/5/35)

DUNKIRK'S MACHINE GUN BANDITS
On July 2, 1935 at 2:00 PM, a lone bandit entered the Merchant's National Bank, Dunkirk, N.Y. escaping with all the cage and vault money. While the lone bandit entered the bank, five other bandits stood on the sidewalk in front of the bank, maintaining a steady machine gun fire. City Patrolman John Brooks was standing a few doors from the bank, when he spotted the machine guns in the hands of the robbers. He pulled his revolver opening fire, but retreated when a bullet passed through his hat. Windows in nearby stores and the telegraph office were shattered by the gunfire. The bandits fled in a new Buick car with stolen plates.

HUMPHREY CENTER HUNTERS

On December 16, 1935, irate farmers of Humphrey Center heard shots fired and found that a 10-point buck had been killed. It was against the law at the time to shoot a deer in Cattaraugus County. The carcass was found cached in a snow bank for retrieval at a later time. Trooper Frank Easton and Edward Broughton took up the trail and after ten miles of walking through a driving rain, dense woods and heavy snow they got their man. Arrested was Joseph Schmidt, 19, Allegany, N.Y. who paid a $100.00 civil penalty and Anthony Skudlarek, 20, Salamanca, N.Y. who was held for further action.

RANSOMVILLE ARSON

On November 7, 1936, Frank Blanco, age 52 and Floyd Pettibone, age 55 of Buffalo, N.Y. set off an incendiary device that destroyed the barn on the Roy Fonner farm near Ransomville, N.Y. Arrested for First Degree Arson, both men were convicted and sentenced to Attica Prison by Niagara County Court Judge Hopkins to not less than ten years and not more than twenty years. The act was a plot of vengeance against Pettibone's wife, age 22 who twice left him for other men. Mrs. Pettibone was living on the Fonner farm at the time of the fire. Sergeant Richard Gibbons of the New York State Police at Lewiston, N.Y. later arrested Fonner, age 47 and Mrs. Pettibone on charges of adultery. (Batavia Daily News – January 1937)

TRIPLE MARRIAGE

On September 9, 1936, Walter L. Dennis, age 28 of Morganville, N.Y. admitted to three marriages that he did not recall ever getting a divorced from. He stated he first married Catherine Trease in 1924 at Sunbury, Pa and had one child. In 1929, he moved to Arcade, N.Y. where in 1930, he married Pearl Brock having one child with her. Troubles with her family resulted in his leaving her and moving to Morganville, N.Y. Here in 1934, he married Aileen Ruhlman having two children with her. His arrest resulted from the complaint of a Bushville woman to whom he was engaged. He was charged with Bigamy and Child Abandonment.

BABIES ABANDONED

On June 10, 1937, 34-year-old Mary Regina Pfohl, Bloomingdale Road, Akron, N.Y., mother of ten children, was charged with the abandonment of her week old twin daughters, Doris and Delores. Having no means to provide for them and no financial support from the father, she left them in the dooryard of Howard Meredith at Clarence, N.Y. shortly after midnight. She then walked five miles in the rain to her home in Akron. An investigation by Corporal Albert Horton and Trooper Norman Lippert revealed that the girls were born on June 2, 1937 at 62 East Huron Street, Buffalo, N.Y. The babies were taken to Buffalo City Hospital where they were examined and found to be in good health. Mrs. Pfohl was arrested and arraigned before justice Walter Shutt who released her without bail to look after her other children. (Batavia Daily News – June 1937)

ALEXANDER, N.Y. CANNON

On July 5, 1937, Alexander, N.Y. youths Francis Pratt, age 18 and William Eichelberger, age 20 were charged with Disorderly Conduct by Trooper Samuel Vint, when an improvised cannon prematurely exploded sending a sixteen pound sledge hammer through the roof of the liberty hotel 50 feet away owned by Eugene Harrington. Pratt was treated for powder burns and bruises to his hands while Eichelberger was treated for hand bruises. The home made cannon, a two foot long, three inch diameter pipe with an eighth inch hole bored for use as a fuse was being fired in front of the hotel at the corner of Main Street and Broadway, Alexander, N.Y. It was prematurely fired, when the youths were pounding a high explosive charge into the cannon, which was set off by friction caused by a fifteen-inch bolt used as a ramrod. The ramrod was shot several hundred feet into the air with a two-inch depression in the pavement caused from the explosion. Charges were dismissed, when the youths made restitution of $125.00 for damages they caused. (Batavia Daily News – 7/6/37)

On October 20, 1937, a national campaign by the Junior Chamber of Commerce was launched for fingerprinting every man, woman and child over sixteen in the community for the civilian files of the FBI.

JOCKO THE PET DEER

During July 1938, the corral at the rear of the trooper's barracks looked like a private game preserve. In early June, a two-month-old deer the trooper's named "Felix" was found at the Mt. Hope Cemetery, Rochester, N.Y. On July 27th, Clarence Slocum, Lake Road, Niagara County found and turned in a four day old buck fawn that was dubbed "Jocko". When the deer were old enough to fend for themselves, they would be released at Letchworth State Park along with two doe's found at Letchworth and Hamlin, N.Y. Trooper Guy Hamm who cared for the fawns said they are "as tame as kittens". They have been fed from a bottle four to five times daily since their arrival. Other animals at Troop "A" are "Kate", a beagle hound with pups, a goose and gander found in Erie County, a half dozen cats, a flock of pigeons and "Major", a Shetland pony stabled with five saddle horses.

PRATTSBURG BANK ROBBERY

On August 24, 1938, a lone bandit brandishing a revolver entered the Prattsburg State Bank and demanded all the money from teller Otis Waldo. Approximately $700.00 was taken and escape made in a waiting car. Witnesses leading to the arrest of John W. Presho, 49, an Erie, Pa. resident, provided a description of the car. Sergeant Harold Kemp, Corporal Oscar Lazeroff and Trooper Michael Fort stopped him at Newstead, N.Y. He was identified as the driver of the getaway car. Sergeant Harry DeHollander and Corporal Vernon Voight arrested Ward M. Townsend, 42, Bolivar, N.Y. five days later with most of the loot recovered. The case was deemed most unusual, as neither participant knew the other's name. They had met in an Olean, N.Y. barroom, sympathized with each other's money problems and slow delivery of unemployment checks and there laid the plans for the robbery at Prattsburg because of its isolated location. Both were taken to Steuben County where they were held for court appearances.

MISFIRE AT BERGEN, N.Y.

On March 9, 1939, Corporal Donald Girven and Trooper Harry Ashe responded to Bergen, N.Y. to investigate the report of a suicidal person. Ashe was sent to the back door of the residence while Girven entered through the front door. While standing in the doorway, Girven heard the click of a gun that was aimed at him from ten feet away. He jumped back, pulled his weapon and directed the assailant to drop the weapon. He did so immediately and was taken into custody. Examination of the shotgun found it to be fully loaded. He was committed to the Rochester State Hospital.

PUNCHBOARDS

On April 5, 1939 Corporal Donald S. Girven arrested Milton C. Bailey, 25, Hobgood, N.C. for possession of 500 punchboards in violation of gambling laws. Taken before Bergen Justice A.C. Aradine, he pled guilty, was sentenced to 30 days in jail and fined $25.00. The boards valued at about $500.00 would have each brought in an estimated $85.00 in revenues. Bailey stated that nine other's were distributing punchboards in New York after a sales meeting held at Auburn, N.Y. the day before. Many punchboards were of the crooked variety. After placing them in a roadside location, a company man would appear at the location and luckily punch the winning numbers. The confiscated boards were destroyed.

1939 WORLDS FAIR DISPLAY

In 1937, the State Police by invitation made preparations for a comprehensive display at the 1939 World's Fair. The display was open for 12 hours daily from April 30 to October 31, 1939. Troopers were on duty to explain the organization and operation of the state police with the aims and objects of the troopers in accident prevention stressed resulting in a better understanding between drivers and law enforcement. The display was located in the New York State building with background murals displayed depicting several phases of police work. Actual displays of diving gear, radio sets, floodlight outfits, fingerprint and photograph items and inhalators called forth much interest. The actual operation of the teletype machine was a feature attraction. Visitors included law enforcement officials from throughout the United States and many foreign countries resulting in many valuable contacts being established for the exchange information.

(NYSP Annual Reports – 1939)

WYOMING COUNTY RUSTLERS

On August 25, 1939, John Mazierski, 19, Java Center, N.Y. and Charles Fairfield, 18, Arcade, N.Y. were charged with Grand Larceny, when stopped by Troopers Oscar Lazeroff, Paul Mellody, Earl Wilkinson and Norman Lippert while transporting two stolen cows to the Buffalo stockyards to be sold. The cows had been stolen from Edwin Snell of Pike, N.Y. They admitted to stealing cows from the McCormack Farm and Mathew Farm, Java, N.Y. and the Charles Buller and Edward Berwanger Farms, Arcade, N.Y. The cattle brought an average of $75.00 each at the stockyards. They said it was easy money. Farms were scouted during the day, then using their panel truck, would drive into the farm field at night, load the cows and drive away.

CHAPTER SIXTY
1940 to 1943 – TROOP "A" BITS & PIECES

July 1940, Troop manpower at 121.

PRECIOUS SERUM RUSHED

On March 11, 1940, Troopers covered over 100 miles of ice and snow covered roads in three hours to successfully deliver serum to the Corning, N.Y. hospital. 13 year old Betty Jean Grover, 35 Grove Street, Corning required the serum to treat a rare blood infection. The serum flown into Rochester, N.Y. from New York City was picked up by Corporal Donald Girven and rushed to Avon where Trooper Donald Kinne was waiting to continue the relay. He drove through piles of snow and badly drifted roads reaching Dansville where he turned the precious cargo over to Trooper John McDonald who took it to it's final destination. The serum was administered and a transfusion given the next morning, however the young girl died shortly before noon.

TROOPERS BASEBALL

In June 1940, the Troopers baseball team defeated the YMCA 9 to 4 in the city baseball league. Pitcher's Joe Brandstetter, Roman Lawrence & Floyd Emery savored the win. John Long, Emery and Stanley Smith provided big hits. Bob Beswick suffered the YMCA loss.

BERGEN CHICKEN THIEVES ARRESTED
On June 20, 1940, Alvice Starkweather, Bergen, N.Y. was arrested by corporal Donald Girven charged with stealing $20.00 worth of chickens from the Edward Boatfield farm, Leroy, N.Y. He pled guilty before Justice Clarence Crocker who sentenced him to six months in the Genesee County Jail. Starkweather was described as the leader of a trio linked to 22 poultry burglaries in the area. His cohorts, Caleb Crowell and Kenneth Nabor also of Bergen, were charged and sentenced to forty and ninety days in the county jail.

ROBINSON APPOINTED EMERGENCY CO-ORDINATOR
On July 26, 1940, Governor Herbert Lehman appointed Captain Winfield Robinson as co-coordinator for the Western New York area in a new plan to co-ordinate police agencies in the event of any defense emergency.

WELLSVILLE ARSON
On August 14, 1940, Wellsville brothers Robert A. Hunt, age 31 and Louis L. Hunt, age 37 were charged with arson in the friendly burning of Louis' house. Troopers George Wood and Claude Stephens determined that Louis, having financial problems, offered his brother Robert $150.00 to set fire to the house. This amount would be paid as soon as the he collected insurance money that was $1000.00 on the house and $1000.00 for its contents. Both were held for grand jury action.

BLACK MARIA
In October 1941, eleven troopers went for a ride in an undertaker's service car armed with crowbars and sledgehammers. Trooper Paul Mellody wearing a black derby in keeping with the somber motif was at the wheel. As they entered Cheektowaga near the Mt. Cavalry cemetery, the car suddenly drove into the driveway of a two-story house and all the troopers poured out taking posts surrounding the house. A second carload of troopers went immediately to the door using sledges to bash down a steel door. Behind the steel door was a first class betting establishment with 150 patrons present. They immediately took charge of betting slips, a dice table and three slot machines. The strategy of using an undertaker's car was to deceive the many lookouts that the establishment had. The establishment had been active for about two months. Patrons left their cars in a large parking lot on Pine ridge Road and were chauffeured to the emporium. Albert Kirsch, age 42, was charged with maintaining a gambling room and slot machine possession. He pled guilty before Cheektowaga Peace Justice Edmund Szymanski who was brought to the location and fined $75.00. All gambling paraphernalia was confiscated and destroyed.

In 1943, the manpower for each troop was 120 officers and men.

WIDOW GETS AWARD
The New York State Court of Claims awarded $12,450.00 to Angelina Nephew of Redhouse, New York, widow of 31-year old Ronald Nephew who died while in custody. It was alleged that Nephew in an intoxicated condition died several hours after being arrested and beaten by Trooper Florence Driscoll. The court found that Driscoll unlawfully arrested Nephew in connection with a minor mishap and struck him unnecessarily.

PAY RAISE
Effective April 1, 1943, troopers received a $200.00 a year pay raise. Trooper recruits starting pay remained at $900.00 with a $200.00 annual raise until a maximum of $2100.00 was reached. Corporal pay would be $2350.00, Sergeants $2500.00, First Sergeants $2800.00, Lieutenants $3200.00, Inspectors $3400.00 and Captains $4800.00.

GRAND LARCENY

On May 17, 1943, Margaret L. McGarry, 35, former assistant bookkeeper at the Central Motors Company, Batavia, N.Y. was arrested at Waterloo, N.Y. by Troopers Norman Lippert and Paul Mellody charged with Grand Larceny 1st Degree. She was accused in a Grand Jury indictment with absconding with $4,300.00 of the firm's money. Manager Dominic Mancuso found the shortage in her books while she was absent from work.

INSURANCE FRAUD

On May 21, 1943, Troopers William Szymanski and Frank Easton arrested three men for destroying insured property with intent to defraud the insurance carrier. They had schemed to wreck a 1941 Buick Convertible owned by Donald E. White of East Aurora, N.Y. by pushing it over the gorge at Indian Falls, N.Y. The car valued at $1,295.00 was to be reported stolen by White while Robert J. Sullivan of Buffalo and Daniel LaQuay of Alden, N.Y. took the car to Indian Falls and pushed it over the brink. As luck would have it, the car was held from falling into the gorge by two boulders and was found by a local farmer. He notified the troopers who started the investigation before it was reported stolen.

OAKFIELD CRAP GAME RAIDED

On August 29, 1943, troopers raided a billiard room operated by Sebastian Bucceri located on South Pearl Street Road, Oakfield, N.Y. Sergeant Leslie Benway along with Troopers George White, Lyman Fortner and Monty Andrews had received several complaints of gambling at the establishment involving minors. All present were arrested on a charge of Disorderly Conduct for being engaged in an illegal activity, fined $10.00 each by Peace Justice Albert Avery and released. Arrested were Sebastian Bucceri, age 53, Philip Ciaccia, 16, August Stornelli, 17, Joseph Pofi, 24, Anthony Giordano, 26, Joseph DiSalvo, 28, Frank Ballister, 43, John Riggio, 23, James DiSalvo, 27, Joseph Giordana, 22, Thomas Pozzobon, 30, Anthony Puma, 26, Alfred Orsini, 16 and Sebastian Puma, 53. Sebastian Bucceri was later charged with allowing gambling in a licensed billiard room. He was given a four month suspended sentence and his billiard revoked. The billiard room was then converted into a grocery store.

SLOT MACHINE RAID

On November 29, 1943, troopers in a raid at the Doud Post American Legion, Route 33, Rochester, N.Y. confiscated 13 slot machines. Lieutenant Charles LaForge led the raid that included Troopers George Wood, Montagu Andrews and J.J. Brady. Bartender Charles Summers was charged with having illegal gambling devices under his control.

MOTORIST KILLED

On December 6, 1943, Paul Privitera, age 23, Buffalo, N.Y. was killed near Bergen, N.Y., when a rear tire blew out causing him to lose control of the car. Privitera was thrown from the car that rolled over the top of him resulting in his death from a fractured skull. He was traveling to visit his mother, Maria Privitera, 27 Concord Street, Rochester, N.Y. when the accident occurred.

The last horse patrol was used in 1943.

(Batavia Daily News)
(1943 NYSP Annual Reports)

TPR. MIKE FLEMING 1922

1924-SGT ED RIMMER

1931 J.NUGENT / C.L. WATKINS

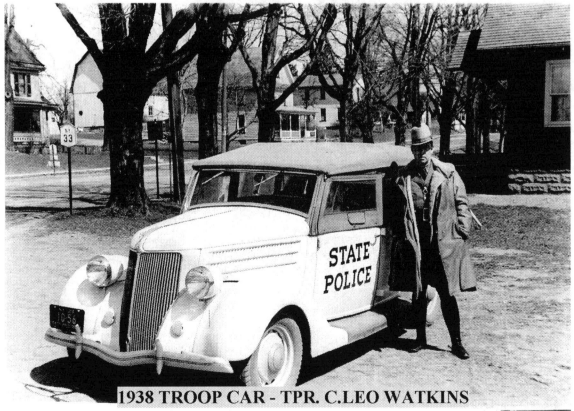

1938 TROOP CAR - TPR. C.LEO WATKINS

1938 - TRIXIE LEMAY - LAST OF TROOP "A" HORSES

Bill Rimmer. Son of the late
stable Sgt. Edw. H. Rimmer.
TPRS. BILL RIMMER / GENE REDDEN - 1941 LEWISTON, NY

CORPORAL ALBERT HORTON-1931

TPR. ANDREW FISHER - 1930

TPR. GEORGE WOOD - 1931

HAROLD KEMP - 1925

1939 KING/QUEEN DETAIL/EAST AURORA

1940 - TPR. CLARENCE PASTO

TPR. PAUL MELLODY - 1929

1920S - TPR. PERCY LEITNER

TROOP "A" HEADQUARTERS 1935

1931 - YORKSHIRE -G.WHITE/ C.WATKINS/T.MARTIN

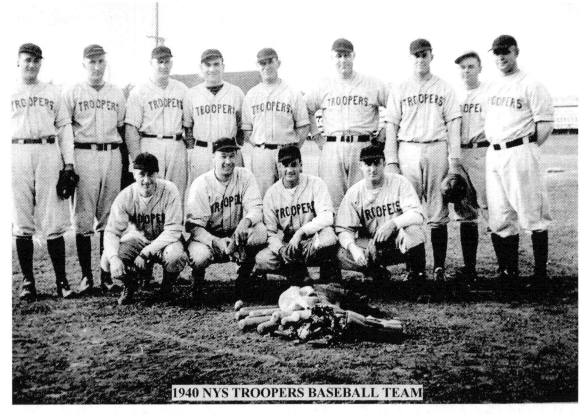

1940 NYS TROOPERS BASEBALL TEAM

BOOK IX – TROOPER PROFILES

CHAPTER SIXTY-ONE
MONTAGU ANDREWS

Monty as he was known, was born in Braintree, England on February 15, 1893 where he attended Essex public school. During WW I, he served a five year enlistment with the Royal Fusiliers serving in France and Belgium. He held the Meritorious Service and Victory Medals. He came to the United States after the war and in 1925, joined the State Police. He resigned in 1928 to take employment, as a Sergeant of Security for the Delaware, Lackawanna & Western Railroad. He returned to the State Police in 1931 and was placed in charge of organizing an identification bureau. He attended a fingerprinting school at the Chicago School of Applied Science studying photography and fingerprints and was a member of the International Association of Identification. He was known throughout Western New York for his expertise that helped solve thousands of cases. He also started and maintained a fingerprint and photograph file which contained 15,000 identifications. He retired on July 1, 1954 taking employment in the Security Department at Batavia Downs Race Track. In 1962, he took a position as Lieutenant of Security with the Buffalo, N.Y. based security firm of E.J. Burke. He was married to the former Theresa Aquino who died in 1960. He died on December 28, 1972 at age 79. Surviving were sons Gordon and Montagu Jr. and daughter, Shirley Wallace. He is buried at Maple Lawn Cemetery, Bethany, New York.

CHAPTER SIXTY-TWO
CORPORAL HOWARD C. BLANDING

1936 to 1946

A COLLECTION OF MEMORIES

Howard C. Blanding was born at East Aurora, New York graduating from East Aurora High School. He was employed at Fisher-Price Toys, East Aurora, as a Band saw operator from 1934-1936. His elementary education was at South Wales, New York where he lived for many years. He responded to an advertisement-seeking troopers in the local newspaper. The examination for the position of Trooper was only conducted at Albany, New York. If you passed the examination, you would have to return to Albany for a physical examination at a later time. Candidates had to be 5'10", weight in proportion to their height, possess a high school diploma and have a clean record. The enlistment was for two years with a $900.00 starting pay. A $200.00 per year increment was provided until a top salary of $1,900.00 was obtained after five years.

Blanding was notified of a vacancy and enlisted in the New York State Police in the autumn of 1936 and was assigned at the Castile, New York Station with Sergeant Charles Z. McDonald in charge. The Troop Commander was Captain Winfield W. Robinson and First Sergeant was Joseph W. Brandstetter. During January and February 1937, he attended six weeks of classes at the State Police School, Troy, New York. Troopers roomed at the Hotel Troy where classes were conducted. Blanding felt that the schooling received gave recruits the basics and understanding of the law, but the real training was obtained by being assigned to work with a Sergeant or a senior trooper for several months prior to being assigned a patrol station of your own. This procedure is still in existence.

After completing the Police School training, Blanding returned for duty at the Castile Station where he patrolled in an automobile until spring 1937. He recalled that troopers never completely unpacked their bags, because they didn't stay at any one station for very long. The idea at the time was for the troopers not to get acquainted with people in the community, because it may influence their judgment in enforcing the law.

All uniforms and equipment was provided by the state. The winter uniform included a full-length sheepskin coat weighing 35 pounds and a seal skin hat. Spurs were worn at all times as part of the uniform. The firearm was a Colt New Service .45 Caliber revolver. Every shot fired from the gun had to be accounted for in a special report. The original 1917 orders were adhered to in that a trooper never took his weapon from the holster unless to clean it or if you intended to use it and if it was pulled, you had better use it. The summer uniform included a Stetson hat. Uniforms were no doubt all wool, but not uncomfortable.

Blanding recalled that many of the new troopers started out on motorcycle patrol, which over the years accounted for many injured troopers until motorcycles were abandoned in favor of cars only. I had owned several motorcycles prior to my entry into the State Police. In the wintertime I rode one to and from work. I also rode one to Florida in the early 30's hitting a cow on the open range in Georgia, at full speed. Trixie LeMay was the cycle instructor givng lessons in the corral behind the barracks.

Sergeants for the most part were permanently stationed and in many cases the troopers working with them lived with the sergeant and his family as boarders. Meals were eaten at restaurants except when the troopers were quartered at Troop Headquarters, when the state ran out of money. During this time, a few horses were still maintained at troop Headquarters for crowd control, parades and fair details. This gave the recruits something to do while still at the barracks, such as cleaning horses and stables while at the same learning many aspects of the job from Stable Sergeant, Trooper Guy Hamm, an old timer.

Automobiles were the old open, 4 door phaetons with hot water heaters, a convertible roof and side curtains. They were great in the summer time, if it wasn't raining, but in the wintertime, they were mighty cold with snow blowing through the curtains and hot water heater of little value. Many back roads were never plowed so consequently, much time was spent shoveling snow and putting on tire chains. To the best of his recollection, both Ford and Chevrolet made Phaetons.

There were only a couple models of the Harley Motorcycle available at the time with troopers using the 74 cubic inch model with no windshields or other frills unless you bought them yourself. Most of the motorcycle duty was from April thru October, when road traffic was at its highest peak averaging about 15,000 miles a summer. Troopers wore their Stetsons while on the motorcycle and with no windshields at high speeds, the hats blew off or would wind up out of shape. With only a motorcycle, a trooper would have to depend on local constables and police for automobile use, when necessary for transporting prisoners. Trooper automobile patrols were usually quite a distance away and not available. There were plenty of cycles for the patrols that were limited to busy traffic areas.

If an arrest was made, prisoners were taken immediately before a Justice of the Peace where minor violations were handled at once and sentence imposed. Major cases were referred to the Bureau of Criminal Investigation (BCI) at Batavia, New York and investigators dispatched to the scene. Except for major felonies, the trooper handled investigations.

If a trooper were assigned to outpost duty, he would live in a civilian home somewhere in a rural area with a "STATE POLICE" signs in the front yard. He would patrol that area during the summer months supervised by the Zone Lieutenant. In 1942, Blanding was at an outpost in Sheridan, NY residing with Don & Betty Zieser.

With no modern radio equipment, Troopers were located by accommodating telephone operators who were familiar with the various stops and checkpoints troopers frequented. Friends of troopers at various points would take messages and were great in locating a trooper in case of an emergency.

The workday consisted of duty 24 hours a day for a month, then a 3-day pass. You were not allowed to drive your personal automobile or wear civilian clothing during this time unless you were on a pass or vacation. Troopers were usually stationed a considerable distance from their homes. A change in duty station could occur at a moment's notice and changes were frequent. During summer months, troopers could not take their days off on weekends or holidays. All troopers got a one-month vacation, which had to be taken during the winter months. Troop Commanders had complete authority to discipline as they saw fit and could terminate a trooper's employment without any recourse. You just packed your bags and left.

Trooper Blanding served at the following stations during his career

STATION	FROM – TO	SUPERVISOR
Wanakah, New York Precinct Headquarters	Spring 1937/Summer 1939 Spring 1946 Motorcycle duty	Lieutenant Lawrence C. Nelson commanding and Sergeant Arthur L. Rich in charge.
Angola, New York	Summer, Fall and Winter of 1937 Motorcycle duty	Sergeant Charles R. Stanton in charge.
Churchville, New York	Spring and Summer 1938 Motorcycle duty	Sergeant Donald S. Girven in charge.
Pittsford, New York	Summer 1938 Motorcycle duty	Sergeant William L. Ireland in charge.
East Avon, New York Precinct Headquarters	Fall 1938 Motorcycle duty	Lieutenant Gerald D. Vaine in charge and Corporal Theodore F. Martin the station Supervisor.
Friendship, New York Precinct Headquarters	Winter 1938 – 1939 Automobile patrol	Lieutenant William J. George in charge and Sergeant Charles E. Stanton the station supervisor
Batavia, New York	Spring 1939, Automobile patrol	
Lewiston, New York	Spring 1940 Motorcycle patrol	Sergeant Herbert G. Southworth in charge.
Clarence, New York	Summer 1940 -- Motorcycle duty.	
Westfield, New York	Summer 1940 - Motorcycle duty.	
Sheridan, New York	Summer 1941 - Motorcycle duty	

The United States was heavily involved in World War II and there was a sense of patriotic duty to serve in the military. On July 1, 1942, Blanding enlisted in the United States Coast Guard as a Boatswains Mate receiving his training at the Coast Guard Academy, New London, Connecticut. He graduated from Officer Training School and was assigned to the US Navy in the Pacific theatre. He served with the 7th Invasion Fleet aboard the USSPC-469 during the Philippine Liberation and the Okinawa and Iwo Jima operations. Blanding considered himself in the Navy , as the Coast Guard was a part of the Navy during the war. His discharge listed his time served, as in the U.S. Naval Service.

On January 16, 1946, he returned to duty with the state police and was promoted to the rank of Corporal. From January 21 to February 2, 1946, he along with other military veterans attended a refresher course at the state police school. On May 1, 1946, Corporal Blanding went on G.I. Leave ending his career with the State Police.

He was happy as a trooper before the war because he practically grew up in it. When he came home and found himself sleeping in a barracks or precinct, he said to himself " What the hell am I doing here. I just finished living on a ship for over a year and I should be with my family". He thought he should live like a human being again, able to spend time with the family. He recalled the following interesting situations he was involved with or had direct knowledge of involving the troopers.

He recalled working on the Cattaraugus Indian Reservation at all hours of the day and night, when the troopers were the only law and most of the Indian residents did not think kindly of troopers. There was constant need for a trooper on the reservation. Arrests were made car theft, larceny, assaults and for shooting one another. Fortunately, we had an old retired mail carrier that delivered mail on the reservation for years and knew every one of reservation residents. We would get him up at all hours of the night to help us locate people we sought. You would ask an Indian where someone lived or could be located and the standard answer was that they never knew. You might be talking to the guy you were looking for. The FBI was supposed to handle felonies, but they were not interested unless the victim was dead. The Sheriff's Dept wanted no part of the reservation.

He was assigned to duty at the Syracuse State Fair which about two weeks in duration. The workday consisted of long exhausting hours on duty and we confined to a barracks for the few hours we were off duty. The barracks was on the fair grounds and the only air conditioning was a fan, if you had one. He remembered shooting a diseased cat in one of the horse stables. This resulted in a pile of paperwork for discharging the issue firearm.

Probably one of my most useful accomplishments was the investigation and successful completion of one of the first convictions under the new criminal negligence with a motor vehicle law. A drunken driver hit a car head on near the Village of Eden, which contained a family returning from Christmas shopping in Buffalo. Two children were killed and others badly injured. The drunken driver, Francis O'Shaughnessy was represented by Senator Walter Mahoney and used every trick possible to avoid appearing in court. We had 25 witnesses who were subpoenaed several times to appear in court and the defendant would be absent, sick or some other excuse. On the last occasion the Judge ordered me to take county Coroner Dr. DeDominicis to Rochester to a hospital where the defendant was supposed to be and bring him back to Buffalo. We located him in the hospital and the Medical Examiner gave him a quick check over and ordered him to get dressed and we took him back to Buffalo and put him in jail where he was available for trial. He was convicted and sentenced to five years, one of the first such convictions under the new law.

For several years, Trooper Roman J. Laurence worked diligently, mostly alone, to better the working conditions in the state police and eventually was dismissed for his efforts. The attitude at the time was not to ask questions and cause problems, rather do as you were told. State Assemblyman Leo

Lawrence made the statement that "If the troopers want an eight hour day, let them join a municipal force. If they don't like their jobs, let them get out." It was because of Roman Laurence's efforts that were responsible for the establishment of the Trooper's Police Benevolent Association. (PBA)

Laurence's dismissal from the State Police was based on the following incident. A Navy Captain left his cap in a restaurant near Leroy, New York and called asking the troopers to recover it for him. Trooper Laurence found the cap and mailed it to the Captain, giving his home as the return address and not indicating he was a trooper. The Captain sent a $5.00 check to Mr. Laurence whose wife presumed it to be a contribution to the newly formed PBA and deposited it to that account. This was considered "accepting a gratuity for performance of duty" resulting in his being fired. Laurence later joined the Corning, New York Police Department where he became Chief.

Corporal Blanding concluded with the following comments:

During his tenure, there were only about 100 troopers in Troop "A". Due to the system of frequent transfers, a trooper would probably have worked with at least 90% of your fellow troopers in a very few years and would have been familiar with all of them. The troopers were a tight knit organization held together through telephone, teletype and personal contact in the field, not unlike the military. He felt that troopers were highly respected by everyone, the camaraderie was great and they were proud to wear the uniform. The reputation of the troopers established during the Steel Strikes at Lackawanna, New York, the Auburn Prison Uprising and the Milk Strikes made everyone respect the big night sticks carried and used so efficiently by the old troopers, usually from the saddle of a big horse. This saved all of those young troopers that followed lots of trouble because when troopers arrived on the scene, trouble stopped.

In 1939, I was part of the Thousand Island grand opening detail to provide security for President Roosevelt. We were confined to our rooms in Watertown with no civilian clothes available. Trooper C. Leo Watkins sent out for a few bottles of Molson Beer and we drank to our hearts content making the best of the situation. Actually, it was more than a few.

On November 8, 1939, Trooper Blanding was part of the detail assigned to escort the Byrd Snow Cruiser through Western New York. It was a monstrosity that completely covered a two-lane road. As he recalled, the Snow Cruiser was headed East on Route 5 & 20 and was in Troop A territory for a couple days. Lieutenant Lawrence Nelson was in charge of security.

CHAPTER SIXTY-THREE
EDITH CHAMBERLAIN

WIFE OF EDWIN
1929 TO 1936

Edith Chamberlain nee Dean was born at Hartland, New York. Her father owned a store at Hartland's Corners and that is where she met Ed. They married in 1933 and had two daughters.

The Chamberlain family was originally from Hinsdale, New York with nine children in the family. An older brother, Devillo, was in the troopers when Ed enlisted in 1929. In the summertime, Ed would patrol on a motorcycle and in the wintertime, on horseback. When Captain Robinson found out that

Ed had a girlfriend in Hartland, he was transferred to Sheridan, New York. Ed left the troopers in 1936, when their first child was born. He took a position at the Harrison Radiator Company, Lockport, New York. The pay was a lot better and he would come home nights. He worked twelve-hour shifts at Harrison, from 6 AM to 6PM or 6 PM to 6 AM.

Her recollections of the job are few. She recalled Ed working with Kaye (Bing) Crosby from Spencerport, Tom Corbett from Batavia and Frank Easton of Cuba, N.Y. Ed was stationed with Jerome Nugent at Sheridan, when Nugent was killed. He hit a big dog with his motorcycle and was thrown from the cycle. He had been recently married and his wife was following behind when the accident happened. Ed really loved the State Police and the people he worked with. The working conditions weren't conducive to family life. Ed was always working or would be on call. The troopers had to stay at the stations during their off time to answer complaints or emergencies, as they were on call 24 hours a day.

She recalled that Captain Robinson had a cabin built somewhere in Vermont and Ed along with Earl Wilkinson and Don Kinney would go there to work on it.

Edith met Trixie Lemay on several occasions. They enjoyed the trooper dinners at the Elk's and Moose Clubs in Batavia where Trixie would play the piano. Everyone would sing along and have a great time. Troopers were a very close-knit group. Two or three wives would get together and stay at a motel in Batavia for a day or two of shopping and gossiping.

Ed was an avid hunter and fisherman, as well as an expert marksman. He died on September 16, 1992 at age 85.

CHAPTER SIXTY-FOUR
TROOPER JOHN C. DOELL

1936 to 1945

John C. Doell was born at Rochester, New York where he attended Aquinas High School graduating in 1927. While there, he was a member of the first ever school golf team. He joined the State Police on December 16, 1936

The following are some of his recollections, as a trooper.

When he first reported to Batavia, he recalled there were four horses and a pony in the corral. The Captain's white horse named Grey Dawn, a mean bastard horse named Mary and others with names unrecalled.

When he first entered the State Police, he was issued a sheepskin overcoat that came down to his ankles. "I was assigned at the Clarence station and was wearing the coat, when Sergeant George Wood came in and asked if that was the best they could do for me. He then gave me his coat which I wore until I resigned".

In 1937, he was assigned to the Clarence station where he worked with John Chambers. He recalled patrolling the Clarence and Akron, New York areas with most of the arrestees being taken before Justice of the Peace Walter Shutt. Troopers at one time rented office space from Judge Shutt.

He recalled two brothers that were troopers, Devillo H. (1928-46) and Edwin B.(1929-36) Chamberlain from Cattaraugus County. Ed had a girlfriend in Niagara County and when Captain Robinson found out about her, he transferred him to Westfield, New York. Both brothers were excellent marksman. Edwin left the troopers taking a job in the security department at Harrison Radiator Company, Lockport, New York, where he worked for 32 years. Devillo retired and ran a grocery store at West Clarksville, New York.

While assigned to Batavia, he read a report written by John G. Macdonald about his investigation into a death where a guy died from a decapitated head. Another report read as follows: A guy was in the kitchen while his wife was ironing and they were having an argument. He took out his old wang and put it on the ironing board and his wife promptly placed her hot iron on it and pressed it. He said that was one thing about the job, you would read some of the reports and get a real chuckle.

During World War II, many men were lost to the military with few patrols on the road. Charlie Cobb was the First Sergeant with Charlie McDonald the night desk officer. McDonald was transferred to Letchworth replaced by Trixie Lemay. Doell, John Long, Donald Girven, John Cole and Percy Leitner were assigned to barracks doing paper work. In order to free them up for roadwork, the state hired three women to do the office work. He remembered that one was Viola Schwingel who took the job he was doing. Another was Berniece Skelton who worked upstairs in the BCI office. It worked out well, as the women were most proficient.

Doell remembered that in 1937, his annual salary was $1100.00. He was supposed to get a $200.00 increase in 1938, but it was suspended because the state didn't have any money. When he resigned, he was making $2700.00 a year that included a cost of living increase. Base pay was $2150.00 for corporal, $2300.00 for sergeant, $2400.00 for First Sergeant and Troop Clerk, $3200.00 for Lieutenant and $3800.00 for Captain. You didn't live lavishly, but you got by.

Doell said that he knew he wasn't going to last long when they transferred him to Liberty. He was told it was a summer resort area and he would be there for the summer only. He had heard the same story before, when they sent Norm Lippert and Frank Easton to New York City to work. They were told to take their toothbrush and razor, as they would be back in a couple of days. Well, they wound up there for two years. He thought the same thing was going to happen to him. That's the way the State Police did business in those days.

He stated that it was the terrible working conditions that led to his resignation. He married in 1935 and lived with his wife in Batavia, New York. He was assigned at Batavia Headquarters where he did necessary record keeping. There was a reserve system in place where he was on duty all night. When Thomas E. Dewey got elected Governor, the system went from a two man to a four-man reserve. The number of troopers at the barracks was depleted to the point that we were working all the time. We were lucky to get one, maybe two nights off a week. In 1945, Troop "C" had been depleted of manpower since many were away on military duty. Two troopers from Troops "A", "D", "G" and "K" were reassigned to Troop "C" for summer duty. Doell was one of those selected. He was assigned at Liberty outside of Ferndale, New York for about a week and a half when he decided he didn't want to stay any longer. He was there from June 3 to 10, 1945. The first weekend there, he was ready to go to bed after working all day, when he received instructions to investigate a death. Before he went to sleep again two days later, he investigated two other deaths. When he got up, he said the hell with this and returned to Batavia where he resigned. At that time, a three-day pass would be used for two days travel, as it was 300 miles one way with no interstate roads to travel. Being a trooper meant you had no time for a life with your family. Doell stated he could dig ditches, make as much money and be home nights. The main reason for leaving was that he just got sick and tired of working all the time. His replacement was Jesse Moulthrop who wanted to go there in the first place, because he had relatives in the area.

Doell resigned from the State Police on June 15, 1945 and went to work for the American Surety Company in New York City on October 1, 1945.

CHAPTER SIXTY-FIVE
SERGEANT MICHAEL J. FLEMING

1920 to 1925

Michael J. Fleming was born on June 19, 1889 growing up in Buffalo, N.Y. He attended Buffalo Public Schools through the 8th grade quitting school to work along with family members for the New York Central Railroad. The family resided at 2017 Bailey Avenue and 39 Burgard Place, Buffalo, N.Y.

On September 28, 1917, he enlisted in the US Army with basic training at Fort Dix, New Jersey. He was then assigned at Allentown, Pennsylvania for advanced training in chemical warfare. In November 1917, he was assigned to the 1ST Army Expeditionary Forces stationed at Chateauroux, France. He was promoted to PFC on May 1, 1918, Corporal on September 11, 1918, Sergeant on January 1, 1919 and Battalion Sergeant Major on February 1, 1919 of the Chemical Warfare Service. He was honorably discharged on April 9, 1919 returning to his job with the railroad.

Fleming took the examination for trooper in April 1921 and was appointed to the New York State Police on August 15, 1921 along with Albert L. Buck, Forestport, N.Y., Frederick O. Weise, 277 Mills Street, Buffalo, N.Y., Casimir J. Knitter, Webster Place, Buffalo, N.Y. and Earl E. Zimmerman, 155 Clinton Street, Tonawanda, N.Y. Initial duty was at Batavia, N.Y. doing barracks chores and becoming oriented with the troopers routine. Trooper Fleming attended the first classes at the State Police School with sessions held at Troy, N.Y. from November 1 to November 30, 1921. Upon graduation, he returned to Troop "A" where he was assigned to various posts, as was the routine at the time. A majority of his career was serving in Genesee and Monroe Counties where he attained the rank of Sergeant. He resigned in 1925 taking a position with the United States Treasury Department, as a Prohibition Agent. Several investigations he conducted are noted below, as well as other chapters throughout this book.

On December 8, 1923, Corporal Fleming and Trooper Earl Foley acting on the report of stolen cars traveling along the main highway through Stafford, N.Y. conducted an all night road check by stopping every car traveling the highway. At about 11:30PM, Louis Samerio, 263 Oak Street and Carmine Terlo, 235 Seneca Street, Buffalo, N.Y. were stopped and found to possess revolvers concealed on their person. They were arrested when their stories about the car they were driving appeared suspicious. This eventually led to a gang of international car thieves being arrested and the recovery of several stolen cars.

On April 7, 1924, Corporal Fleming and Trooper Otto Bahr charged 22- year old John Parsons, 191 Sherbourne Street and 19- year old Jack John Lever, Toronto, Ontario, Canada with violation of Federal Immigration Laws. Both had extensive criminal records in Canada and were on parole. They were detained and turned over to Canadian Authorities.

On April 14, 1924, Corporal Fleming was in charge of a detail that was the forerunner in a crusade to stop the operation of alleged gambling and illegal sale of liquor in the Village of Leroy, N.Y. Accompanied by Mayor Ward and Leroy Police Officers Docking and Dampier, a gambling operation on the second floor of the Paladino building located on Main Street was raided. A card game with $49.00 on the table was in progress resulting in the arrest of the following who identified themselves as Alexander J. Noel, John Wallace, Charles Lambert, Harry Rider, Alfred J. Burling, Ivan Fagan, Michael Maloy, Joseph Michals and Arthur Hewitt. Police Justice Macpherson was brought to the location and court proceedings held. Noel pled guilty, was fined $50.00 and released. All but one of the other participants pled guilty to Disorderly Conduct, were fined $15.00 and released. One man making a food delivery pled not guilty and was released until police looked into his story. Whiskey and wine found at the scene were confiscated and turned over to prohibition agents.

On June 9, 1924, Corporal Fleming and Trooper Otto Bahr arrested Robert J. Clarke, age 18, Oakfield, N.Y. for attempting to pass a forged check for $185.00 at the Bank of Corfu. The check when presented had the name Almon W. Orr, a South Alabama merchant signed to it. Clarke was arraigned before Pembroke Justice Mallory and held on $1000.00 bail for Grand Jury.

On June 17, 1924, Sergeants Sam Dunlap and Fleming seized a truck carrying 75 cases of Canadian ale on the Main Road east of Batavia, N.Y. A loaded 45-caliber revolver was found in the truck. Arrested were Frank Mackri, age 26, Watkins, N.Y. and Frank Sitara, age 41, Endicott, N.Y. Both were turned over to prohibition agents and the ale confiscated. A fine was paid for the weapons possession.

On July 14, 1924, Sergeant Fleming, Corporal Richard Gibbons and Trooper Porter conducted raids at roadside hotels charging twenty-three persons with violating the Saturday Night Closing Law. The troopers entered a hotel at Forks, N.Y. operated by Frank Kauffman where patrons were "having a hilarious time dancing and drinking". All were fined $10.00. Also raided was a hotel on Transit Road, Amherst, N.Y. operated by Peter Ducasse. All were arrested with Ducasse paying a $50.00 fine before Justice G.E. Ouchie of Williamsville.

During March 1924, Fleming was part of the investigative team at the Linden Murders that to this day have been unsolved. (Linden Murders are detailed in Book V)

On November 28, 1925, Fleming was appointed a Prohibition Agent in the Internal Revenue Service. His appointment notice read "You are to enforce the National Prohibition Act and all Internal Revenue Laws relating to the manufacture, sale, transportation, control, and taxation of intoxicating liquors." His starting rate of compensation was $1860.00 yearly, which was almost double his state police salary. Fleming's aggressive style and arrest record, eventually, earned him high praise and promotion in May 1927, as the Agent in Charge of the Buffalo, N.Y. office. He had been assigned to the Malone, Watertown, N.Y. areas. His expertise was utilized, when he was assigned temporarily to the Chicago, Illinois office where the legendary "Elliott Ness" was assigned. Prohibition was repealed in 1933, however Fleming left the service in 1932 because of pending legislation that would repeal of the Volstead Act placing his job in jeopardy. His impending marriage to Margaret Fekete may have also influenced his decision to seek employment that would keep him closer to home. Following are some excerpts from his daily log.

"May 4, 1927, accompanied Inspectors Ford & Mathews and Agent Combs to Jamestown, N.Y. executing a search warrant at 134 Institute Street seizing 1 pint of home brew and 3 gallons of cider. The next day, traveled to Olean, N.Y. executing a search warrant at 608 West State Street seizing 12 pints of cider and 3 pints of whiskey and later, at Sunset Inn, RFD, Olean, N.Y. 1 quart & 1 pint of cider. On May 7, attended a hearing before Commissioner Charles E. Doane at Buffalo, N.Y."

May 17, 1927, 9:00AM, Investigated complaints at Clayville, N.Y., then proceeded to the Palm Hotel, Suquoit, N.Y. where Agent Neil purchased a glass of cider for 10 cents. Seized 60 gallons of hard cider. Proceeded to the Eugene Collins Hotel, Yorkville, N.Y. purchasing hard cider. Traveled to Utica, N.Y. to investigate the report of a still at the Fabor Trunk Factory. No violation found. Stayed at Yates Hotel, Utica, N.Y. at a cost of $2.50.

June 1927, working under cover on wildcat breweries at Rochester, N.Y.

August 5, 1927, executed search warrant at 25 Chapel Street, Mt. Morris, N.Y. seizing whiskey and coloring. Proceeded to the Van Tweel Farm, Helendale Road, Irondequoit, N.Y. closing a brewery and seizing all equipment. Later, proceeded to 1335 & 1353 Emerson Street, Rochester, N.Y. seizing stills and related equipment.

During the week of August 15, 1927, raided the following Rochester, N.Y. wild cat breweries and establishments:

1499 Lexington Avenue, Richter's Garage, 816 Monroe Avenue, 290 Parkway, 160 Lyell Avenue, Knox Club, 3835 Goodman Avenue, 109 Hartford Street, 21 Market Street, 375 Weaver Street, 440 Oak Street, 107 Exchange Street, 211 Caledonia, Street, 359 Plymouth Avenue, 57 Bartlett Street and 938 Clinton Street.

In 1932, he accepted a position as "Keeper" at the Erie County Penitentiary (ECP) located in Alden, N.Y. This position was less dangerous than any of his previous positions in law enforcement. During this employment, he resided at 100 Buell Street, Akron, N.Y. Having earned a reputation of fairness and common sense, he was promoted several times eventually to a supervisory position which earned him housing privileges located adjacent to the Penitentiary. He retired with distinction in 1955.

Michael J. Fleming died on March 16, 1960 at age 71. He was survived by his wife, Margaret nee Fekete, daughter Mina (Ryan) and son Michael C. Fleming.

CHAPTER SIXTY-SIX
ALBERT S. HORTON

Albert S. Horton was born on August 25, 1902 at Newfane, N.Y. where he attended public schools. He worked at a local felt company along with his father and brother in a job that he did not care for. He answered an advertisement for the position of trooper in the New York State Police easily passing the examination that was given. On June 15, 1927, he was appointed to a position in the New York State Troopers. He remained a member of the state police until his retirement on March 15, 1953.

Albert Horton attended the State Police Academy graduating on February 16, 1929. Following normal procedure, he was assigned at various locations throughout the troop. The theory of regular transfers within the troop was to familiarize the trooper with the entire geographic area of his responsibility. On June 1, 1930, he was designated as the Troop "A" blacksmith. On July 1, 1930, he was promoted to the rank of Corporal. Horton was assigned to the newly formed Bureau of Criminal Investigation (BCI) on June 2, 1937. During September 1944, he was elevated to the temporary rank of Provisional Sergeant. Those members on active military duty upon return were reinstated to the rank held prior to leaving for active duty. From 1947 until his retirement, he was assigned as Officer in Charge of the Darien, N.Y. sub-station. On December 1, 1951, he was appointed to the permanent rank of sergeant.

During the Auburn Prison riots of July 1929, Trooper Horton was one of the first from Troop "A" detailed to help restore order. Inmates and guards were killed and injured during the melee. He continued to provide security for several months after the riot until reconstruction of the partially burned facility was completed.

On April 21, 1930, Troopers Albert Horton and Earl Wilkinson arrested 24-year-old Maynard R. Glor of Attica, N.Y. for Reckless Driving. Glor, while traveling south on the Alexander Road was attempting to pass a car, when he sideswiped a vehicle driven by Clara Heidenrich, forcing her into a ditch that resulted in injury. Glor pled guilty to the charge before Alexander Justice George Curtiss, paid a $20.00 fine and was released.

During January 1937, Corporal Horton and Trooper Frank Hackett arrested eighteen persons for violating an eight-ton bridge weight limit at the Horseshoe Lake overpass. Warnings went unheeded making enforcement necessary. Construction of Route 5 caused a re-routing of traffic. An alternate route had been provided, but truckers chose not to drive the few extra miles. All paid fines of $10.00 before Stafford Justice William Tyrrell

On June 6, 1938, a series of forgeries were solved with the arrest of Roy A. Rex, age 37 of Knapps Creek and Joseph P. Keller, age 38 of Buffalo, N.Y. Horton and Vernon Voight ended the six month crime spree that netted the pair several thousand dollars in cash, a truck and farm implements. Checks had been forged at Williamsville, Silver Creek, Dunkirk, Allegany and Olean. Both men were charged with Forgery 2nd Degree and held for Grand Jury action.

On September 6, 1942, Corporal Horton arrested Karl Metz, caretaker of the Spring Garden Association Club, Two Rod Road, Porterville, N.Y. for providing alcohol to minors. Metz was serving drinks at his home located on club property to schoolchildren. Several complaints had been received of children coming home in an intoxicated condition. Metz pled guilty to the charge before Marilla Justice Ernest Kelsey who sentenced him to 90 days in jail.

On May 9, 1950 while assigned at Darien, Horton and Trooper Charles Schwarzenholzer detained a male hitchhiker on Route 20. Not satisfied with responses to inquiries, he was charged with a minor violation. Continued investigation identified him as Paul Brown alias Martin J. Brown from New England. When confronted, he readily admitted his true identity. He was being sought nation wide for the hatchet murder eight days earlier of Yvonne Lavallee, age 41 at Worcester, Massachusetts. He admitted to assaulting her, but said he wasn't aware that she had died. He waived extradition and was turned over to Massachusetts's authorities.

Other investigations that Albert Horton participated in will be found throughout this book.

Albert married Mona Hurren in 1928, residing with his parents at Newfane until relocating to Batavia, N.Y. Prior to purchasing a house at 61 Redfield Parkway, Batavia, N.Y., it is said that permission was required from Captain Robinson, as Robinson was a Redfield Parkway resident. They raised three children, Albert T., Gary A. and Jeanine. Mona, Albert and Jeanine have since passed away and son Gary is the Genesee County, N.Y. Public Defender.

After retirement, he took employment, as Chief of Security at the Carborundum Metals Inc., Akron, N.Y. and as the Genesee County Court Officer.

He died on December 20, 1982 at age 80. Burial was at Grandview Cemetery, Batavia, N.Y.

Form 79. T-8-29-6000 (1D-117)

STATE OF NEW YORK

EXECUTIVE DEPARTMENT DIVISION OF STATE POLICE

NEW YORK STATE TROOPERS

TO ALL WHO SHALL SEE THESE PRESENTS, GREETING:

Know Ye, *that reposing special trust and confidence in the fidelity, valor, good conduct and abilities of* _____ Albert S. Horton _____

I do, by these presents constitute and appoint him a _____ Corporal _____ *of* TROOP "A", Batavia _____ *of the* NEW YORK STATE TROOPERS, EXECUTIVE DEPARTMENT, DIVISION OF STATE POLICE *to rank as such from the* first *day of* June *nineteen hundred and* thirty

He is, therefore, carefully and diligently to discharge the duties of the said office to which he is warranted with honor and fidelity, by doing and performing all manner of things thereunto belonging.

And all members of the Division of State Police, under his command are strictly charged and required to respect and be obedient to his orders as a non-commissioned officer of his grade and position.

And he is to observe and follow such orders and directions, from time to time, as he shall receive from His Excellency, The Governor of the State of New York, from me or from some other superior officer set over him, according to the laws, and rules and regulations made and adopted for the organization, discipline and conduct of the Division of State Police, for which this is his sufficient warrant.

Given *under my hand and the Seal of the Division of State Police at the Capitol in the* City of Albany, N. Y., this fifteenth *day of* June _____, *in the year of our Lord, one thousand nine hundred and* thirty _____

ATTEST

Captain, Commanding Troop "A"

Batavia, N. Y.

(SEAL)

By order of
Major John A. Warner, Superintendent.

Deputy Superintendent

CHAPTER 67

HAROLD L. KEMP

CHAPTER SIXTY-SEVEN
HAROLD L. KEMP

1924 TO 1951

Harold L. Kemp was born at Andover, New York in 1895 where he attended school. His first employment was in the Andover Silk Mill. He served in World War I and received the Purple Heart for gas wounds suffered while serving with the 305th Infantry, 77th Division at Chateau Thierry, France. He married the former Marian A. Murphy of Depew, N.Y.

He joined the NYS Police on July 1, 1924 and was assigned at Clarence, Randolph, Newfane, Knowlesville and Batavia. He attended the State Police Academy during February 1925. In 1927, he was promoted to Sergeant and assigned to Webster where he remained until 1932, when he was transferred to Pittsford. In 1937, he was appointed to the Bureau of Criminal Investigation (BCI) and assigned at Batavia. On September 1, 1943 he was promoted to Lieutenant and sent to Malone, N.Y. where he served until February 1947, when he returned to Batavia, as an Inspector. He retired on May 1, 1951 taking a security position with the Todd Company Inc., Rochester, N.Y.

Noted below are a few of his recollections, as a trooper.

On May 24, 1933, he captured 24 year old Ross Caccamise who six days earlier had shot and killed Edmund P. VandeWater in the Bulls Head post office. After eluding authorities, Caccamise robbed three people in a general store at Lakeside, Wayne County and fled into a wooded area. A posse soon surrounded him, but was held at bay by gunfire. Kemp disregarding the gunfire entered the woods taking Caccamise into custody. He was convicted of the murder and on June 14, 1934, and was executed in Sing Sing Prison's electric chair.

Kemp was credited with uncovering a crime in a case that had earlier been written off, as an accident. On September 3, 1936, Parole Officer Irving Green was returning two youths captured in Ohio to a detention center at Industry, N.Y. While traveling along, they were involved in an accident near Scottsville, N.Y. that resulted in Green being killed. Kemp didn't feel things fell into place properly so continued the investigation. Under intense questioning, both youths admitted to plotting an escape. They had hit Green over the head with the heel of a shoe prior to the car going out of control. Both were indicted on a 1st Degree Murder charge.

He was instrumental in solving a series of Rochester area burglaries that occurred during 1935. On one occasion, stolen property included a truckload of eggs, several turkeys and $5,000.00 in bonds stolen from the home of Stanley Brodie. Arrested was a Rochester, N.Y. dentist, Aloysius M. Smeja, his son Eugene A. Smeja and Clark Leonard. All were convicted of Burglary, a felony. The dentist was given a suspended sentence. His son was sentenced to a term of one to five-years in prison and Leonard a sentenced to a five-year prison term.

Another investigation led to the arrest of John H. Pepper, the Lindley Town Supervisor, Steuben County, N.Y. indicted on 322 counts of Forgery and Larceny for misappropriating $20,000.00 of town funds.

On March 20, 1939, Kemp's investigation led to the arrest of George & John Trout, Horseheads, N.Y. brothers who admitted to 87 burglaries in the Southern Tier area. Both were convicted after trial and sentenced to terms at Attica Prison.

Kemp described his career with the state police as "reasonably pleasant work". You always run up against the idea that nobody likes a policeman and it's your job to keep them from doing wrong".

Harold L. Kemp died at age 99 on February 10, 1995.

CHAPTER SIXTY-EIGHT
FRANK A. LACHNICHT

1929 TO 1952

Frank A. Lachnicht was born in Batavia, New York on September 1, 1903 where he attended public school. He served two years in the US Navy being awarded two medals for heroism, the Navy Expeditionary Force Medal and Yangtze Medal. He played a heroic role in fighting a 16-hour fire on a Chinese steamer in Foochow Harbor in 1927 and was part of a force that traveled inland to rescue a Catholic Mission threatened by radical Chinese Army elements. In June 1942, he enlisted in the Navy again as a Chief Petty Officer, and during the North African Invasion, his ship was sunk. His exploits, as a Navy diver were legendary.

He enlisted in the State Police on September 16, 1929, always assigned to Western New York, primarily the Batavia area. He retired on disability on February 1, 1952. He suffered critical injuries when crushed between a row of trees and an automobile on the Dublin Road, Bergen, New York on August 14, 1949. While conducting a plain clothes investigation, he jumped on the running board of a car he was attempting to stop. The driver intentionally drove into the trees knocking him off.

The Batavia Daily News in an editorial tribute said, " He was the type of individual who was always selected for the most difficult assignments in law enforcement, welcomed the opportunity and was equal to the challenge." His colleagues were quick to acknowledge that, when confronted with hazardous details, they were always comforted and enheartened, when Frank Lachnicht was along.

He died on November 3, 1967 at age 64 years at his home.

He had two sons, Frank who retired from the Batavia Police Department and George who retired from the New York State Police.

CHAPTER SIXTY-NINE
TRIXIE LEMAY – THE GENTLE GIANT

Richard F. Lemay was born at Troy, N.Y. in 1902.

Trixie, as he was affectionately known, was in the Regular Army from 1918 until 1921 stationed at Baltimore, Maryland. From 1921 to 1923, he conducted Lemays Novelty Orchestra in Troy, N.Y. He entered the state police in 1923 having the reputation as, the biggest man in the state police weighing in at 300 pounds on his 6'1" frame. He was a piano player and songster and was always available for a short or long tune. He had a reputation for stopping and chatting with everyone he came in contact with and his friendly smile and demeanor won many friends. One man said that he wouldn't trade him in for two 140-pound troopers, as they don't make them better than Trixie.

During the time of the Linden Murders, Trixie was assigned to the area to provide protection and calm to a terrified community. Roads being unpaved at the time, Trixie would constantly wear out tires on his motorcycle returning weekly to Batavia for a replacement and a bath, as tubs were generally to small to hold him.

Trixie retired in 1947, residing at Stafford, N.Y. where he was elected a Justice of the Peace. He died on April 2, 1956 at age of 55.

CHAPTER SEVENTY
TECHNICAL SERGEANT JOHN M. LONG

A COLLECTION OF MEMORIES 1929 TO 1969

Sergeant John M. Long, Troop designation # H20 was the longest continuous serviced New York State Trooper in Troop "A" serving from July 1929 to December 1969.

He was born at Buffalo, New York on August 22, 1903 where he attended public school. He was an excellent baseball player playing for a muny league team known as the Apaches, as a shortstop. He then played with the Rich Ice Cream team, now Rich Products and the Buffalo Harold's. He later played semi pro ball with the Easter Brands. He was also a member of the 121st Cavalry Regiment of the New York State National Guard.

Sergeant Long was acquainted with a former trooper named Stanley Maciewski who talked him into taking the examination for trooper. It took almost two years after passing the test, but he was sworn in as a State Trooper on July 21, 1929. The salary at the time was $900.00 compared to $13050.00 at the time of his retirement.

The following are some of Sergeant. Longs recollections:

In the summer of 1929, Long worked with Senior Trooper Cliff Lee assigned at Savonna, N.Y., Steuben County. In the winter 1929, he was stationed with Trooper Oscar Lazeroff at Fillmore, N.Y., Allegany County.

On December 11, 1929, Long and Oscar Lazeroff were ordered to return to Batavia, N.Y. and from there would be going to Auburn Prison, where inmates were rioting. They traveled by horse from Fillmore to Warsaw, N.Y. where they stayed overnight. During the night, there was a sleet storm, so the next morning, they located a blacksmith and had cork put on the horses shoes. They started out for Batavia walking every bit of the way through the slush. Late in the afternoon, it started to freeze up with icicles forming on their coon fur hats. A few passing cars would splash them adding to their misery. When they finally arrived at Batavia, the slickers they wore were frozen stiff and had to be cracked to get them off. Their feet were soaked with water and slush oozing between the toes. Sergeant Eddie Rimmer saw them coming and had two other troopers tend to their horses while they thawed out. The next day, they were sent to Auburn Prison where they were assigned until early spring 1930. Duty consisted of walking the prison wall for six hours at a time while the burned portion of the prison was rebuilt. The troopers were quartered at the local armory.

From 1930 until July 1, 1936, he worked patrol by horse, car and motorcycle while assigned at the Bath, Castile, Pittsford, East Avon, Gaines, Lewiston, Clarence, Friendship, Alden, Athol Springs and the Randolph stations.

Long recalled that while working horse patrol at Fillmore, the troopers loved to stop at a little country hotel in Caneadea called the Kelly House. Two sisters ran it, the Kelly's, who put out the most delicious meals. They would give you a steak dinner with all the trimmings at a cost of 50 cents a meal.

While assigned to Athol Springs, he and Trooper John Rowe worked with and became good friends with Angola Town Constable Sam Catalano. Sam had a car so the three of them would patrol in Sam's car. Sam later became founder and owner of the Evans Builders Supply Company on Lake Shore Road at Evans Center, N.Y.

While working at Clarence, he recalled that troopers rented rooms from Walter Shutt, a Clarence Florist and Justice of the Peace. Another location was a motel owned by Al Hughes where troopers would stay and make recommendations to travelers looking for a decent place to rest.

Civilian staff at Batavia were Larry Callan, the long time Troop "A" Chef who would put out some of the most delicious meals that you ever tasted. Beatrice O'Grady, born in Ireland whose many duties were helping Larry and keeping the barracks in presentable order, ably assisted him. (Her son, Jerome joined the State Police in 1962 and went on to be a Deputy Superintendent)

In 1933, Long was assigned at Pittsford, N.Y. with the local fire station as the office and quarters. The accommodations were outstanding and he became friends with two full time fireman, Philly Criss and Fireman Helmer. Sergeant Harold Kemp was in charge while there.

Because of their horse skills, John Long riding "Lizzie" and Leo Mellody riding "Ashland" were selected to compete in the pair's class at the state fair. The competition was excellent and riding the two bay horses, won first place and the blue ribbon. They also competed in the four-horse competition along with Corporal Earl Wilkinson and Trooper Frank Easton and to their pleasure, won the event, which consisted of walk, trot, canter and gallop.

Every fall, the troopers were invited to run a flat race at the annual Geneseo Horse Show. Trooper Long rode a horse named "Tommy Tucker" and Earl Wilkinson rode "Amy". Both were beautiful long legged bay horses that were full of pep. Amy had won several races at Geneseo in previous years and was the favorite. When starter Chandler Wells of Buffalo, N.Y. called the race, Tommy Tucker left like a shot and continued to lead into the home stretch. Amy known as a closer was coming on fast and near the finish line, caught up to Tommy Tucker. Giving a last burst of energy, Tommy Tucker surged ahead winning by a head. Trooper Long was presented with a silver plated plate donated by Mary Abigail Chiverick of Buffalo, N.Y.

CHAPTER SEVENTY-ONE
EDWARD A. RIMMER

Edward A. Rimmer, a native of Batavia, N.Y. was born April 9, 1881 where he attended public school. In 1898, he enlisted in the US Army Cavalry at Ft. Riley, Kansas. He served during the Spanish American War, the Philippine Insurrection and the Boxer Rebellion in China. While stationed at Luzon in the Philippines, he was the island rifle champion. After discharge from the military, he married Catherine Moran (born in Ireland) and raised three sons; Edward J., George M. and William A. Rimmer. Ed enlisted in the New York State Troopers on August 1, 1918 serving until his retirement in 1935. He was known throughout the troop, as the stable sergeant. His son William enlisted in the state police in 1938 serving with distinction until 1962. In the early days, troopers were called on for assistance in every imaginable circumstance. Some of those that Ed was involved are noted below.

The first mention of Ed Rimmer in the Batavia Daily News was for the recovery of a stolen Ford car on January 29, 1919. Found in the car were several new tires and tubes, horse-blankets, hammers, jimmies, jacks and other yegg (burglar) tools.

In July 1919, he and sergeant Ed Miller disarmed an insane person who had physically thrown his family from the house and threatened to kill the troopers. While Miller conversed with the man, Rimmer entered through a rear door and disarmed him. He was committed to an asylum.

On May 24, 1920, Trooper Rimmer and Corporal Gerald Sullivan found a working still in Corfu, N.Y. The still was destroyed and whiskey along with the defendant turned over to federal authorities for prosecution.

In 1923, Corporal Rimmer won the title of Troop "A" champion marksman beating out twenty-five other troopers and officers with a score of 438 out of a possible 500. The competition was held annually on Thanksgiving Day at the trooper's rifle range in the gravel pit located on the Charles Bolt farm across from the barracks. First prize of $45.00 went to Rimmer, second place to Oscar White and third place to Corporal Homer Harrison.

On July 14, 1924, Sergeant Rimmer led a squad of troopers who performed before the Genesee County Gentlemen's Driving Club at Exposition Park. The horsemen did fancy and roman riding as well as pyramid riding and other feats of skill.

In September 1930, Sergeant Edward Rimmer was selected as Marshall of the parade of Catholic men of Genesee, Wyoming and Orleans Counties. Every church was represented and it made a memorable day for those that watched the Sunday afternoon affair down Batavia's Main Street.

Other exploits will be found throughout this book. He entered disability retirement in 1935. He resided at 154 Ross Street, Batavia, N.Y. He died on June 2, 1964 at age 83 and is buried in St. Joseph's Cemetery.

CHAPTER SEVENTY-TWO
GEORGE S. WOOD

George S. Wood was born at Burt, N.Y. on July 1, 1904 and was a 1925 graduate of Genesee Wesleyan Seminary at Lima, N.Y. Enlisting in the State Police on August 16, 1929, he was promoted to Corporal on July 1,1936, the new BCI unit in 1937 and Sergeant on February 16, 1947. On May 4, 1961, George was elevated to Senior Investigator. He concluded a 40-year career on December 30, 1969. He died on August 10, 1977 at age 73. George Wood resided at 30 Washington Street, Batavia, N.Y. with his wife, the former Rowena Kendall. They had four children, Charles W., Denniston K., George E. (also a trooper) and Rowena Klinge.

The following are some of his humorous recollections:

While searching for an illegal still during prohibition, he observed a rabbit that wasn't acting normally. It would move slowly in a crooked line and fall over, get up and fall over. He followed the rabbit, which led him to mash for the still that the rabbit had been eating. The rabbit was drunk.

He arrested a man for being intoxicated and when he asked for the man's name, he would say what sounded like it's all right. Trooper Wood replied by saying, I know it's all right, but what is your name. It turned out the man's name was Sol Wright.

At the end of a jury trial at which he testified, Trooper Wood was present, when the jury foreman said that a verdict had been reached. The foreman, of Italian decent said, judge, he a good fella, lawyer, he a good fella, trooper, he a good fella too. We find the defendant not guilty, if he promise not to do it again.

While away from home and renting a room in a private home, the landlady owned a parrot that was kept in a cage near the dining table. The trooper's hated the parrot, because it would shake feathers and birdseed on their meal plates. The troopers didn't get back from patrol until after midnight each night. The landlady was always asleep so the troopers would lift the parrot's cover and whisper, "you're a son of a bitch." The parrot was soon saying it all the time. The landlady was embarrassed and apologetic and couldn't imagine where the bird had learned such language.

During a raid on a speakeasy, it was found that the owner was spiking the drinks with lye. Trooper Wood asked if his customers didn't complain about a burning in their throats. In a gravely voice, he replied no, they're steel workers and like it that way.

While having difficulty subduing a man, Trooper Wood's partner, Pete Beck pulled his gun and told the man he would shoot him in the foot, if he continued to resist. The man responded in a shaky voice that he was pointing the pistol at his head. The trooper said, yes I know, I have a very poor aim.

When he got married, George wanted to elope, as he was apprehensive about what tricks his fellow troopers might pull. He had good reason. When Frank Easton was to be married, he was handcuffed to his bunk bed at the Barracks almost missing the wedding. When John Long was married, they raided a cockfight and brought the birds back to the barracks. They were released in Long's bed while he was asleep.

BOOK X – INJURED & KILLED

CHAPTER SEVENTY-THREE
INJURY TO WESTERN NEW YORK

TROOPERS WHILE ON DUTY

05/31/19 - Patrick J. Haggerty
Hunters for an escaped negro convict near Watkins, New York yesterday mistook Trooper Patrick J. Haggerty for the man they were looking for and shot him in the right leg with a .32 calibre revolver. He was taken to St. Jerome's Hospital, Batavia, New York where the bullet was removed. The bullet had passed through the thigh bone into the stomach and upward. Haggerty remained at the hospital for several days recovering from the wound.

06/05/19 - Samuel Griffin
Trooper Samuel Griffin suffered multiple fractures of the jawbone and severe bruises the result of a motorcycle accident. He was speeding to escape a coming thunderstorm, when he hit the curb and flew onto the lawn of the First Baptist Church, East Main Street, Batavia, New York. He was trying to avoid a collision with a car driven by J. F. Post of Pearl Street road that was turning into the church driveway. Frank Thomas, a witness summoned a passing motorist who took Griffin to St. Jerome's hospital where he was treated and admitted.

1920 and 01/14/31 - Thomas L. Corbett
Trooper Thomas L. Corbett suffered a hip injury and partial loss of use of one hand when he struck a bridge rail with his motorcycle while escorting Governor Alfred E. Smith on the Lewiston – Youngstown Highway.

On 01/14/31, Corbett received a broken back and pelvis when involved in an accident while a passenger in a car driven by Trooper William Silage near Caledonia, N.Y. As a result, he was placed on disability retirement. He remained hospitalized until his death two years later.

09/04/22 - Leslie Benway
While operating a motorcycle, Corporal Leslie Benway suffered two fractures of the left leg and bruises while sidecar passenger Trooper Raymond Clark received severe bruises when thrown from the motorcycle after crashing into the rear of a touring car near Temperance Hill. Their attention had been diverted to a previous accident and failed to notice the touring car in front of them. Benway was admitted to the Batavia Hospital.

08/24/22 - James R. Burke
Trooper James R.Burke was injured when his motorcycle was sideswiped at Pembroke, N.Y. by a car driven by Frank Halper of Buffalo, N.Y. Burke was attempting to pull Halper over for driving in a reckless manner when he was hit. As Burke pulled alongside, Halper turned sharply into the motorcycle causing heavy damage and rendering Burke unconscious. Burke was taken to St. Jerome's Hospital for treatment. Halper was arrested and taken before Pembroke Justice Mallory. He pled guilty to Reckless Driving. He was fined $5.00, given a 60 day suspended sentence and ordered to pay for damages to the motorcycle.

08/16/20 - John Curley /John Howard
Troopers John Howard and John Curley escaped serious injury when their motorcycle and sidecar collided with a horse owned by George Tollner of Tonawanda, N.Y. The cycle rolled over three times

tossing the troopers more than twenty feet in the air. Howard was knocked unconscious and received several severe cuts and bruises. Both returned to duty the next morning.

07/26/24 - C.L. Tryon/Carl L. Rasmussen

While escorting an ambulance through Leroy, N.Y., Troopers Tryon and Rasmussen were thrown from their motorcycle as they avoided striking children crossing in front of them. Tryon suffered severe finger cuts down to the bone and Rasmussen received minor cuts and bruises. They got back on the motorcycle and continued the hospital escort to Batavia, N.Y.

07/09/25 - Leon Balling

Trooper Leon M. Balling was seriously burned when the gasoline tank of his motorcycle exploded at a roadside filling station between Hamburg and Collins, N.Y. He was admitted to Our Lady of Victory Hospital, Lackawanna, N.Y. where he was listed in serious condition. Balling survived the injuries, however they required him to enter disability retirement.

05/28/26 - Harold J. DeBrine

Trooper Harold J. DeBrine, a passenger in a ford automobile driven by Corporal James C. Wolcott was injured in an automobile accident near Siver Creek, N.Y. Wolcott was unable to stop and struck a car driven by Joseph Correado who had driven his automobile across the road directly in front of them. Both vehicles were heavily damaged. DeBrine suffered a double fracture of the pelvis, cuts and bruises and was admitted to Brooks Memorial Hospital, Dunkirk, N.Y. No one else was seriously injured. On 11/13/26, DeBrine was awarded $4000.00 in civil damages by a Supreme Court Jury in Mayville, N.Y.

08/22/27 - Walter Croadsdale

Lieutenant Walter Croadsdale, age 34 was fatally injured near Lafayette, N.Y., when his automobile struck a highway road roller. He succumbed to his injuries at Crouse-Irving Hospital, Syracuse, N.Y. where he had been transported. Croadsdale was born and raised at Oswego, N.Y. enlisting in the State Police in 7/2/1917 after a tour in the US Army. It was reported that the road roller owned by the contracting company of J.L. Dugan of Newburgh, N.Y., was parked on the highway without warning lights or lanterns. He was an original Campman.

07/09/28 - Harry Adams

Corporal Harry Adams was slightly injured and his companion, Trooper Robert F. Damon suffered broken ribs and a dislocated collarbone when the steering mechanism failed sending their speeding motorcycle into a tree. The accident happened at Portland, N.Y. while responding to an accident in Westfield, N.Y. Damon was admitted to the Dunkirk, N.Y. hospital where he remained for several days.

03/30/29 - Fred N. Sponable

Sergeant Fred N. Sponable, age 43 was the target of five shots with one striking him in the leg. He drove himself to Newark, N.Y. hospital for treatment. While driving along the Newark-Palmyra Road, Sponable observed a touring car parked without lights. As he approached, he observed a male and female in the car. The male occupant shouted something and started shooting. Two shots went wild, one struck the troopers holster, one went through his coat and one struck him in the leg. The perpetrator then fled.

On July 8, 1929, Sponable suffered serious back injuries, when he jumped from his car after the lights went out and he was headed for a ditch. He was confined to Geneva General Hospital.

1930 - Edward Rimmer

Sergeant Edward Rimmer was seriously injured, when he was crushed in a stall by a horse.

06/16/30 - Lyman D. Fortner
Trooper Lyman D. Fortner, 26 Law Street, Batavia, N.Y., accidently shot himself between the first and second fingers of the left hand, when a dog he was about to destroy jumped, jarring his hand discharging the weapon. Fortner and Trooper John Cole were at the George Yunker farm where the dog had killed several sheep, when the accident occurred.

09/07/34 - William S. McNaughton
Trooper Willam S. McNaughton suffered a skull fracture when his motorcycle crashed on the East Aurora- Springbrook road. He was unconscious for several days at Mercy Hospital, Buffalo, N.Y. A resident of Albion, N.Y., he never returned to duty going on disability retirement.

04/21/35 – Richard "Trixie" Lemay
Trooper Richard Lemay had complained of a sore back since being struck with a missle during milk strike duty a year earlier. X-ray examination revealed a fracture of the coccyx, a curved bone at the end of the spinal column. Surgery was performed.

07/29/35 - Anthony F. Laurence
Trooper Anthony F. Laurence, age 28, brother of Trooper Roman Laurence was killed, when his motorcycle struck a tree on the Bolton Road north of Lake George. He was the tallest member of the Troop standing 6'6" tall.

09/30/37 - W.D.Easton
Trooper W. D. Easton, age 23 suffered a broken finger, cuts and bruises, when he was thrown from his motorcycle in a collision with an automobile in Caledonia, N.Y. The car was backing onto the roadway attempting to make a U turn at the time.

/00/37 – Judson Peck
Trooper Judson Peck, age 32, Churchville outpost, was admitted to Rochester General Hospital with a possible skull fracture, a broken nose and left shoulder injury. He was thrown from his motorcycle when it hit a rut in the Gough Road throwing him from the cycle.

4/20/40 - Harry DeHollander
Sergeant Harry DeHollander, age 41, 32 Montclair Avenue, Batavia, N.Y. suffered a fractured skull when he was thrown form his automobile after running off the road and striking a hydrant. He was taken to Bethesda Hospital, Hornell, N.Y. where he was admitted.

10/26/41 – Laurence D. MacCall
Laurence D. McCall, age 27, Dalton, N.Y. suffered a fractured pelvis, fractured skull, multiple body bruises and lacerations after striking an automobile with his motorcycle. He was patrolling Route 31 just east of Medina, N.Y., when a car driven by Arthur House, age 61, Medina, N.Y. turned left in front of him. McCall hit the car head-on and was thrown from the motorcycle. House was charged with Reckless Driving. McCall recovered from his injuries returning to duty.

CHAPTER SEVENTY-FOUR
WESTERN NEW YORK TROOPERS

KILLED IN THE LINE OF DUTY

James B. Losco – Enlisted 16 March 1924 – Died 7 July 1925 in a motorcycle accident while returning to his barracks. He was passing an oil truck in a curve on Clinton Street, Gardenville, N.Y., when a tire blew out on his motorcycle. He was unable to gain control   striking an approaching bus head-on. At age 23, he was the first trooper in Troop "A" to lose his life. Born and raised in New York City, he served in the US Army in France during World War I. He was renowned as a great pistol marksman having won numerous national awards.

Robert Roy – Enlisted 15 October 1926 – Died on September 8,1927 from shotgun wounds to the head while serving a warrant on Wilmont Leroy Wagner at Caneadea, N.Y. He and Trooper Arnold Rasmussen had allowed Wagner to change his clothes while out of their sight. Prior to entering the State Police, Trooper Roy had been a member of the Royal Canadian Mounted Police and was an accomplished author writing under the name "Rob Roy".

Arnold T. Rasmussen – Enlisted 16 July 1927 – Died on September 8, 1927 while serving a warrant on Wilmont Leroy Wagner at Caneadea, N.Y. from shotgun wounds to the head. He was in recruit training and had not yet attended the State Police School. He was 23 years old.

Homer J. Harrison – Enlisted 16 May 1921 – Died on June 19, 1933 when he drowned in Silver Lake, Castile, N.Y. He was fishing with his two sons and Trooper Harold Beach when the boat capsized. His body was recovered an hour later. He was 41 years old. Sergeant Harrison had been commander of the Castile Outpost since 1925. He was a veteran of World War I serving in France, as a canoneer.

Jerome B. Nugent – Enlisted 1 May 1929 – Died on 14 October 1933 of a fractured skull, when he was thrown from his motorcycle after striking a large dog on the Forestville - Sheridan Road near Sheridan, N.Y. He was taken to Brooke Memorial Hospital, Dunkirk, N.Y., but died without gaining consciousness. He was age 25 and newly married.

Thomas L. Corbett – Enlisted 16 Jul 1921 – Died 14 October 1933 the result of injuries received from an on-duty auto accident. On January 14, 1931, Corbett was a passenger in a state police car driven by Trooper William Silage that ran off the road overturning. Corbett suffered a broken back and crushed pelvis. He was placed on disability retirement on 01 August 1931.

Earl R. Wilkinson – Enlisted 1 June 1929 – Died on May 24, 1942 while on active duty in a military airplane crash near Houlton, Maine. He was the son in law of long time Peace Justice E. Harry Miller of East Pembroke, N.Y.

Harry Adams – Enlisted 16 August 1923 – Died on September 1, 1951 after being struck by an auto while investigating an accident on the Sawyer Road, Carlton, Orleans County, N.Y. He was 55 years old and served as the Albion Station Commander.

James B. Conrad – Enlisted 18 June 1962 – Died instantly on November 11, 1966 after striking a tractor trailer that had made a left hand turn into his path near Bath, N.Y. Conrad was 30 years old and was survived by several children.

Richard L. Weltz – Enlisted 18 June 1964 – Died on March 17, 1970 when he apparently fell asleep driving off the road striking a tree and telephone pole on Route 219 near Hamburg, N.Y. He was returning from a pistol match at the time. He was an outstanding marksman having won many national and international awards. He was 30 years old.

Robert Van Hall – Enlisted – Died on December 5, 1980 when shot during a drug arrest at Corning, N.Y. He along with Investigator William Gorenflo were conducting an undercover investigation, when they stopped and confronted two brothers who immediately opened fire. Van Hall died at the scene. The assailants were captured a short time later.

Thomas L. Buck – Enlisted 6 May 1968 – Died on March 19,1981 after contracting hepatitis during an arrest at Hanover, N.Y. He was securing a hypodermic needle as evidence, when he punctured his finger. In early 1972, he was diagnosed with infectious hepatitis. Continued episodes of liver dysfunction resulted in his entering into disability retirement on August 1, 1979. He died at age 36 on March 19, 1981

Gary E. Kubasiak – Enlisted 6 September 1973 – Died on August 30, 1982 from shotgun wounds suffered while investigating a domestic complaint at Dayton, N.Y. He and Trooper Timothy Howard responded to the scene of a domestic dispute where there was a history of mental health problems. Kubasiak, also the Troop A canine handler knowing the subject entered the residence with his dog Donovan and without warning, was shot fatally in the chest.

Calvin P. Kurdys – Enlisted 29 June 1970 – Died on September 15, 1987 when struck by a speeding car while on radar duty on the NYS Thruway at Pembroke, N.Y. He was the pick-up man at a radar site, when radar detected an automobile traveling at 100 mile per hour. Trooper Kurdys stepped to the edge of the highway in an effort to stop the vehicle, when it lost control striking him killing him instantly. As a result, the radar operations as they were conducted at the time were permanently terminated.

BOOK XI – MISCELLANEOUS

CHAPTER SEVENTY-FIVE
THE CONSTABULARY

The following metrical praise of the State Troopers came from the pen and heart of Miss Minna Irving after she had been obliged several times to turn to the men of Troop K for legal aid. It appeared some months ago in "The New York Sun" from which it is reprinted.

Along the country road he rides
In fair or stormy weather,
The splendid steed that he bestrides
And he are pals together,
A criminal may run away
With darkness to abet him,
The uniformed in grey
Is sure to go and get him.

The farm and hamlets far and near,
In every direction,
And cabins in the outlands dread,
Are under his protection,
No more I hesitate to stray,
Along the woodland's border,
For he patrols it every day;
And he is law and order.

As brave and gallant as a knight,
Of old romances he passes,
His horse's hoofs make music light,
Upon the wayside grasses,
Clear hazel are his fearless eyes,
Twin pools of love and laughter,
I watch him o'er the distant rise
And oh! My heart goes after.

(August 1920 issue of State Trooper Magazine)

CHAPTER SEVENTY-SIX
TROOPERS SONG
THE PURPLE AND THE GREY

Although there are many colors
That prove our loyal ties
And sent us forth to struggle
With faith that never dies

There's a blend that's most familiar
And cheers us on our way
It's a badge that stands for justice
It's the purple and the grey

As the grey of dawn betokens
The line twixt day and night
And black and white are symbols
That stand for wrong and right

So the state police advances
To cast dark wrong away
And the sign that stands for triumph
Is the neutral garb of grey

When the deepening shadows lengthen
O'er the hilltops in the west
And bring the purple twilight
As a soothing balm of rest

A band of brave grey riders
Protect and guard the way
And reflect the shades of evening
In the purple and the grey.

Written by Eleanor Louise Porter for the
New York State Police in about 1927.

CHAPTER SEVENTY-SEVEN
WHILE WE ARE RIDING TO DUTY

Written by Eleanor Louise Porter and sung to the
tune of Marching Through Georgia.

Bring the good old fashioned mount,
Or start the motor car,
Swing into the highways broad,

To meet the call afar,
Have a purpose strong and sure,
That nothing else can mar,
While we are riding to duty!

Chorus
Hoorah! Hoorah! The purple and the grey
Hoorah! Hoorah! We meet the cares of day,

When the summons calls us, we are eager to obey,
While we are riding to duty!
Chandler's sturdy, grey-clad boys,
Will ever meet the test, with his high and lofty aims,
We'll always do the best,
It matters not where paths may lead,
Or what the stern behest,
While we are riding to duty!

(April 1921 issue of A Journal of Law and Order)

CHAPTER SEVENTY-EIGHT
STATE POLICE STATIONS THAT
EXISTED AT VARIOUS LOCATIONS

THROUGHOUT TROOP "A" TAKEN FROM AN OLD BLOTTER FOUND DURING RE-MODELING.

STATION	DATE OPENED	DATE CLOSED
ALBION	24 OCT 1946	PRESENT
ALDEN	03 JUN 1933	30 OCT 1942
ALLEGANY	05 MAR 1931	07 APR 1979
ALEXANDER	09 AUG 1953	31 JAN 1963
ANGOLA	06 MAR 1931	01 SEP 1949
ATHOL SPRINGS	01 FEB 1930	31 DEC 1971
AVON	01 MAR 1931	20 DEC 1965
BATAVIA	22 NOV 1917	PRESENT
BATH	14 FEB 1964	SEP 67(TROOP E)
BELFAST	11 AUG 1953	02 JUN 1963
BEMUS POINT	06 MAR 1931	03 OCT 1941
BERGEN	06 NOV 1953	31 JAN 1963
BLAKELY CORNERS	26 MAR 1942	26 DEC 1953

BOLIVAR	07 MAR 1931	21 OCT 1939
BROCKTON	07 MAR 1931	04 NOV 1941
CANISTEO	01 MAR 1931	07 JUL 1943
CASTILE	6 MAR 1931	13 MAR 1968
CHAUTAUQUA	23 JUN 1931	27 AUG 1961
CHURCHVILLE	9 MAR 1931	30 MAR 1944
CLARENCE	7 MAR 1931	PRESENT
CLARKSON	1 AUG 1946	SEP 1967(TROOP E)
CLYMER	6 JUN 1976	20 JAN 1982
COHOCTON	27 JUL 1935	10 JAN 1940
DANSVILLE	1 JAN 1933	4 SEP 1934
DARIEN	31 MAR 1947	8 AUG 1953
EAST AURORA	27 DEC 1953	31 DEC 1971
EVANS CENTER	18 OCT 1932	5 SEP 1942
FALCONER	12 NOV 1959	PRESENT
FILLMORE	11 MAR 1973	PRESENT
FRANKLINVILLE	5 MAR 1931	PRESENT
FREDONIA	1 APR 1964	PRESENT
FRIENDSHIP	30 DEC 1930	17 JUL 1945
GAINES	1 JAN 1932	23 OCT 1946
GRAND ISLAND	30 SEP 1954	30 APR 1963
GROVELAND	8 AUG 1931	23 NOV 1932
HENRIETTA	31 MAR 1944	SEP 1967(TROOP E)
JOHNSON CENTER	29 JUL 1931	13 NOV 1932
LEWISTON	22 MAY 1933	PRESENT
LIMA	7 JUL 1930	31 DEC 1932
LIMESTONE	7 JUL 1931	1 SEP 1934
MARTINVILLE	18 APR 1931	15 AUG 1944
MEDINA	26 JAN 1935	1 MAY 1937
MT.MORRIS	23 JUN 1935	12 JAN 1944
NEWFANE	8 MAR 1931	16 NOV 1953
NIAGARA FALLS	31 MAR 1951	30 SEP 1952
NORTH HORNELL	12 JAN 1944	25 JUN 1962
NORTH TONAWANDA	16 AUG 1944	9 NOV 1948
OLEAN	20 AUG 1919	5 MAR 1931
ORCHARD PARK	1 JAN 1972	19 JUN 1976
PAINTED POST	27 APR 1931	SEP 1967(TROOP E)
PITTSFORD	16 MAR 1931	31 MAR 1944
RANDOLPH	28 MAR 1933	11 NOV 1959
RANSOMVILLE	20 JUL 1931	16 AUG 1932
SHERIDAN	19 JUL 1931	27 AUG 1943
SHONOGO	10 MAY 1932	29 JUN 1932
SILVER CREEK	19 OCT 1961	31 MAR 1964
SPENCERPORT	8 MAR 1931	15 SEP 1936
SPRINGBROOK	12 MAR 1931	7 NOV 1940
VARYSBURG	7 MAR 1931	8 OCT 1941
WARSAW	13 MAR 1968	PRESENT
WAYLAND	11 JAN 1940	15 JUN 1966

WEBSTER   2 JUN 1933   14 MAY 1963
WELLSVILLE   18 JUL 1945   PRESENT
WESTFIELD   12 AUG 1936   1 APR 1964
WEST HENRIETTA   8 MAR 1936   PRESENT
BUFFALO STRIKES   21 JUL 1922
ROCHESTER RIOTS (ARMORY) 25 JUL 1964 TO 8 AUG 1964
     (PUBLIC SAFETY BLDG)   29 JUL 1964 TO 3 AUG 1964

CHAPTER SEVENTY-NINE
TROOP "A" FIRST SERGEANTS

09/01/1917 - 12/31/1917	James F. Skiff - Promoted to Lieutenant
1/01/1918 - 09/15/1919	Edward B. Miller – Resigned for family business
9/15/1919 - 03/31/1920	Walter Croadsdale – Promoted to Lieutenant
04/01/1920 - 05/31/1921	John M. Keeley – Promoted to Lieutenant
06/01/1921 - 02/16/1924	William F. George – Promoted to Lieutenant.
02/17/1924	Joseph E. Holcomb
1924 - 09/01/1925	Oscar White – resigned, went with US Border Patrol
1925	Richard L. Gibbons (One month only- preferred and returned to road duty)
10/01/1925 -09/01/1937	Joseph W. Brandstetter (Promoted to newly formed position of Traffic Sergeant)
1937 – 1953	Charles E. Cobb (Acting F/Sgt-promoted to Sgt. in 1939 when Sgt. Michael Serve retired) 1953 To
1953 - 0/31/1961	Charles Z. Mc Donald
12/14/1961 - 07/20/1966	Howard D. Smith
07/21/1966 - 01/04/1968	Anthony Malovich
01/05/1968 - 07/27/1978	Vernon J. Clayson
08/01/1978 - 10/26/1988	Thomas C. Smith
11/26/1988 - 06/26/1996	Edward H. Kusmierczyk
1996 – 2003	William F. Urbanski
2003 To Pres	Frank Broderick

CHAPTER EIGHTY
1939 TROOP "A" MANPOWER
DISBURSEMENT

Troop Commander – Captain Winfield W. Robinson
Troop Clerk -   Sgt. Samuel Dunlop
First Sergeant - Sgt. Charles E. Cobb

Quartermaster -   Sgt. Leslie C. Benway
Night Desk Officer -   Sgt. Charles Z. Macdonald

The Eleven County Troop Area Was Divided Into Four Precincts:

Precinct # 1 -   Lt. Lawrence C. Nelson In Charge
Erie Co. – Wanakah   Sgt. Arthur L. Rich
Chautauqua Co.- Westfield   Sgt. Clifford H. Lee
Niagara Co. – Lewiston   Sgt. Herbert G. Southworth
Patrol Stations – Angola, Clarence, Springbrook, Alden, Westfield, Sheridan, Chautauqua & Newfane

Precinct # 2 -   Sgt. Charles E. Cobb In Charge
Genesee Co. – Batavia   Sgt. Charles E. Cobb
Orleans Co. - Gaines   Sgt. Harry Adams
Patrol Stations At Medina & Gaines.

Precinct # 3 –   Lt. Gerald D.Vaine In Charge
Livingston Co.   Avon   Sgt. John D. Krick
Monroe Co. – Pittsford   Sgt. William L. Ireland
Steuben Co. – Erwins   Sgt. Charles G. Burnett
Patrol Stations – Mt. Morris, Erwins, Canisteo, Cohocton, Pittsford, Webster, Spencerport, Churchville & Scottsville.

Precinct # 4 –   Lt. William J. George In Charge
Wyoming Co. – Castile   Sgt. Richard Gibbons
Allegany Co – Friendship   Sgt. Charles Stanton
Steuben Co. -   Tpr. John G. McDonald
Patrol Stations – Bolivar, Letchworth Park, Castile, Allegany, Randolph & Franklinville.

Bureau Of Criminal Investigation
Lt. Inspector Eugene F. Hoyt in Charge.
Sgt. Harry M. DeHollander – Second In Command
Investigators

Sgt. Harold L. Debrine	Sgt. Harold L. Kemp	Sgt. Edward J. Doody
Cpl. Albert S. Horton	Cpl. Paul J. Mellody	Cpl. Vernon R. Voight
Cpl. Earl R. Wilkinson	Cpl. George S. Wood	Cpl. Oscar Lazeroff
Cpl. Norman H. Lippert	Tpr. William J. Szymanski	Tpr. Michael L. Fort

Identification Experts - Tpr. Clarence J. Pasto & Tpr. Montagu Andrews.

CHAPTER EIGHTY-ONE
DEPARTMENT OF STATE POLICE
ARREST STATISTICS – 1918 TO 1942

YEAR	HIGHWAY LAW ARRESTS	PENAL LAW ARRESTS	PATROL HORSE MILES	PATROL AUTO CYCLE	NVESTIGATIONS WITHOUT ARREST
1918	1960	2311	333,039	433,239	4,836
1919	1527	2744	243,332	705,206	2,859
1920	7724	2928	242,647	721,022	28,265
1921	8473	4191	286,850	1,217,014	22,798
1922	5300	5497	247,589	1,590,983	18,109
1923	9077	5089	310,028	1,768,130	13,992

MOTOR
VEHICLE LAW (REPLACED HIGHWAY LAW)

1924	14,461	8462	235,044	2,547,297	14,962
1925	14,773	10,961	222,582	3,210,813	15,903
1926	10,999	11,680	228,275	3,587,696	16,088
1927	19,343	14,348	230,619	4,882,513	19,383
1928	20,649	12,467	208,564	5,161,702	45,500

VEHICLE &
TRAFFIC LAW (REPLACED MOTOR VEHICLE LAW)

1929	27,039	12,836	221,148	5,313,715	54,506
1930	37,986	16,861	171,888	6,458,430	80,082
1931	29,945	18,036	142,212	6,832,819	36,016
1932	30,272	16,533	83,052	8,268,130	30,378
1933	29,463	16,695	107,594	8,578,393	28,118
1934	34,469	15,990	74,637	8,383,472	29,274
1935	36,208	16,817	48,559	8,537,512	29,376
1936	31,229	18,835	29,424	8,858,658	30,151
1937	42,315	21,116	23,541	10,237,435	35,175
1938	41,300	18,586	30,941	10,279,314	35,980
1939	40,874	17,391	34,903	11,179,314	35,028
1940	42,248	21,806	39,522	12,620,138	39,843
1941	52,924	17,520	26,711	16,139,834	45,691
1942	34,743	12,726	22,894	14,705,684	28,325

(STATISTICS FROM THE NEW YORK STATE POLICE ANNUAL REPORTS.)

ODDS & ENDS

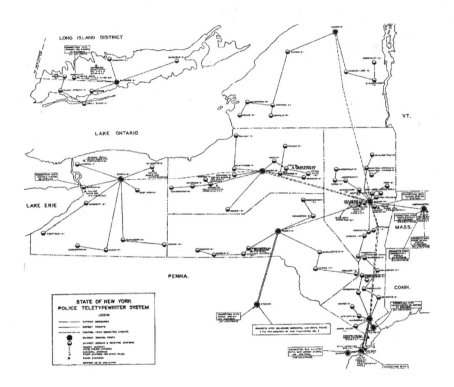

THE AMERICAN CITY

This detail of New York State Troopers was assigned to escort the Prince of Wales during his recent New York visit.

They Guarded the Prince of Wales

The best was none too good for the Prince of Wales. Hence, the special guard of four New York State Troopers and a Harley-Davidson Police Motorcycle.

Nor is the best too good for the 1891 cities and towns that use Harley-Davidsons for police service. This famous mount—on proved records of economy, durability and year-'round dependability—has become indispensable to the efficient, modern police department.

One Harley-Davidson does more to rid a community of speeding, reckless driving and crime than a dozen patrolmen. Speeders and crooks prefer towns that are less up-to-date—where there are no police motorcycles.

Be Sure to See the New "Stream-Line" HARLEY-DAVIDSON

27 improvements on the 1925 models. More speed—more power. Lower riding position. Yet the price is reduced! New "Stream-Line" model is the finest Harley-Davidson ever built.

Ask your dealer or write us for special literature on Police Motorcycles—*Free.*

HARLEY-DAVIDSON MOTOR CO.
DEPT. M   MILWAUKEE, WIS.

208

764   FILE 14   SP BATAVIA   MAY 18-34
TO   SP PRECINCTS, HAMBURG, LEWISTON, EAST AVON AND FRIENDSHIP

THIS MARRIAGE RACKET BUSINESS IN TROOP "A" IS STARTING UP AGAIN. A REQUEST HAS COME IN THIS MORNING FOR A TEN DAY LEAVE OF ABSENCE IN JUNE FOR THE FOOLISH PURPOSE OF GETTING MARRIED. ALL MEMBERS OF THE TROOP HAD A GOOD LONG VACATION THIS PAST WINTER AND EARLY THIS SPRING WITH FULL PAY AND THEY CERTAINLY HAD ALL THE TIME OFF THEY ARE ENTITLED TO. THIS IS GOING TO BE A VERY BUSY SUMMER, WITH LITTLE OFF DUTY LEAVES AND IT CERTAINLY IS A POOR TIME TO THINK ABOUT GETTING MARRIED. SUCH LEAVES ARE VERY UNFAIR TO OTHER MEMBERS OF THE TROOP, AS IT MEANS THAT SOMEBODY HAS TO PUT IN EXTRA HOURS TO MAKE UP FOR THE SIMPLE ONE WHO IS GOING THROUGH MATRIMONY. THE PROPER TIME FOR THESE WEDDINGS WILL BE WHEN THE ANNUAL VACATIONS COME ON NEXT NOVEMBER. ANYONE WHO INSISTS ON A LEAVE OF ABSENCE THIS SUMMER CAN EASY GET THE TIME OFF BY PRESENTING THEIR RESIGNATION, WHICH I WILL BE MOST HAPPY AND DELIGHTED TO APPROVE.

THIS ORDER TO BE PLACED ON ALL BULLETIN BOARDS AND ACTING DESK OFFICER WILL ACKNOWLEDGE RECEIPT OF IT.

AUTH W.W. ROBINSON, CAPTAIN   FIRST SGT. BRANDSTETTER   9:40 AM

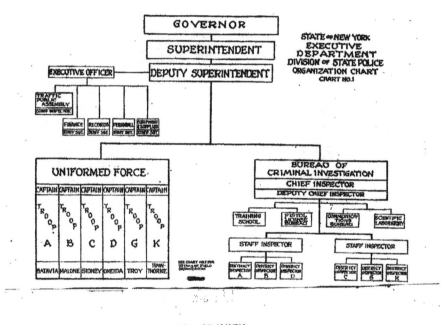

STATE OF NEW YORK
EXECUTIVE DEPARTMENT
DIVISION OF STATE POLICE
ORGANIZATION CHART
CHART NO.1

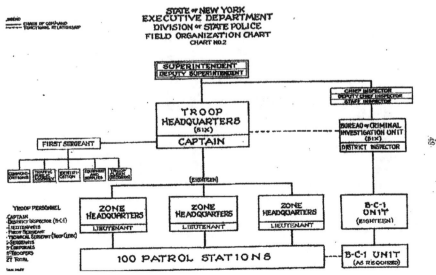

STATE OF NEW YORK
EXECUTIVE DEPARTMENT
DIVISION OF STATE POLICE
FIELD ORGANIZATION CHART
CHART NO.2

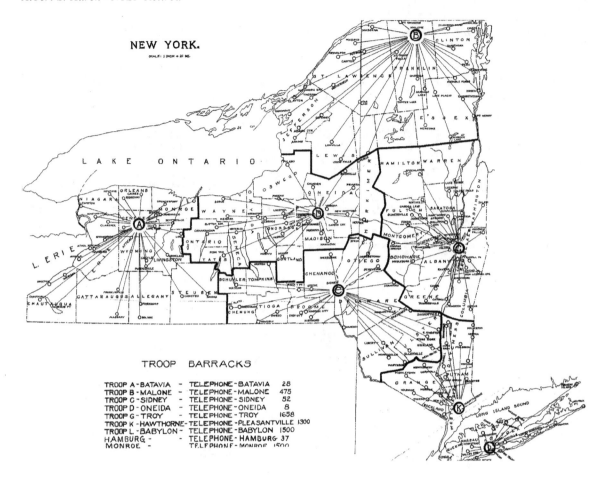

NEW YORK.
SCALE: 1 INCH = 21 MI.

TROOP BARRACKS

TROOP A - BATAVIA   - TELEPHONE - BATAVIA   28
TROOP B - MALONE   - TELEPHONE - MALONE   475
TROOP C - SIDNEY   - TELEPHONE - SIDNEY   52
TROOP D - ONEIDA   - TELEPHONE - ONEIDA   8
TROOP G - TROY   - TELEPHONE - TROY   1658
TROOP K - HAWTHORNE - TELEPHONE - PLEASANTVILLE 1300
TROOP L - BABYLON   - TELEPHONE - BABYLON   1500
HAMBURG -   - TELEPHONE - HAMBURG   37
MONROE -   TELEPHONE - MONROE   1500

Vol. 1

Sheriff William Bennett
Livingston Co,
Geneseo, N.Y.

No.

JOHN A. WARNER - Superintendent
GEO. P. DUTTON - Deputy Superintendent

ALBERT B. MOORE - Chief Inspector
DR. BRADLEY H. KIRSCHBERG - Laboratory Director

BUREAU OF CRIMINAL INVESTIGATION
NEW YORK STATE POLICE
SCHENECTADY **DECEMBER** NEW YORK

The B. C. I. Bulletin is issued every month by the Bureau of Criminal Investigation of the New York State Police to acquaint and familiarize all Law Enforcement Officials with the workings of our Bureau and the Laboratory. We invite any questions on the application of applied sciences to crime investigation or any issue as to the decision of the courts on the expert testimony.

* * * * * * * * * * * * * *

As far back as we can remember police always formed the most popular target for public criticism. No other branch of the governmental machinery has been so often abused as that group of men to whom the people in general entrust their safety, property, and lives. There seems to be however, a general mental revolution and in going over our correspondence which reaches the Superintendent, the Chief Inspector, and the different troop Commanders, we are indeed pleased to note that letters of criticism are completely fading out and expressions of approval and appreciation are becoming more evident. From the daily mail of our Superintendent the following has been selected for the present issue of the bulletin.

OFFICE OF THE DISTRICT ATTORNEY
OF LIVINGSTON COUNTY
GENESEO NEW YORK

October 30, 1936

Major John A. Warner
Superintendent
New York State Police
Capitol
Albany, N.Y.

Dear Major Warner:

We have just had a demonstration in Livingston County of the effectiveness of the Bureau of Criminal Investigation of the New York State Police.

A man was found dead with a broken neck, in a little shack in which he lived alone in the town of Ossian, Livingston County. The conclusion of most people was that there was no foul play and that he had received the injury in a fall. Evidence of anything but an accident was meagre.

However, Inspector Hoyt of the Bureau of Criminal Investigation came into the country with a detail of men and did most remarkable work in solving the case. I was with them most of yesterday and was very much impressed with the effective and rapid manner in which they did the work.

This convinces me more than ever that the creation of this bureau is a decided step forward in criminal apprehension and detection. It is a valuable aid to prosecuting and peace officers.

I want you to know that I very much appreciate the work that Inspector Hoyt and his men did in this case and that insofar as the Livingston County District Attorney's office is concerned I will at all

-2-

times welcome the aid and assistance of this bureau. I feel that it is only fair that you should know of the valuable work they did in this case.

                              Cordially,

                        (Sgd) Elliott A. Horton

                              District Attorney

* * * * * * * * * * * * * * * *

The above letter, while it bespeaks the sincere appreciation of an energetic, progressive and socially minded District Attorney, conveys to those of us who are familiar with the case even more than that. For it expresses Inspector Hoyt's ability to use scientific aids in the investigation of a crime. No simple matter was the tracing of the truth in this case. The inquiring mind of the criminal investigator would not accomplish very much without the hearty cooperation of the Director of Livingston County Laboratory, Dr. Gustav Salbach. Both Inspector Hoyt whose study of the case indicated that it was not an accident, Dr. Salbach whose careful study and experimental investigation following the autopsy which he performed on the body of John Fronk led to reach a conclusion supporting Inspector Hoyt, and our friend, District Attorney Horton, presented most desirable and perfectly blended ensemble of a Police Investigator, a Scientist, and a Prosecutor. Such cooperation is the very thing we need.

* * * * * * * * * * * * * * * *

In this particular case the Bureau was faced with the question, "Was it an accident or was it murder?" We are not particularly interested in the subdivisions of homicide. The question of whether it is murder, manslaughter, or death resulting from culpable negligence is obviously very important but ultimately it is up to the District Attorney to determine the particular section of the Penal Law under which he desires to prosecute a case. The Bureau and all the other criminal investigators approach the task from a rather different standpoint; namely that the life of an individual belongs to the state and that the destruction of such life except under conditions which are manifestly clear and evident calls for an investigation. Hence we have coroners, medical examiners, coroners physicians, and health officers whose duty is to investigate any death if no physician can honestly sign the death certificate. Police and the District Attorneys go one step further. This is especially true in that very debatable question "Was it Suicide or Was it Murder?" The mind of a clever murderer often times prepares the scenery and lays the proper background to throw off the scent even experienced criminal investigators. In one instance science comes again to the rescue and that is in the case of death resulting from the use of a firearm. Fingerprints of the murderer can be rubbed off the fatal weapon; the fingerprints of the victim can be fairly well imprinted on it. The position of the firearm when found, the character of the wound, the presence of powder marks, and the location of the bullet may baffle even the medical examiner, but the presence of the invisible to the eye but visible to the microscopic chemist particles of condensed by-products resulting from the firing of a weapon on the hands of the suspect, usually on the right hand, and conversely, their absence on the hands of the suicide will tell the grim and tragic story. Known under quite a number of names such as Lunge's reagent or Guttman's reagent, the reaction has been known for many years to the microscopic chemists. It depends entirely upon the color reaction which results in the firing of the weapon and creates nitrites and nitrates. The modus operandi of the test together with many others will be shown very shortly in our forthcoming first number of Technical Notes and criminal investigators and especially coroners and coroners physicians should familiarize themselves with the test in question.

Unfortunately, there are a great many other cases which often times baffle coroners and pathologists. Fortunately, they do not happen very often but the truth should always be established. Thus a short time ago a physician died under such suspicious circumstances that an alert District Attorney ordered a thorough toxicological ex-

-3-

amination of the organs. The report of the Laboratory was negative and the subsequent examination of the history of the case revealed that the man unquestionably died from leukemia. On the other hand in an article by Dr. Anton Werkgartner (Inst.f.Gerichtl.Med.,Univ. Wien.,Arch.Kriminol.,1935,97,1.)we find two cases which had all the manifestations of murder, yet proved to be suicides.In one case, a woman was found sitting on a stool, dead, with one hatchet in her left hand and the other between the underarm and the abdomen. She inflicted on herself three major wounds, one in the middle of the forehead, one in the left temporal region, and one in the right. In another case the woman actually stood up and had given herself several blows on the head with the broad side of a chopper.

Only most honest police investigation will prevent the unnecessary arrest of a suspect and only most thorough knowledge of the technique of autopsy, pathology, and anatomy will reveal the truth.

* * * * * * * * * * * * * * * *

The staff of the Laboratory cheerfully welcomes the arrival of its new member. Below we take the liberty of introducing the new addition to our Laboratory, a specially constructed comparison microscope of Bausch & Lomb. You will note two adjustments for the manipulation of the bullet, the coarse and the fine, instead of only one adjustment which is the customary arrangement. The reader will also note the facility with which the bar holding the camera can be removed from its vertical position and placed in a manner allowing horizontal photographs. The Director of the Laboratory spent considerable time with the Nestor of microchemists, Prof. E. Chamot of Cornell University and as a result of the conference our comparison microscope instead of having the usual 10 to 22 magnification has special adjustments allowing it to be increased to 100. That allows the use of the microscope for comparing and control in the study of most minute specimens such as dust, fragments of fabrics,small metallic particles, cement, sand and nearly everything else.

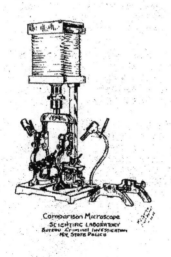

Comparison Microscope
SCIENTIFIC LABORATORY
Bureau Criminal Investigation
N.Y. State Police

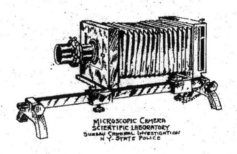

MICROSCOPIC CAMERA
SCIENTIFIC LABORATORY
Bureau Criminal Investigation
N.Y. State Police

* * * * * * * * * * * * * * * *

From Health News weekly bulletin of State Department of Health October 12th, 1936.

"Prompt and alert action by Sergeant J.D.Krick, a state trooper detailed to Allegany, Cattaraugus county, led to the apprehension recently of five negroes who were charged with possessing and transporting marihuana cigarettes in violation of the Public Health Law. This is an outstanding example of the fine cooperation which

-4-

state troopers have accorded the State Department of Health in its control of narcotic drugs.

Sergeant Krick had been informed that five negroes traveling by motor were suspected of distributing narcotic drugs in southern tier counties. The car had been registered in Buffalo and had been under surveillance by state troopers in the vicinity of Olean.

On September 11, Sergeant Krick while on patrol apprehended the five negroes and examined both the car and its occupants who were found to have in their possession five dozen marihuana cigarettes. On arraignment, the men pleaded guilty before Justice of the Peace Roland H. Pratt of Little Valley, New York, who imposed fines totaling $105."

* * * * * * * * * * * * *

We highly appreciate the attitude of the Health Department and are very glad that Sgt.J.D.Krick of Troop A has been successful in the apprehension of the culprits, although we feel that we simply did our duty. We will admit however that the question of enforcement of Section 1751 especially in relation to the possession of marihuana is becoming quite a complicated problem. Complicated both from the legal, the correction for which is not within our jurisdiction, and the laboratory standpoints. The latter however, we are glad to report, is progressing satisfactorily. Referring to the legalistic aspects of the enforcement of Section 1751 P.L. we have witnessed recently a quasi-serious and quasi-comical instance. The Hon.Anthony LaBelle,City Judge of Saratoga Springs, refused to sit as Committing Magistrate on the charge of possession, which is a misdemeanor punishable with imprisonment for not more than one year; a fine of not more than $500; or both. Our friend, the Judge maintained that should he find the defendant guilty and impose "both the imprisonment and fine" and the financial condition of the defendant would not allow him to pay the fine it would be mandatory for the Judge to sentence the man to 365 days imprisonment plus 500 days,making 865 days. Judge LaBelle claimed he had no jurisdiction and held the defendant for the Grand Jury. At the request of the Narcotic Supervisor, Mr. Frank Smith, the Bureau of Criminal Investigation prepared an inquiry which was submitted by Commissioner of Health to Attorney General for ruling. We quote excerpts from Attorney General's letter. At this time we do not know what action Commissioner of Health will take.

"With regard to the particular prosecution referred to in the memoranda attached to your letter, it seems clear that the City Court of Saratoga Springs has jurisdiction to hear, try and determine every misdemeanor committed within the corporate limits of the city, and impose the sentence prescribed by law. (Saratoga Springs City Charter, Section 51).

It appears to be well settled that the City Court of Saratoga Springs would have jurisdiction of a defendant charged with a misdemeanor under Section 1751, and would have authority upon conviction to impose the punishment provided by that Section regardless of the former provision limiting Courts of Special Sessions to imposing sentences not exceeding a fine of $50.00, imprisonment for six months, or both. (In re:Bray,12 N.Y.Supp.366; People v. Mittleman, 150 Misc. 394; People v. Kraft, 229 App.Div.281; People v. Monahan, 257 N.Y. 388.)

To remove any possible jurisdictional doubts, my suggestion would be that you amend Section 1751 of the P.L. by removing therefrom the second sentence relating to the misdemeanor charge, and add a new section,to be Section 1751-a,containing the matter removed from Section 1751. Section 56 of the Code of Criminal Procedure should then be amended by the addition of a Subdivision 35-b, to read "All violations of the provisions of section seventeen hundred fifty one-a of the penal law". There would then be no doubt as to the exclusive jurisdiction of Courts of Special Sessions of violations other than such as constitute felonies."

214

Form 16a. 4-17-25-20,000 (63-5663)

STATE OF NEW YORK — DEPT. STATE POLICE

SUMMONS

To ....

You are hereby summoned to appear before .... Justice of the Peace of the Town of .... Street, in the Village of .... of .... 192...... at .... M., to answer a charge made against you for violation of Section .... Paragraph .... Article .... of the .... Law of the State of New York, committed at .... and upon your failure to appear a warrant will be issued for your arrest. Dated at .... N. Y., this .... day of .... 192......

.... Rank .... Troop .... Dept. State Police

Date .... 192...... Time .... M.
Name ....
Address .... St.
Vehicle License No. ....
Chauffeur } License No. ....
Operator }
Owner of Vehicle ....
.... 192...... M.
Returnable at ....
Before Justice ....
Address .... St.
Issued by ....
Write description of vehicle and violation on reverse side of this stub.

Form 16-A. 5-22-22-5000 (33-4136)

STATE OF NEW YORK

NEW YORK STATE TROOPERS
DEPARTMENT OF STATE POLICE

SUMMONS

To .... You are hereby summoned to appear before .... Justice of the Peace of the Town of .... at his Office .... Street, in the Village of .... on the .... day of .... 192...... at .... M, to answer a charge made against you for violation of .... and upon your failure to appear a warrant will be issued for your arrest. Dated at .... this .... day of .... 192......

.... Trooper, Dept. State Police

Time Issued .... 192...... M.
Name ....
Address .... St.
License No. ....
Owner of Car ....
Address ....
Returnable before Justice ....
Address ....
Date Returnable ....
Time Returnable ....
Trooper ....

M. FLEMING -1922

1929 - TROOPER ED CHAMBERLAIN

Form No. 4. 5-6-31-15,000 (1D-7652)

STATE OF NEW YORK
EXECUTIVE DEPARTMENT

NEW YORK STATE TROOPERS
DIVISION OF STATE POLICE

APPLICATION
READ CAREFULLY AND ANSWER EACH QUESTION CORRECTLY

NOTE:—The Law requires each applicant to be a citizen of the United States; to pass a mental and physical examination; to be of good moral character and between the ages of 21 and 40 years. Applicant must be a practical horseman not less than 5 feet 8 inches in height without shoes, and weigh not less than 140 pounds stripped. Height and weight standards are strictly adhered to and no waivers whatsoever allowed—IF YOU DO NOT MEASURE UP TO OUR STANDARD YOU ARE NOT ELIGIBLE FOR APPOINTMENT. The enlistment period is two years. RECEIPT OF THIS APPLICATION WILL NOT BE ACKNOWLEDGED. Preference will be given applicants who have honorable discharge from Army, Navy, Marine Corps or National Guard.

This application must be filled out in INK in applicant's own handwriting and forwarded to the Superintendent, Division of State Police, Albany, N. Y.

..............................19....
(Date)

Name in full ....

Present residence address ....
(No.)   (Street)   (City and state)

Present business address ....
(No.)   (Street)   (City and state)

Present employer's name ....

What position do you hold .... How long held ....

Born at .... County .... State ....
(City or town)

Date of birth .... Present age .... yrs. .... mo.
(Month) (Day) (Year)

Married or single .... number of persons dependent upon you for support ....

EDUCATION

School attended	Years	Grade reached

MILITARY SERVICE

Organization	Length of service	Grade reached

(OVER)

Form 29. 7-30-35-20,000 (1D-961)

STATE OF NEW YORK

NEW YORK STATE TROOPERS

EXECUTIVE DEPARTMENT

DIVISION OF STATE POLICE

PATROL REPORT

Trooper...Horse No..........................Auto No...........................

Trooper...Horse No..........................Cycle No...........................

Left...Date..........................Time...........................

Arrived...Date..........................Time...........................

Stopping at...Hotel Phone No...........................

Will stop at...Hotel..........................N. Y. 24 hours later

Will stop at...Hotel..........................N. Y. 48 hours later

VILLAGES PASSED THROUGH: SPECIAL REMARKS

....

....

....

....

....

....

Mileage: Horse..................Auto..................M-Cycle..................Train..................Boat..................

Foot..................Trolley..................Auto Bus..................

POST MARKS

....

....

....

....

....

....

....

....

....

....

....

1938 PATROL CAR

TROOPER ANDY FISHER - 1920S

TROOP A GARAGE - MOTORCYCLE REPAIR

1925 - SMOKEY JOE DEAVENS

1936-J.E.HARRER/TILLIE

1938 ERIE COUNTY FAIR DETAIL

1938 CYCLE SCHOOL - LEMAY-MERRING-McGAUGHEY-DOELL-BRADY-WELCH-WRIGHT

1938 ANDOVER TOWN HALL

BIBLIOGRAPHY

REFERENCE:
COMMITTEE FOR A STATE POLICE ANNUAL REPORT
DAWN DAYS OF THE STATE POLICE
GREY RIDERS, THE BOOK
HISTORY OF THE NYSP
HUMAN DETECTIVE CASES MAGAZINE – 11/1944
JUSTICE FOR ALL, THE BOOK
NATIONAL JOURNAL OF LAW & ORDER – 1922
NYSP ANNUAL REPORTS
STATE TROOPER MAGAZINE – 1920S
W.W. ROBINSON LETTER – 5/28/27

NEWSPAPERS:
BATAVIA DAILY NEWS
BINGHAMPTON NEWS
BUFFALO TIMES
OLEAN TIMES UNION
ONEIDA DISPATCH
ROCHESTER DEMOCRAT & CHRONICLE
ROCHESTER TIMES UNION
ROME DAILY SENTINEL
SYRACUSE HERALD
SYRACUSE POST STANDARD
SYRACUSE TIMES UNION

PUBLIC LIBRARIES:
AUBURN PUBLIC LIBRARY
BATAVIA RICHMOND PUBLIC LIBRARY
BOONEVILLE PUBLIC LIBRARY
ERIE COUNTY LIBRARY
HORNELL PUBLIC LIBRARY
MEDINA LIBRARY
OLEAN PUBLIC LIBRARY
ONEIDA PUBLIC LIBRARY
ONONDAGA COUNTY HISTORY DEPARTMENT
ROCHESTER PUBLIC LIBRARY
ROME LIBRARY
SYRACUSE PUBLIC LIBRARY
UTICA PUBLIC LIBRARY

COUNTY CLERK'S OFFICES:

ALLEGANY COUNTY
CATTARAUGUS COUNTY
ERIE COUNTY
GENESEE COUNTY
LIVINGSTON COUNTY
NIAGARA COUNTY
ORLEANS COUNTY
WAYNE COUNTY
WYOMING COUNTY

PERSONAL INTERVIEWS:
BLANDING, HOWARD – CPL., NYSP RETIRED
CHAMBERLAIN, EDITH – SPOUSE OF EDWIN
DOELL, JOHN – CPL., NYSP DECEASED
FLEMING, MICHAEL C. – CONSTRUCTION ENGINEER
HORTON, GARY – GENESEE COUNTY PUBLIC DEFENDER
LONG, JOHN – SGT., NYSP DECEASED

ABOUT THE AUTHOR

Albert S. Kurek has spent 40 years in law enforcement. He served in the United States Marine Corp from 1957 to 1960, the New York State Police from 1962 to 1985 and as a Special Agent with the Defense Security Service from 1985 to 2002. A lifelong resident of Western New York, he is a graduate of Genesee Community College and State University College at Buffalo, N.Y.